IN THE BATH

CONQUERING THE CHANNEL IN A PIECE OF PLUMBING

BY

TIM FITZHIGHAM

preface
publishing

The FitzHigham Papers: Volume V

Published by Preface 2008

10 9 8 7 6 5 4 3 2 1

Copyright © Tim FitzHigham, 2008

Tim FitzHigham has asserted his right to be identified as the author of this work under the Copyright, Designs and Patents Act 1988

First published in Great Britain in 2008 by
Preface Publishing, an imprint of the Random House Group
1 Queen Anne's Gate
London SW1H 9BT

www.rbooks.co.uk
www.prefacepublishing.co.uk

Addresses for companies within The Random House Group Limited
can be found at www.randomhouse.co.uk/offices

The Random House Group Limited Reg. No. 954009

A CIP catalogue record for this book is available from the British Library

ISBN 9781848090255

The Random House Group Limited supports The Forest Stewardship
Council (FSC), the leading international forest certification organisation. All
our titles that are printed on Greenpeace-approved FSC-certified paper carry
the FSC logo. Our paper procurement policy can be found at
www.rbooks.co.uk/environment

Mixed Sources
Product group from well-managed
forests and other controlled sources
www.fsc.org Cert no. TT-COC-2139
© 1996 Forest Stewardship Council
FSC

Typeset in Great Britain by Palimpsest Book Production Limited,
Grangemouth, Stirlingshire
Printed and bound in Great Britain by Clays Ltd, St Ives Plc

PRAISE FOR THE STAGE SHOW, *IN THE BATH: UNPLUGGED*:

'One of the most moving and compelling tales you'll hear anywhere.' *Scotsman*

'The audience barely stops laughing as FitzHigham narrates jokes at an intense pace.' *Metro*

'Take a delightfully daft idea and add a delightfully posh performer and what do you have? A delightfully nice hour.' *Evening Standard* (Critic's Choice)

'A must see.' *Independent*

CONCERN FOR TIM FITZHIGHAM:

'By his own admission Tim is bonkers, which says it all really. But I respect him very much for being who he is, and not at all afraid of it! Tim and I go back a long way, we were pals at junior school, and as he so rightly remembered for a short period of time we had the same shoes. Tim is the kind of person who you would never dream of saying "keep smiling" to... he already is!'
ELLEN MACARTHUR

'Many people have foolish adventures, few make them so consistently hilarious, all in all the perfect British Eccentric.' DARA O'BRIAIN

'When I first met Tim I thought, "OH my God." Then I got to know him and thought, "Oh MY God." Then I heard he was writing a book and I thought, "OH MY GOD!" BUY THIS BOOK!' NEIL MORRISSEY

'The most heroic achievement since the invention of the "Crapper". Buy this book! Then read it in the bath.' SIMON KIRBY, MD of Thomas Crapper & Co

'There are few people in this life with the drive and the old-fashioned British pluck to achieve something like this. There are fewer still with the wit and charisma to tell their story with such gleeful hilarity. Tim is a rare talent indeed, brave, determined and the very embodiment of the great English eccentric. He is a true adventurer in the Giles Wemmbley-Hogg spirit. May God bless him and all who sail in him.' MARCUS BRIGSTOCKE

'This book reveals a hitherto unknown light on the consequences of youthful COLD BATHS... I have read the book which I commend you to do also, preferably in the bathroom!!' SIR CHRISTOPHER BENSON, Master of the Company of Watermen and Lightermen of the River Thames 2004–2005

'The fragile spirit of British eccentricity lies in the horned hands of this idiot. God help us!' SUGGS

'It's journeys like the bath trip that put the Great in Great Britain. This is what we do best. When I first heard about Tim's bath I laughed so hard I nearly fell overboard.' PAUL LUDWIG, Bargemaster to Her Majesty the Queen

'A barkingly mad, noble adventure – a brilliantly told tale.'
PETER BENNETT-JONES, Chairperson of Comic Relief

'There's a fine line between madness and genius – Tim has well and truly crossed it . . . Now none of the rest of us ever have to [make this journey]. Ever.'
RICHARD HAMMOND

OTHER BOOKS BY THE SAME AUTHOR

FICTION

BIOGRAPHY

VOLUME III: Pig Keeping in the West Indies
VOLUME IV: Paper Boat
VOLUME VII: The Man Who Discovered the Kama Sutra
VOLUME VIII: My Cufflinks Box: Its Vital Importance

GENERAL
A Splendid Haul
Willets and the Dark Tunnel
Poetry: A Word of Guidance
Keeping Pig Keepers
Pennyquick and the Fallen Men
Black Death in The Family
The Correct Uses of Gin
Moses Chamawam and the Great Ice Robbery
Lepers' Squints: A Monograph
Mistakes in Medieval Wool Gathering
The Conker: A Failed Experiment in Diet
My Top One Hundred Conker Recipes
The Decline in Domestic Manners Since 1270

OTHER PUBLISHED BOOKS BY THE SAME AUTHOR

. . .

For my family,
here and gone.

A blank page.

Every manual should have one.

CONTENTS

FOREWORD

This is the true story of how out of hand things can become from a very simple starting point. It covers the two summers when I tried to become the first person in history to successfully row the English Channel in a bath. I pursued this aim with the innocence and drive of a five-year-old and the mess this created is contained in the following volume.

I've tried to remember the events of those two summers and the intervening winter as well as I can. I may have mixed up a sand-bank here or a tide or date there but I've tried to decipher my notes of the time (written with very badly damaged hands) to the best of my abilities to capture the story as truthfully as possible. I apologise in advance for any mistakes I've made, but the truth of the bath remains, like the trip itself, eccentric. I do hope you enjoy reading it.

There are a few people to thank, in no order and leaving most of the more important ones out: my friends and other animals. PBJ, Janette, Mary and all at PBJ. Charlie Viney and all at Mulcahy & Viney. Patient Trevor and all at Preface. Jeremy, Karon and Joe.

The theatres, kind reviewers and audiences that have kept me out of gaol all these years. The clowns who make it such a joy to make people laugh and have guided me endlessly. The Clan. St Chad's College. LFH. The team of hardened drinkers who inspire me. The bar staff who inspire them. And, the bath team – this is our story.

Finally, I'd like to thank the skippers of all the massive tankers and container ships in the English Channel that narrowly missed me.

Signed under the moon with the ice rapidly melting in the glass.

Tim FitzHigham
Tangiers, 1843
(on 26 February 2008)

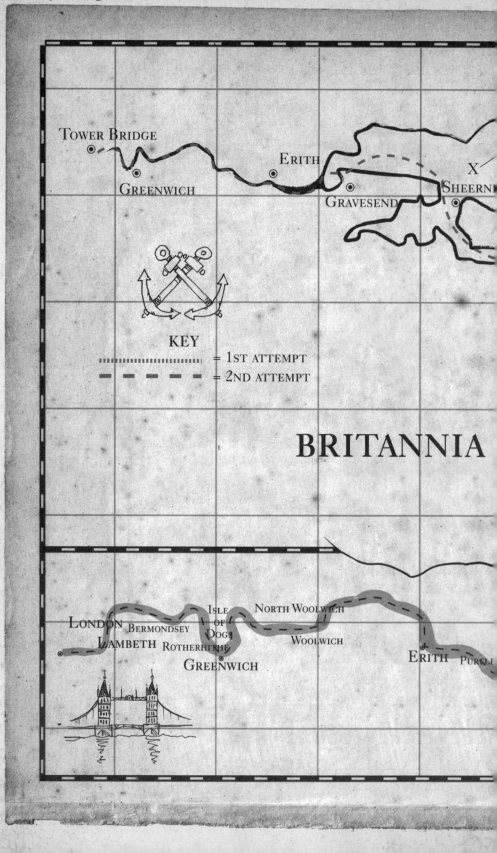

TOWER BRIDGE

ERITH

GREENWICH

GRAVESEND

SHEERN...

X

KEY

••••••••••••••••• = 1ST ATTEMPT

— — — — — = 2ND ATTEMPT

BRITANNIA

LONDON   BERMONDSEY   ISLE   NORTH WOOLWICH
                      OF
LAMBETH   ROTHERHITHE DOGS   WOOLWICH

GREENWICH   ERITH   PURFL...

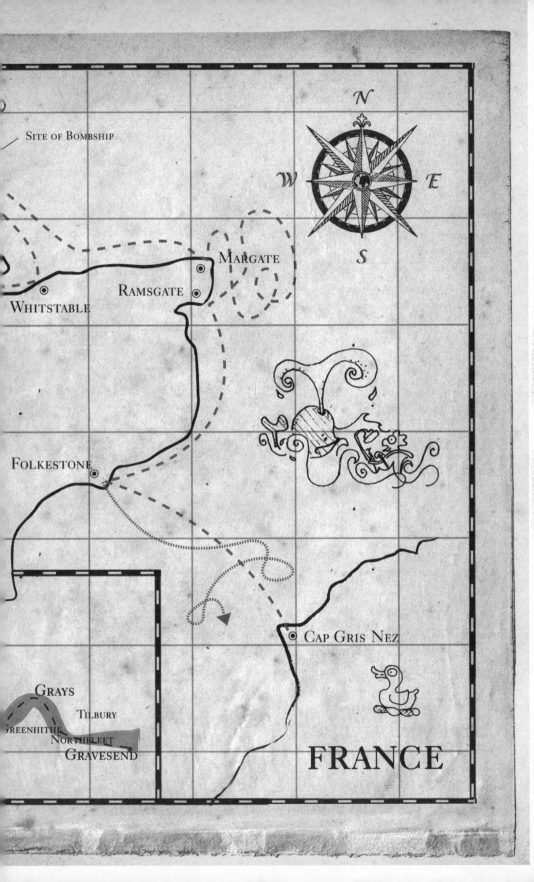

MUCH SIMPLE PLEASURE

There are few things in life as good as the warm embrace of a well-drawn bath. Steam swirled soporifically around my nostrils, rising up to form complex weather systems round the dead hanging plant above me.

I lay back, waves gently lapping the islands of my knees, thinking of the most luxurious bath time I'd been involved in. Easy: a huge bath I'd shared with three beautiful women, playing hunt the soap.

I was three and they were four, two and one respectively.

I'd been bathing for many years semi-professionally. It started in Norfolk. I was born in what is now the lunatic asylum in King's Lynn. There seems to be some confusion about the exact date it changed but at the time I arrived there, I'm told people are fairly sure it was the maternity unit. I was taken back to a large bath in the fen. The fens of Norfolk are a flat land with big sunsets. They were claimed out of the sea by Dutch engineers in the 1600s using clever dikes and are now a slightly tamed version of a swamp. In the 1970s, when I was born, not many people lived there and socially it was still run like medieval England. There was a Lord, who lived a long way away, a Sir, who might live closer or even run things locally and, failing both of these, there'd be a Squire who would run, and probably own, your village. Where we lived wasn't even a village, it was much smaller and more chaotic. Places too tiny and eccentric to be villages in Norfolk are called droves. Being a really little one of those, it didn't even have a squire. In the absence of sane alternatives, our happy drove made do with my dad.

I loved bath time in Norfolk. I was normally found in, what I remember as, a permanently sunlit orchard. I'd be playing, well, more sitting or bouncing, before being taken up for my bath. My mum and I had songs for everything and there was a bathing one, too.

The Norfolk house we were living in had been gradually slipping into the fen for years. Normally they build houses in the fens on large oak rafts but somehow someone had forgotten this. Many of the walls leaned quite badly and there were rooms that were shut off from us as they'd gone under. Our house was miles inland but sinking fast. When I was two, my sister arrived and joined me in bouncing and baths. I gave her my favourite bouncing chair and Dad converted an old wooden beer barrel into a castle for me. In line with my designs (I was three at the time so they may not have passed an architectural course) he even cut gothic windows into it. I moved in with a large ginger stray – a cat I loved called Oscar.

By the time my barrel got gothic windows, the main house was faring less well. The wall near the main staircase was leaning nine feet to the perpendicular. Dad finally accepted this might be a bit unsafe. Accompanied by much booing and hissing from me we left the bath in Norfolk to sink gently into the fen, along with the house that surrounded it, and moved to Derbyshire. Dad took the large oak gateposts from Norfolk with us and made the dining-room table from them. The bath in Derbyshire was much smaller, more awkward and much, much colder. The countryside was also considerably higher with numerous humps and mountains. At first I didn't like it and registered my protest by painting violently on walls all over the house when no one was looking. I found hills very frightening as in Norfolk I'd never met them.

However, over many baths, snow-laden mornings in winter, gorgeous mists hanging over stone walls in spring, warm, sunny summers and golden-leafed autumns I came to love Derbyshire. It was a very happy place. My grandparents on my dad's side lived there and my granny was one of the funniest, most beautiful things in the world to me. She and her oldest friend Elsie had me in non-stop tears of laughter with stories, songs and jokes. One was all about how they'd been drilled in the war to defend Derbyshire with an antique Gatling gun, no instructions and some rather soggy ammunition. Somehow it went off and the ensuing chaos of the story made me laugh till I hurt. The memory of Granny telling how she and Elsie flailed around behind the butt of this mighty weapon trying to work out how to stop it as it spewed ammunition all over the Derbyshire countryside still makes me smile, even now.

Derbyshire became too much of a distraction from my baths, so we moved to Hertfordshire as Mum got a post there. She's a priest and her career has given my dad some great moments. Striding up to people at parties who didn't know what Mum did, he'd open with, 'as I said to the vicar in bed last night . . .' before looking on at the total bafflement that met him. Now she's been made a canon it's led him to a rich seam including anything ending with 'you're fired', many lines involving short or long fuses as required and several others which, if you ever meet him, will not be more than a few seconds away.

In the holidays I'd go on bathing tours, great plumbing progresses of the country, staying with eccentric relatives who only had outdoor wells, godparents who taught me to surf and debonair great-uncles and -aunts who would take me out for lunch and let me read books. Hot steam wrapped about my ears.

Throughout all these holidays and various baths, I'd always come back to the one in Hertfordshire. My parents' Hertfordshire bath is the finest I've ever found. It's huge and wide and really comfy. Not so big that it's impossible to keep hot, but not so small that you need a degree in yoga to use it. It has no complicated or ostentatious plumbing; it's just a really solid, decent bath – rather like my parents. This was the bath in which I now found myself.

Coming round from dozing lazily I attempted the most complicated of bath-based manoeuvres: letting some water out of the plug while simultaneously topping up the bath with new, hotter water. It didn't work very well. It never does for me. I lay back into the hot, watery arms and turned my mind to my current problem – a problem that was dogging me with cat-like stealth.

In 2003 I'd broken the world's oldest maritime record kayaking down the River Thames in a boat entirely made of paper. I'd discovered the original record in a footnote while reading a book on poets in the reign of James I (or VI, I'm not going to take sides on the issue here). The record had been set in 1619 when the Thames Water Poet, John Taylor, made it 40 miles down the river in a paper boat using two large dried fish for the oars. This record had slightly obsessed me for years. So, during a very wet March, in the worst weather seen on the Thames in 40 years, I'd set out to go 41 miles and raise £500 for a charity called Comic Relief. When I stepped off my 100% recycled paper boat, 384 years after John Taylor, I'd gone 160 miles in what was rapidly becoming a soggy mass of papier mâché held together with gaffer tape and luck. The paper boat finish was televised on four continents and raised in excess of £10,000 for the charity. This was way beyond anything I'd thought remotely possible and ignited in me a passion for boats, water and adventure that I didn't know I had. Admittedly, I'd always done things slightly differently from those around me, but a succession of teachers, friends and relations had tried to keep this tendency in check. I'd been more embarrassed that I seemed to see the world sideways than proud of it. The triumph of the paper boat was that I normally kept my imagination under wraps. This time I'd let it fly and the results were great.

Bath water nibbled seductively at my earlobes as the problem raged round my head. I was reflecting, with all the brilliance of a cracked mirror, on how to follow up the adventure in the paper boat. The problem was: what could I do next? Anything seemed possible but I just couldn't decide what. If the world was my oyster, I was having difficulty opening the shell.

The paper-boat adventure had been a hugely successful, joyous trip into the absurd. It had combined the three things I loved most: outdoor adventure, raising some cash for a cause and making people laugh. It had challenged me and taught me something new. Before the paper boat, I'd never been in a kayak and certainly never dreamt I'd get to take one the whole length of the mighty River Thames. However, when the journey finished, it had left a hole.

To that point, I'd spent my life wandering around bumping into experiences, feeling a bit lost and trying to find something useful to do. I'd made a career out of temporary jobs, while I tried to escape towards doing something in comedy or acting. I'd been lucky; I'd loved it all (with the possible exception of a very brief, dyspeptic spell cleaning drains with no proper equipment).

Trying to find something to do in life had in itself been a great life. However, in the wake of the paper-boat trip it now felt something was missing. Being out on the water in the middle of challenge had made me smile and, desperate as a frisky bullock demanding entry to a pasture of cows nine months before breeding season, I wanted more.

Legend records a graveyard where elderly elephants instinctively go to lie down and die. Similarly, whenever I need to think really hard, I always head to my parents' Hertfordshire bath, draw it and lie down. Many of my best and worst plans had come to me in the bath that now cosseted me. I looked up at the dead plant in the hanging basket for inspiration: none came. And the bath water had got cold again. With only mildly less success than before, I attempted to top up the bath again.

What could I do?

I took a sip from the now warm glass of gin left on the table next to me. As I reached over to put it back, it knocked against the bath. There was a muffled thud. It was as though the bath had spoken. I tapped it again. There was a cast-iron work of genius nestling beneath my buttocks. I'd do something with a bath. People always seem to be sitting in bathfuls of beans for charity: no challenge there.

Then in a flash it hit me. I could row it. A Noël Coward song about a man rowing an India Rubber bath across Lake Windermere ripped into my head.

Like Archimedes before me, in that instant, I discovered something that I wanted to do. I would take a bath, put oars on it and row it across the English Channel. I felt called, driven, motivated. I would become to sanitaryware what the Wright Brothers were to aviation. I would be the Captain Webb of baths. Synapses in my brain snapped and whirred into life. Fireworks of ideas shot out of the bath and bounced off the walls in the tiny bathroom. I was hooked.

I've become aware over many years and countless projects that I have the potential to become a little obsessive about things. It's something I've always tried hard to control, so now, when an idea comes to me I normally give it ten minutes' thought to try and talk myself out of it. Within ten short minutes, the bath plan had totally taken hold. This idea was not only a goer, it was a belter.

I burst into the drawing room to see my parents not even sketching; they looked up, shocked. I left the drawing room and returned to the bathroom. Putting on a dressing gown to cover my nudity I left the bathroom again and re-burst into the drawing room. 'I'm going to row the English Channel in a bath for Sport Relief.'

Mum sat looking a bit stunned. Dad responded first, 'Well, your great-grandmother was the first lady to swim from Folkestone to Dover, or was it Dover to Folkestone . . . or perhaps it was Ramsgate?'

'Really, Dad?'

'Yes she was called Lilius; although in the draconian times when she did it, swimming costumes were so big she probably floated most of the way on an enormous pair of bloomers. Still if you make it, it'll be another first for the family.'

Dad smiled, Mum still looked a bit shocked. I closed the door and triumphantly dripped back to the bathroom, leaving my parents feeling much, I suspected, like a less mathematical version of Mr and Mrs Archimedes.

A litter of questions popped up. I had no money to fund the project and above all, didn't have a spare bath. My first attempt to get one was not a resounding success.

'Dad, you know I need a bath to row the Channel . . .'

'Yes . . .'

'Can I borrow the one in the bathroom?'

'No.'

CHAPTER ONE

VIBRATING PIPES

'I climbed Mount Everest – from the inside.'

Spike Milligan

Back at my desk, problems and questions carpet-bombed me. I didn't know anything about the sea, would that be important? Would it be possible to make a bath really float? What was the procedure for rowing the Channel? Was there anything legal that had to be done? These and many more questions entered the fray until the dogfight of problems diving and weaving above me had developed into a real scrap.

At the time I was working off and on in a temp job for the civil service. After work one night, I met up with an old friend called Jack. I'd been trying to keep the bath idea a secret, as I didn't really have much of a clue how to proceed at that stage, but seeing Jack I suddenly blurted out, 'I'm going to row the English Channel in a bath for Sport Relief.'

Jack looked on wide-eyed, similar, I imagine, to a frog that's swallowed a wasp. He rallied and in a voice pitched much higher than his normal one responded, 'Off you go then . . .'

Sipping his beer, his eyes relaxed and the incisive brain I've always rated him for hummed and revved into a higher gear.

'How are you going to pay for it?'

'Erm . . . I hadn't really thought about that in huge detail.'

'I'll get you a list of bathroom companies. One of them might sponsor it.'

With Jack-like efficiency the list arrived the next day. I started at the top and began phoning bathroom companies. No one was interested. A third thought I was mad, another third that I wasn't serious and the third third thought both.

My phone rang, it was Jack: 'Have you got the list?'

'Yes. I've been phoning them all day. It's not going very well . . .'

'Have you got to the last page yet?'

'No, why?'

'Have a look at the "T" section.'

'Oh my . . . are they still in business?'

'It seems so – I think they might be the ones for you.'

'I'll give them a ring . . .'

I put down the phone and picked it up again immediately. The ring tone on the other end seemed to take longer than a BT engineer but finally a female voice answered, 'Good afternoon, Thomas Crapper and Company, how may I help you?'

Stifling a giggle, I put on the stentorian voice I'd been perfecting in tests for the civil service, 'I'd like to speak to someone in charge . . .'

'I'll put you through. May I ask what it's about?'

'I'd like a bath.'

After some holding music, rather pleasingly Flanders and Swann, a soft midland accent rolled into my ear, 'Good afternoon, Warwick Knott, General Manager, how can I help?'

'I'd like one of your baths please.'

'Certainly, what sort of bath would you like?'

'A strong one; I need it to withstand the English Channel.'

'What?'

'I'd like to row the Channel in it.'

'Oh good . . . I'll put you through to the Managing Director.'

After more Flanders and Swann, a clipped officer's voice arrived with martial precision at the end of the line, 'May I help you?'

'I'd like one of your baths please.'

'Certainly, what sort of bath would you like?'

'A strong one; I need it to withstand the English Channel.'

'What?'

'I'd like to row the Channel in it.'

'Very funny, Ronnie, I've really got to go, I've got quite a lot to get done this afternoon. Goodbye.'

The line went dead. I paused. Who was Ronnie? I picked up the phone and dialled again. The same female voice answered.

'Good afternoon, Thomas Crapper and Company, how may I help you?'

'It's me again, I seem to have got cut off, please can you put me through to the Managing Director again?'

'Certainly.'

'And tell him I don't know who Ronnie is . . .'

The officer's voice came back on the line.

'I'm sorry, I thought you were a friend of mine. Now what can I do for you?'

'I want one of your baths to row across the English Channel to raise money for a charity called Sport Relief.'

'That was what I thought you said the first time . . .'

I waited for another rebuttal.

'If you're really serious about this, I think you'd better come and see me.'

'Perfect. How about the day after tomorrow? Where are you?'

'Just outside Stratford upon Avon.'

Two days later I drove up to Stratford, looked at the instructions I'd been given, then left Stratford and headed south. Somewhere on the way I missed the turning. Somewhere on the way back I missed it again but on the third time found the understated gateway I was looking for. I drove up the track. On the left was a cricket pavilion and in front of that, following the original designs laid down by God, a pitch. To one side of it were cricketing nets and a tree: so far, so perfectly English. On the right of the track were fields with a stream running through them and various sheep masticating nonchalantly and discussing the effects of unexpected car arrivals on ovine digestion.

Pulling into the car park I was unable to park. Baths overran all the parking spaces. There must have been 200 parked there in all. I'd reached the bath version of the Promised Land. Over the other side of the baths, ahead of me and slightly to the left, was a double gate to some sort of stabling. To the right of the gate, another smaller drive and a large rhododendron bush, was another smaller building. A plum-coloured sign announced to the world that this was the head office of the world's greatest bathroom company: Thomas Crapper & Company. Crapper's Head Office was as eccentric and beautiful as you might expect. Beneath the sign was the main entrance. Either side of the door, where other lesser companies would have stone lions, bulls or other animals proudly standing rampant, stood two massive, stunning Victorian urinals. The overall effect was clear: you have found the HQ of an ablution legend.

I rang the bell. A Bond girl answered the door. I took a guess and assumed her to be the owner of the voice that had first picked up the phone.

'Good afternoon, Thomas Crapper and Company, how may I help you?' confirmed it.

'I'm here to see the Managing Director, it's about a bath.'

'Oh, sorry, he's out for lunch at the moment . . . oh, no wait, here he is now . . .'

I turned around and saw, coming down the drive towards me, a bearded man, in his mid to late thirties, riding a penny-farthing bicycle. One enormous, oversized wheel at the front, one tiny one at the back, seemingly added as an afterthought – they are lethal death contraptions, famously fiendishly difficult to ride. The bicycle we now know as normal, with two wheels of the same size, is actually called 'the safety bicycle' and was invented due to the huge numbers of penny-farthing-related deaths in the Victorian era. The most experienced person I'd ever seen on a penny-farthing was an old photographer in Derbyshire. He used to wobble round the village fêtes and garden parties of my youth in an entirely unconvincing manner. However, riding down the track towards me was the apotheosis of penny-farthing riding. This was a steady, commanding performance. The bearded man even took the speed bump at the end of the track without flinching. In that moment I knew we'd get on.

He slowed down and dismounted with episcopal serenity and, holding the penny-farthing in one hand, extended his other to me.

'You must be Tim. I'm Simon Kirby.'

We then entered the lavatorial equivalent of the old curiosity shop, and turned right up a staircase. At the top was a tiny office engulfed by an enormous desk. Simon sat on one side of it and I squeezed in behind the other.

'Now, what do you mean you want to row the Channel in a bath?'

'Just that. I want to try it to raise cash for a charity.'

'Seriously, are you serious?'

'Very.'

'Right! How can we help?'

I outlined what I wanted from Simon and he agreed with all of it.

'I'll do some maths and be in touch. I'm supposed to say, "I only wish I could come with you in the bath", but nothing would make me want to do that.'

With that he gave me a tour of the offices and various sheds of the Crapper empire before I left for the drive back to London.

Driving back, it dawned on me I needed to make a very important call. A significant problem had been growing steadily in my mind: I knew nothing about the sea or anything to do with maritime navigation. It was becoming obvious to even my very dim intellect that this would be something of a handicap so I'd need help.

I picked up the phone and dialled the Royal Navy and by mistake got put through to an Admiral, Rear or Vice – I'm not sure which. Several members of the family had been in the Navy and I'd always been taught that it was naval courtesy when talking to a sailor to start the conversation with the question: 'How are your futtocks old man?' I had no idea what a futtock was but did not wish to be discourteous so as the voice on the end of the telephone said 'Hello,' I launched in.

'How are your futtocks old man?'

There was a wheezing chuckle before the voice said, 'At their furthest reach dear boy, at their furthest reach.'

I paused. Now what? I was having a conversation that I didn't understand a word of. 'I need advice on rowing the English Channel.'

'Then I'd say you'd come to the right place.'

After this slightly odd beginning, our conversation went amazingly well. We really got on. I inferred that the man on the end of the phone had actually, or was soon to be, retired from the Navy but seemed very keen to help. Then came the awkward bit. We'd been talking for about half an hour about wind, sea and currents, none of which I'd really understood, and still I hadn't mentioned the bath. I really needed this man's help so didn't want to scare him off but I also had to tell the truth. Finally I took the bullet squarely by the horns.

'This boat that we're talking about trying to get across the English Channel . . . I should probably tell you, it's a bath.'

The line went dead. I'd really blown it. I'd lost him. I was just about to hang up when the line crackled into life.

'Well, same rules of navigation apply dear boy, I'm on board.'

I now had an Admiral (Rear or Vice) (probably ret.) to help. Later that week I was with another old sailor and told him I'd used the question, 'How are your futtocks old man?'

Instinctively he replied, 'At their furthest reach dear boy, at their furthest reach.'

I looked at him, with much the same ranid expression Jack had used in observing me earlier in the month. 'That's exactly what he said.'

'Well, it's a bit old-fashioned but he said it because it's the correct naval response to the question, "How are your futtocks old man?"'

'That's fantastic but what does it actually mean?'

'Well, that's the thing, Tim, nobody actually knows.'

There it was: an almost forgotten Britain in a nutshell. The Admiral and I had just begun a conversation with phrases that neither of us understood but that both of us were too polite and locked in etiquette to admit we didn't understand. The bath project was going to be great.

The Admiral (ret.) suggested I find someone else to advise me as well as him. He had to be away quite a bit over the next few months and would be uncontactable. During these times he wanted to be sure that someone would be there to help me. This was a great idea; the only question was who? Someone would have to take me from a total maritime novice to being capable of taking on the Channel. They would need top naval knowledge and the patience of a saint: two qualities very rarely compatible.

Thinking it through over the next couple of days, a single name bounded into my head. I'd known Dominic Hurndall for years. He had been in the Navy and risen to the rank of Lieutenant Commander before leaving to attend various top-level beer-based discussions with me at university. At college, Dom was something of an enigma. While I'd spend summer holidays playing around, losing temp jobs and teaching, Dom would go back into the Royal Navy and protect my freedom to do so. He made me laugh with tales of windsurfing gone wrong and his determined attempts to take up the trumpet. However, when it came to maritime stuff, Dom was the most knowledgeable person I knew.

In distinguished competitions he'd raced against my friends' older brothers. They all rated him as a truly great sailor. Once, he successfully skippered a boat to victory in the prestigious Fastnet Race.

The fact Dom had an ability, consistently proved at college, of being able to calmly explain stuff to me without wanting to throw me out of a window was also truly important. It was becoming very obvious that without Dom, I'd really struggle on the bath trip. I picked up my phone.

'Dom, are you about for a beer?'

Even though he's a very old and close friend, as I bumped into the table inside the door of the pub, I realised I was oddly nervous about seeing Dom. The more I'd thought about it the less possible the bath project seemed without him. This had to go well.

Returning to the table with beers, we began chatting about all sorts of stuff. In fact everything under the sun that didn't involve baths or Channels. Eventually, I thought I'd just have to bite the bull and said, 'I've got a plan . . . sort of charity thing . . . a bit like the paper boat . . . but I'm going to need your help.'

'What is it?'

'Well . . . I want to row the Channel and I know nothing about the sea.'

'Should be fairly straightforward. I could teach you what you'd need to know.'

'Hmmm . . . I want to row the Channel in a bath.'

Dom looked as shocked as Jack. Then laughed out loud.

'That's a brilliant wheeze. It's going to be tough and I'm not sure you'll make it but I'd love to help.'

Dom had joined the team and I'd found an officer to run plumbing command.

'Have you checked with the French? They own half the Channel.'
'Good point. I'll get on to that . . .'
'Another beer?'

I'd invented a new maxim, 'hard drinking leads to success at sea', and attempting to prove it, the next night I met up with a man called Douglas. I didn't know Douglas well. He'd been to a talk I'd given about the paper-boat trip and after it, he gave me his card. He was some sort of boat designer and said that if ever I needed his help I only had to ask. Before going to the pub that evening I finally checked out the website address on his card with my coal-fired laptop. It turned out Douglas was not just some sort of boat designer but a multi-award-winning boat designer. Asking a reputable boat designer to put his reputation on the line for a floating Crapper bath was a big call. Asking a multi-award winner at the top of his profession to do it would be almost impossible.

We met in a pub just off Lots Road near the harbour in Chelsea. I bought beers and sat down opposite Douglas. In our short acquaintance I'd already become aware that he was one of life's most cheerful people. Every time I'd seen or spoken to him he'd had a huge smile on his face. He seemed a man consistently one beat away from a gut-wrenching peal of laughter.

We talked about all sorts of stuff, found common ground and drank lots of beer. Several beers in, I thought it might be time to chance my arm.

'You know how you said you'd be up for helping if I had another idea?'
'Absolutely.'
'Well . . . I've got one.'
'What is it now: a paper sail? A loo-roll Armada?'
'I want to row the Channel in a bath.'
There was a beat. Silence. Douglas burst into hysterics. He came up gasping for breath. 'Brilliant. I'm in. What do you need?'
'Well, do you think a bath can actually float and do this?'
'Erm . . . I don't know. Have you got a pen?'
Together we drew countless designs on beer mats for the rest of the night. The more beer we drank the sillier the designs became and the more we laughed. Design mark 2B made us laugh so much

we hurt doing Hamlet impressions in the style of Sean Connery, Roger Moore and Mrs Thatcher. Via several versions of the mark 8, we finally finished the night on a totally implausible design: the mark 12E.

Two days later my phone rang. It was Douglas.

'Mate, I've really got it.'

'Still? Oh dear. My hangover's just clearing.'

'No, I've got the design. I've been working on design 12E.'

'Was that the good one?'

'Absolutely.'

'Perfect.'

'I'll pop it in the post.'

'Brilliant work, mate. Fancy a beer after work?'

'Great idea . . .'

Waking up somewhat later I remembered Dom's words about checking with the French. Now I had the designs of one of the country's leading boat designers, I was bound to be fine. I tried to look up the French Coastguard and was somewhat surprised that I couldn't find one. I phoned the French Embassy.

A slick diplomatic Gallic voice answered the phone, 'Bonjour, the Embassy of France.'

'Ah, bonjour, excuse me for asking but where is the French Coastguard?'

'At the coast. Guarding.'

'Perfect. Of course. Do you have any contact details for them?'

'But of course.' He rattled off the contact details of the French Navy.

'Erm . . . I don't think I want the Navy, I rather need the civil Coastguard.'

'We have no civil Coastguard in France.'

'I don't mind if they're rude, I just need to . . .'

'What?'

'I just need to talk to whoever it is in France that is the equivalent of the British Coastguard.'

'This is the Navy in France.'

'Thank you so much for your time. Or, should I say, merci beaucoup.'

'Pardon?'

'Merci beaucoup. I think it's "thank you" in French.'

'Oh sorry, *bien, desolé*. I didn't understand you. *Au revoir*.'

I thought I'd better check my new information. Perhaps I'd not been clear with the man from the Embassy and he'd got confused. I dialled the Admiral.

'It seems it's the French Navy that I should be talking to about the Channel crossing not the Coastguard.'

'Right. There's no Coastguard in France. They let the French Navy do it. They have to give them something to do. It's not good for national pride to have to disband it so they turned it into a Coastguard. I think it does a few other bits and bobs too.'

'Right-ho, thanks . . . I'll phone them.'

It was 2004 – the 100th anniversary of the Entente Cordiale – or the centenary, in the pre-decimal system of measurement. Signed on 8 April 1904, the Entente Cordiale was a series of agreements between France and the UK attempting to put an end to the rivalry that had dogged the two nations up to that point and usher in a new era of peaceful co-operation[1].

I thought: what better way to celebrate 100 years of love between our two great nations than to row the waterway that separates us in a giant piece of sanitaryware? With the fervour of a terrorist, I wrote to the Prime Minister to tell him of my plan. I didn't hear back. Then I picked up the phone and dialled the French Navy.

'*Bonjour* . . .'

He went on in French. This was something I'd not bargained for. Fairly early in the conversation it became obvious even to me that the French Navy spoke nothing but French. I did GCSE French, or as it should be known 'French for the stupid', and being stupid, passed with flying colours. The course was themed around a series of books: the first one was called *Tricolore*, the second was called *Encore Tricolore*, then they ran out of words to rhyme with 'Tricolour' and for the third book settled on *Tricolore Trois*. As it was written on the book cover as *Tricolore 3* I always suspected it was probably pronounced '*Tricolore* Three' but arguing this with my French teacher would have been less pleasurable than my castration and probably lead to a similar result.

---

[1] Together with the other two of the Triple Ententes (Anglo-Russian and Franco-Russian) it paved the way for World War I but that's not important in the bath story and was certainly not the intention when it was signed.

The *Tricolore* series had irreparably drummed into me how to ask the way to the station: '*Où est la gare?*' I remember repeating the same phrase over and over again, yet at no point in the whole murderous series had I been taught the one phrase that would have been actually useful to me: 'Hello sir, I would like to row the English Channel in a bath, please.'

I tried hard to improvise. I knew the French for 'hello'. I knew the French for 'sir'. I even knew the French for 'I would like'. Surpassing myself linguistically, and in the spirit of the Entente Cordiale and basic politeness, I'd even looked up the French for 'the English Channel'.

The French, somewhat surprisingly, don't like calling it 'the English Channel' but don't seem to feel justifiably able to call it 'the French Channel' either. Mysteriously they call it 'la Manche' which translates as 'the Sleeve'. I discovered later that the same word – the Sleeve – with a slightly different accent shift or a *Carry On* style eyebrow wiggle is also a slang term in France for condoms. In England, slang for condoms is 'French letters'. Knowing this, everything became clear.

'Please' is easy in French and again had been drummed into me, coupled like the passenger carriage to '*Où est la gare?*' So the only hurdle I could see was the verb 'to row'. Cursing myself for not being better at French and desperately flipping through the dictionary I heard the naval man on the end of the phone repeat helplessly, '*Pardonez moi, monsieur, mais je ne comprends pas.*'

I found the 'R' section, ran my finger down the page and apprehensively shut the dictionary. A bead of sweat appeared on my forehead. I felt nervous, self-conscious, dishonest and cagey: the classic signs that a stout-hearted Briton is milliseconds away from attempting French.

In a French accent developed through a lifetime of using English I said, 'Hello sir, I would like to row the English Channel in a bath please.'

What actually arrived in the ear of the French Navy man was, 'Hello sir, I would like to fight a condom across a bath if you please.'

The naval man clung to his mantra like a monk in a whorehouse, '*Pardonez moi, monsieur, mais je ne comprends pas.*'

I had to think fast. The education system of Thatcherite Britain had failed me at the first hurdle. What option was left to me? Politely, I tried slowing down my questions, which did not help. I tried using monosyllabic words[2], which still did not help. Then I tried the age-old trick of the Briton abroad and raised my voice. This really did not help.

Finally, desperate to communicate, I attempted mime to try and get my point across. Innovative mime was my best shot and would have worked had we not been separated from each other by a phone line. I finished in my best French by thanking him for his time and asking if he knew the way to the station before putting the phone down.

I phoned the Admiral back.

'It's no use, Admiral, the French speak nothing but French.'

There was a short pause on the end of the line then his voice rattled into life like a sabre.

'They're lying, Tim!'

'What?'

'The French Navy must by law speak English, as English is the international maritime language of the sea.'

'Has anyone told the French that?'

The line went dead for a moment before he thundered, 'Yes: Nelson. At the battle of Trafalgar.'

I tried to stifle an irresistibly British giggle not knowing if the Admiral was making a joke or not. I got it right. He was serious.

The indignant thunder continued, 'This is rotten behaviour; he was playing a cruel trick on you. The animal is probably now laughing about it down the mess with his other officers. Your mistake was to try and speak French at him in the first place.'

I put down the phone to the Admiral irritated with the cunning officer of the French. However, I decided in the spirit of what I was trying to achieve that I'd play his game for as long as I could. I needed to find someone who spoke French like a native.

I was in London that weekend and left my flat to wander round the corner to grab some milk. On the way back a lady sashayed down the road towards me, looking not unlike Audrey Hepburn

---

[2]It is one of the greatest achievements of the English language that the word mono-syllabic, used to describe words with a single syllable, does itself contain five syllables. I love footnotes.

in *Breakfast at Tiffany's*. She came closer and smiled. I smiled back.

'Liza!'

It was a staggering coincidence – in its defence, all I can say is that London is a very small place sometimes.

'Hello Tim, how are you? Do you fancy a cup of tea? I only live down the road.'

'Lovely idea, I've even got milk, if that helps . . .'

'I'm sure I've probably got some, too, but that's very sweet of you.'

It had been ages and ages since I'd seen Liza. In fact, the last time I'd seen her, she'd been one of history's most radiant and happy brides.

'How is Ed?' I asked of her implausibly tall, stunningly nice husband.

'He's great, although he's out today – he'll be so sad to miss you. Fun bumping into you, I've got loads of news. This way.'

The list of people who are genuinely sad to miss me can normally be limited to the parents of girls I've fallen foul of, staring down the barrels of shotguns and cursing their aim. However, Ed is one of the rare exceptions and I couldn't believe of all the days to bump into Liza I'd managed one when Ed was away. Nevertheless, it is always a blissful joy to see Liza and plus I have a golden rule in life: never turn down the offer of a cup of tea.

Inside, we drank tea, laughed and nattered. There really was loads to catch up on, especially the news that Liza was pregnant. I had missed so much by being away in paper boats. During our second cup, a dark force began to grow on the dull edges of my brain. These forces grew and developed into an army of thought before bursting out of my mouth, 'Liza . . . you speak French don't you?'

'I should, I grew up there.'

That was what I'd been trying to tell myself to remember.

'I even went to school there and everything.'

My mind flashed to Liza's 21st birthday party years before. I knew it! It was in France.

'You couldn't do me a favour could you?'

She laughed. 'As long as it's not running the marathon as I'm not sure that's good for the baby.'

I explained my chronic lack of French and what I was trying to achieve.

'I mean I think it would be semi-OK. I probably could just about be understood if I practised really hard at it but I just want someone who can speak it like a native as we've got to be absolutely clear with them so they can make a judgement on it.'

'I'd love to give them a call.'

This had been a blinding flash of inspiration as although Liza can quite justifiably be compared to Audrey Hepburn in appearance, her voice is even prettier than that. She could put honey into early retirement. If there were a weapon that was guaranteed to charm the hearts of French Naval Command, I'd just found it. She did have a warning though.

'I think it might be tough as they're not really on the same wavelength as us on this sort of thing.'

A day later my phone rang. It was Liza. 'They're not convinced at all. He says he'd like to see some plans.'

Douglas might have been drinking with me the night it was conceived but, as it turned out when the plans arrived, he was justifiably a multi-award winner. The plans were brilliant: totally meticulous down to the last degree. As finely expressed as the sayings and equations of Wittgenstein. He had taken beer-mat design mark 12E, thought through the problems, solved them and made the craft that now appeared on the paper seem more indomitable and seaworthy than the *Ark Royal*.

Pleased at being able to sort this one fast I said, 'Sure, what's the fax number?'

The next day Liza called to tell me the news.

'Right. It's taken quite a bit of talking but he says his advice is clear and it's the advice of his government: they're not happy about you rowing the Channel but that goes for anyone. He said the French government don't like anyone swimming or rowing the Channel at all and their official position is that no one should do it. They can't understand the English fascination with it. However, people ignore that every time they swim or row the Channel. So he says, bearing that in mind, if you're willing to take the risk and promise to have a safety boat near you, there's nothing he will do to stop you.'

'Thank you Liza, that's really good of you. Can you phone him and say I'd like to call to thank him personally.'

'Sure.'

Fifteen minutes later I heard the now familiar foreign dialling tone, then a click.

'Hello. This is Tim FitzHigham just phoning to say thank you for your help.'

'No problem. Sorry I couldn't understand you before, I thought you were Dutch.'

What I wanted to say at that point was not what came out of my mouth: 'Thank you for being so understanding and I promise to undertake this safely.'

'It will be hard but we hope it goes well for you. I'll put some documents on the fax for you.'

'Thank you. I'm looking forward to it.'

His English was not great but at least he was now using it. This all seemed like a huge step in the right direction.

I put down the phone and called Liza back.

'Thank you so much. They even spoke English this time.'

'They like it when you make an effort.'

'They seem fine with everything.'

'I think he was impressed with the plans. That seemed to swing it. However, I feel it's only fair to warn you that although they are fine with it today, the French have been known to change their minds.'

The bath plan was coming together and the spirit of the Entente Cordiale was very much alive and kicking in the 21st century. Hurrah for the French.

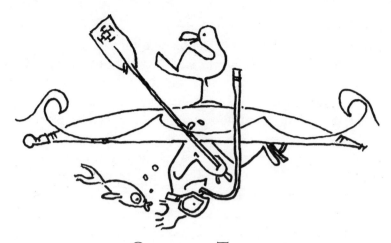

Chapter Two

ROW, ROW, ROW YOUR BATH, GENTLY TO THE SEA . . .

'Give me a camel and I can get anywhere.'

Gordon of Khartoum

From an early age, I'd spent years trying to learn to row. I'm qualified to be a rower: I went to university. That should count. My college was famous for its rowers. While there, I spent weeks during both the Michaelmas and Epiphany terms under the river, obsessed with trying to master rowing. I remember my coach on the riverbank screaming encouragement, as only the truly deluded can, while I heroically turned the boat over and sank it in a variety of impressive ways. I transformed capsizing into an art form: the slow-motion capsize; the one where I'd fake that I was going to capsize on the *left* before righting myself just long enough to hear him shout enthusiastically 'well done', then flipping it over effortlessly on the *right*; and my favourite: capsizing while doing up my shoes. To be that bad takes talent.

Rowing should be a simple and beautiful thing. In an ideal world start with legs fully extended so your bottom is furthest from your feet, push your hands down to lift the blade from off the water (this is known as the release). Then you turn the blade (known as feathering) so that the face of the blade runs parallel to the surface of the water as you move up the stroke to the top of the slide. This is sometimes called the recovery. At the top of the stroke, your sliding seat can't go any further towards your heels. Your buttocks are nearest your feet and your arms outstretched in front of you. In this position square the blades so that they're now at right angles to the water. Then pop the blades down into the water in the glorious moment known as the catch. Pushing your bottom away from your feet you glide down the slide with as much power as possible to the moment known as the finish where your legs will be fully extended again. Push your hands downwards, raise the oar up out of the water and you're back at the release. Simply repeat the process until you've either won the race or crashed into the bank. It involves balance, speed, strength and mental toughness. Rowing is justifiably called the sport of kings.

It didn't seem to matter how many times the above details were explained to me, I could not get it right. Somehow the blades contrived to be feathering when I was trying to catch or I finished as they were at the recovery. Sometimes it was the boat that would make things difficult by demanding my attention at the top of the stroke when I was administering to the finish. Through all these problems I never once blamed my tools.

Once I went out rowing on the coldest day of the year. I kicked snow off the landing stage where they launched the boats. It went into the river in snowball-sized lumps and sank in snowball-sized lumps. Never before had I made it back to the bank without capsizing but my coach thought that this would be my great day. I had managed eight strokes without capsizing the week before (my personal best) and so everything seemed in my favour. It really was freezing cold and there wasn't another boat out that day. I could see my own breath as I pulled out into the centre of the river. I took a couple of strokes and didn't capsize. Just six more and I'd equalled my personal best. The river was racing, carrying me with it. I felt the boat run underneath me, this was how rowing was meant to be. The water made a pleasing sound as I successfully managed another one; in a flash I'd strung an extra three together before attempting the tricky seventh stroke.

With the poise of a prima ballerina I gently rotated the boat just less than 90 degrees right to hold it half above and half below the water's surface. I paused long enough to wave politely at the bank before serenely flipping it the remaining 90 degrees and slipping under the icy water. I gulped for air; only ice came. I was upside down, still attached to the boat, racing downstream in freezing cold water. Would I drown first or die of cold? I managed to get my head above water, gasped down air and swam desperately for the bank.

Clearly worried about me, my coach shouted from the bank, 'Go back for the boat! Don't come back in without it!'

I'd forced that normally mild-mannered man to hit the tone of a drill sergeant. I was too cold to argue so turned back to get frost-bite and fetch the boat.

'If you can find the blades too, that would be good, only with you learning to row we're getting short of them in the boat house!'

I got the boat and one oar back to the bank but was really cold. I knew it was serious when he looked and me and said, 'I think you'd better get back up to college and hope the hot water's on . . .'

I didn't hear the rest of what he said. I knew where I should be: safely in a hot shower, wrapped up in a bosom or buried beneath a mountain of towels. Mainly, safe on land.

That evening, as I went into the dining hall, the rest of college laughed. The clear imprints of my bare feet in the inches of snow formed a path running up from the riverbank to the college. They stood out like neon monuments to stupidity beside the many sensible shoe and welly prints coming home from lectures. It was now commonly known that if there were footprints in the snow, I'd been learning to row again.

When you win a regatta the boat club lets you keep your oars as a mark of respect. It's a big honour. At the end of that year as a mark of irony the Boat Club Captain presented me with a broken oar simply for having survived a capsize on the coldest day of the year. Embarrassingly, following that there was even a college four[3]

---

[3]For those people who don't row, me among them, a four is the most common unit of rowing crews. Single rowers are called scullers. They row in a racing boat made for one called a scull. Two rowers is a pair. Four is a four and eight rowers is an eight. Whoever patented this system was a man of staggering charm.

named after me. The 'Higham First Four'[4] was the slowest crew on the river and finished triumphantly last in every race. I hate irony but I was never even good enough to row for them.

That night I sat swathed in blankets, my still-numb feet in a bowl of hot water, as close as it was possible to be to my radiator. As I drank warm Coca-Cola that night (we were told this prevented the Weil's Disease, rife in the river[5]), I mused that it might have been better if I had died or drowned earlier than face the ignominy of my failure.

If my life had been a Hollywood movie I would have turned it round the next morning, learnt to row, trained to 'Eye of the Tiger', won the Henley regatta and married Jennifer Aniston with Adam Sandler gurning in the background. It wasn't Hollywood. I continued to capsize for three more weeks before I gave up rowing for ever, invented drinking croquet and discovered alcoholism.

Sitting at my desk, I snapped out of the reminiscences of a capsize ninja. The campaign of problem carpet-bombing stepped up another gear. The terrifying memories of my career as a serial sinker reminded me that there was a problem to climb bigger than the Matterhorn: I couldn't row.

I started a list, as there were now so many problems I began to run the risk of not even being able to remember them. Forgetting my problems would in itself be a problem. I put 'Having too many problems and forgetting one of them' at the top of my new list. Underneath this I wrote, 'No money to fund the project'. Beneath that I wrote, 'Not speaking French well enough'. Next on the list was, 'A total lack of even basic knowledge of the sea and maritime matters'. Finally, shuddering, I added, 'I can't row' before slumping back in the chair.

---

[4]The 'Higham First Four' colours were green and palatinate – a kind of pinkie purple – quartered. I was known as Tim Higham at college. FitzHigham simply means 'Son of Higham' and always seemed such a mouthful and so awkward to spell that I didn't use it back then.
[5]The Coca-Cola does not have to be drunk warm but I was cold – also I'm sure having thought about it that another brand of cola would be equally effective but at the time we all thought Coke had magical powers to ward off Weil's Disease. I've suggested this to the Coca-Cola empire as a marketing strategy but am yet to hear back from them: 'Beat Weil's Disease – drink Coke!' (cue jingle).

I've never liked thinking about problems. The main reason for this is that, like a mummy rabbit and a daddy rabbit who love each other very much, when you have two problems very often they suddenly become six. Sure enough just as I was thinking this, a sixth major setback popped out: I was chronically unfit.

I'd had a brief moment of sobriety and fitness during the paper-boat challenge. This was largely inflicted on me by my loving cousin and had been a short flash of sunshine in the violent storm of my utter unfitness. Also, if you've never rowed, you are unaware of the very high level of fitness it requires. Rowers are among the fittest athletes on the planet. This problem was serious, what was I supposed to do?

Jack had now left frog-like shock far behind him and swung into action.

'I've found you a rowing machine, you know one of those training Ergo things, at nearly no cost . . .'

It belonged to a girl we'd known from university who was going abroad and couldn't take it with her. She was a great rower at college and also very beautiful. I get terribly shy around beautiful women and had always found her impossible to talk to. Still, beauty is dulled by age, I thought as I rang the doorbell at her flat in Clapham. Besides, I'd grown up, so wouldn't be shy this time.

When the door opened the eyes that met mine beheld a stammering, nervous apparition that looked like the logical result of breeding a Fraggle with *What-A-Mess*. They blinked, opened again and managed to mix bemusement with a slight giggling twinkle. If anything she'd got more beautiful with time.

'Oh, hi Tim . . . it's upstairs.' She looked at me as I stood stammering on her doorstep. 'Come in.'

We dismantled the Ergo and I took the first bit down to the car. We agreed it would be called Betty. Arriving back at the top of the stairs to fetch the second bit she looked thoughtfully into the distance.

'So, Jack says you're going to row the Channel. That's a really tough challenge – personally, I don't know anyone who's managed that.'

'Erm . . . neither do I, really.'

'I don't remember you being much of a rower at college – in fact Tim, did you even row?'

'No,' I lied.

Thank goodness, she'd obviously left before I took up sinking. I hate lying but thought it was better to leave her with the impression that I was someone with great rowing potential, untapped at college, rather than embarrass myself further with the truth. The door closed on the stunning eyes and I tried to cram the second half of the Ergo into the back of my battered car. At least I now had something to train on. That had to be a step in the right direction.

Driving away, this one positive soon turned negative. I was the worst rower in the history of my college with the balance of a cowpat (in the words of my long-suffering coach). Yet insanely, now I thought I could take on the trickiest single-seat rowing challenge in the world.

The car turned into a rabbit warren as another problem surfaced. I needed to find someone to foot the bill for Jack's 'nearly no cost' and help pay for the Ergo. The Thomas Crapper money was specifically tied up in bathroom products and I'd budgeted nothing for training costs. Bother. Getting out of the car I pulled out my list and wrote 'Hopeless at budgeting' underneath 'Chronically unfit'. On the plus side, both of these qualities do qualify me for one thing: being Chancellor of the Exchequer.

After unpacking the Ergo, I arrived back at my desk and pulled out my phone.

'Hi, is Kenny there?'

Kenny was the kind newspaper editor who fought so hard to help me with the paper-boat project. The paper boat almost failed to happen several times and Kenny had been instrumental in making sure it came off. Through these trials, including my rotting skin and near death, we'd become great mates. He's got a brilliant sense of humour and is the only man I know who is merely four generations removed from a caveman (his ancestor was a nook-dwelling highland shepherd). I felt sure he'd help.

'You've got another plan? Oh good . . .'

He managed to say 'oh good' in a way that combined several emotions: the first, 'not another of your plans, Tim, the last one almost got me sacked'; secondly, 'it's bound to be a cracker – what's the plan this time? Paragliding strapped to a piece of toast?'; and thirdly, 'of course I'll be involved – what do you need?' That's the thing about truly great friends, you know what they mean and can always rely on their help.

'Fancy a beer after work?'

Over a few of London's finest we laughed about the paper boat. If he'd not decided to edit newspapers, he'd have been writing jokes. At one point only two people thought the paper-boat plan could work and both of them currently sat either side of the pub table.

'So what's the plan this time?'

'I want to row the English Channel in a bath.'

'Of course. What do you need?'

With a dry smile, little chuckle and sip of beer Kenny had joined the bath team. Over a couple more beers we discussed the various things I'd been putting in place so far before Kenny said, 'Why stop there, Tim? Why not row it all the way to Tower Bridge? In fact, I bet you one pint of beer you can't make it from France to Tower Bridge in that bath.'

His words were strangely reminiscent of the ones that had almost got me killed in the paper boat but, thinking only of beer, my brain knee-jerked into a response so quickly that it kicked logic in the crotch.

'You're on!'

In my head and not having checked the charts, Tower Bridge didn't seem that far away from Folkestone, Dover or wherever it was that you stopped when you'd rowed the Channel. I pulled out my list and wrote, 'Check where the Channel finishes'.

Later I would discover that in just two ill-chosen words, I'd lengthened the aim of my journey by 170 miles to win a single pint of beer.

Over the next few months I embarked on a gruelling drive to get fit. I looted bookshops and read tonnes of books on fitness. One advocated, 'Always run in trainers'; another, 'Find some comfy boots'; a third, 'Never run in boots'. Spurred on by this clarity I read a fourth, 'Cycling or swimming is good, running is not.'

In darkened corners of bookshops all over the place I found books on rowing technique, too. They seemed just as unified in their thought. One, 'Sliding seats are a must for long-distance rowing'; another, 'Never use a sliding seat for long-distance rowing.' A third, 'Meat cleaver blades are best for rowing at sea', and a fourth, 'Meat cleaver blades are very damaging to your back over long distances, this is especially true when rowing at sea.'

As well as being confused by general fitness and rowing books I also read books on diet. The first one said, 'Always start your day with a bowl of cereal'; another, 'Never eat anything but fruit before midday.' I decided these books were cunningly designed to make me stay in bed till after midday, on the phone to a broker buying shares in a cereal company. I was stumped. No two books had the same advice.

There's a senate of faceless and formless beings that always get quoted by others when the quotee needs validation. This senate is known simply as 'They'. They say 'a little knowledge is a dangerous thing' but the same also seemed to be true of too much opinion in a field that demands more clear research. I'd taken to eating both cereal and fruit before midday just to be on the safe side.

I sat in the old barn at my parents' house looking at the piles of totally confusing and expensive books (I hadn't budgeted for them either). If there's no clear lead on how to get fit, there's no wonder we have an obesity problem in this country.

I gazed over at where I'd proudly assembled Betty the Ergo. During all the months I'd been reading about getting fit, Betty had been sitting unused. I was becoming PhD-level educated on the confusing subject of getting fit but had absolutely no practical knowledge. To think this over further, I went to the pub.

That Thursday night I was going to stay with my friend James in Putney. Jimmie is a very safe bet to talk to about fitness as he regards any form of physical exercise at best as insulting and at worst permanently damaging. As often happens in families, his brother is a super-fit soldier. Jimmie had just got back from weeks away touring as an actor and as usual was full of great stories. After a good night drinking and nattering we went back to his flat. Following more laughter and a nightcap I dropped into bed. I was sleeping in the room his older brother had stayed in a few days before.

I woke up the next morning with a hangover they wrote about in the Bible and, through eyelids lined with sand, glanced over at the bedside table. On it was a book called *Fit for Life* by Sir Ranulph Fiennes. This was one fitness book I'd not read.

With my head beating like a marching band and Jimmie groaning in the room down the corridor, I slowly began to read the first chapter. Midway through, I suddenly got the urge to make a cup of hot tea with lashings of milk and sugar. Then following the advice in *Fit for Life* Chapter 3 about having as little milk as you can and no sugar in tea, I took the milky sugared tea back to the kitchen and made the first cup of black tea I can ever remember having.

I poured in the water. Steam rose off the nefarious dark brew below. Tentatively I lifted the cup to my lips. There are people who would rather lose a testicle than drink tea black and I was among them. I took a slurp. It wasn't too bad, but hard to tell with just a slurp. I blew over the surface of the tea then took a bigger slurp. Like a wine connoisseur I swilled it round my mouth to try and work it out. It was much more bitter than I'd expected. A third gulp passed my lips. My mind was made up. I liked it. It felt somehow pure. In just three sips of tea that book had struck more of a chord with me than all the others put together. Like St Paul on the road to Damascus, I'd been transformed, only in Putney with a huge hangover.

As I went back to bed with my gorgeous black tea and read the rest of the book, the single chord turned into a number-one hit. It's a regime suggested by a man I've always admired. This gave me inspiration through example. It's also a very practical set of guidelines and suggestions. It gives you advice to achieve whatever stage of fitness is appropriate to you. The main thing I liked about it was the suggestion that you should find what works for you and, most importantly, stick to it.

Finally, with *Fit for Life* manacled to my side, I started training in earnest. I only realised the terrifying level of my chronic unfitness when I started to train. Betty the Ergo was an incredibly cruel mistress. I started gently. I'd arrive in the old barn at my parents' and spend some time stretching. Then I'd spend time begging Betty not to hurt me too much, before mounting her and doing 3,000-metre distances. It may sound like a lot but 3,000 metres is a relatively short distance. It's the blink of an eye to someone seriously wanting to row the Channel but I wanted to build up my ability to do this and not pull any muscles, tendons etc before attempting longer distances.

I didn't have rower's shoulders, or, in fact, strong shoulders of any sort, and my lower back wasn't used to Ergos – this is traditionally the area that gets a lot of punishment in rowing. So many people I knew had started training on macho impenetrable distances, pulled something in the first week and had to give up rowing for ages. To keep any hope of rowing the Channel alive, this could not happen to me.

After a while I progressed to 6,000-metre distances. At this point I added weights, more stretching and running, to build all the various muscles and support the Ergo training. Betty was the most unflinchingly vindictive of women. I discovered quickly that one of the main challenges of an Ergo is mental.

Finally, I was up to pulling decent times at 10,000 metres with running, stretching and weights. This was the regime I kept up, pounding away as much as possible to try and maintain the level of fitness I'd achieved. At the time I was working in another temp job at the Foreign Office in London in an attempt to pay off various booksellers. I had to leave the house at 6.30 a.m. and arrived back in at 8 p.m. It was one of the more demoralising things to come in from a full day at work and realise I'd got 10,000 gruelling metres to pull on the Ergo.

There was another significant problem. As well as training and temping I had a very precious girlfriend.

It was a very hot day in late summer when I'd first seen her. I was staying with a cousin who was studying for a Masters. I'd gone to pick him up after college one evening. In a meadow behind one of the halls of residence some people he knew had organised a lazy game of rounders. I hadn't realised we'd be seeing anyone else so was still in a pair of eccentric bright orange tartan trousers. I was testing them to see if he and I could get away with them as the new family tartan. As we lived in the middle of nowhere (nowhere being deepest rural Wiltshire) I'd assumed I could test them in private.

I wasn't sure I could meet his friends wearing something quite so inexplicable but he insisted, supportively, 'What are you talking about? I've barely ever seen you wear something appropriate.'

We arrived at a barbeque; a friend of his was cooking. As the greatest smell on earth filled the air, my cousin introduced me to his friends and there she was. My cousin smiled ingeniously and left us. I followed my usual protocol on these occasions of stammering, trying to disguise it with a joke and looking at the floor. She laughed at the joke and at the same time unleashed a devastating smile. She was blonde, foreign and was studying at the college too.

We were called over to play lazy rounders. Oddly enough, lazy rounders is a game I'm normally quite good at. The main reason for this is that I'm left handed and very often there are fewer fielders in the place where I want to hit the ball and in lazy rounders no one can be bothered to move around so I normally manage to score fairly well. We were on the same team and she teased me and laughed throughout the game but, I noted with interest, smiled quietly when I scored.

After everyone got bored of rounders and dispersed to eat, chat and drink, the gentle haze of a hot English summer evening descended on the meadow. I threw her a rugby ball; she caught it and threw it back. Probably as a girl, it's not the most romantic thing to have a rugby ball thrown in your direction but such are the peculiar courtship rituals of the English gentleman.

Within weeks, something of a land-speed record for me, we'd got together. Scared by how effortlessly well it was going I conformed to a horrid, shameful stereotype and bolted.

Oddly, and in a series of genuine coincidences, similar to bumping into Liza that day with the milk, I'd kept bumping into her on Valentine's Day each year. In Battersea one Valentine's, I popped out to buy some bread and arriving at the baker's, the only other person in there was her. Other, greater thinkers would have seen this as an omen; I merely filed this under 'Odd' in my head and buttled on with life.

I always move fast in affairs of the heart and a mere two years after first bolting I finally asked her out for supper. Within a day we were totally happy and inseparably together. There hadn't been a single moment of unhappiness since then, just rather sickeningly joy, happiness and smiles.

She had been with me throughout the paper-boat adventure and was now preparing for the bath trip. I'm not sure either of us realised quite what an inconvenience to us spending time together it would be but throughout it all she had been brilliantly under-standing and selflessly, guilt-inducingly supportive. In the foreign land that created her, they clearly made women well. What a girl.

Betty had finished giving me the pounding of my life for the evening. Later, as my muscles tingled, like fingers on a frosty morning, I lay back in bed. This was an arduous period of training. I listened to the birds. I was positive. Probably due to the previously unseen levels of exercise-induced happy hormones running round my brain, although it could have been because my punishing training regime was going really well. I was now getting very fit.

There was just one slight oversight in my indomitable training regime. I'd still not actually trained in a boat.

CHAPTER THREE

IN A BEAUTIFUL PEA GREEN BOAT

'Rowing seems to me to be a monotonous pursuit, and somehow wasteful
to be making all that effort and be going in the wrong direction.'

Peter Ustinov

With my training going so well, I turned my attention to other matters. During lunch hours at the Foreign Office, I'd been hunting for a boat maker to turn the plan Douglas and I had made into a reality. Many boat makers had not believed it possible and most had laughed me off the phone. Some had not even taken my calls. Without a boat maker to help me adapt the bath I was stuck. I didn't know a keel from a stern; I certainly couldn't adapt a bathtub to withstand the high seas.

As a result of the paper-boat trip I'd been made an Honorary Freeman of the ancient Company of Watermen and Lightermen of the River Thames. This may not mean a lot to many people but on the river it's important. The Watermen are respected. They have trained for seven years to gain the right to captain freight and passengers up and down the Thames.

I like being a Waterman as it's not some glorified old buffers' club but a hard-working organisation. Currently, the European Union is trying to strip them of their rights in order to make the Thames less safe. However, hopefully the common sense of hundreds of years will win out in the end. Watermen know everyone on the Thames.

I stood outside the Foreign Office in King Charles Street under the statue of Clive of India with my phone pressed to my ear and called Waterman's Hall.

After a brief chat and catch up with the assistant clerk, she put me through to the Clerk of the Watermen. He's the Company's chief administrator on a day-to-day basis and through the paper boat, I'd got to know him quite well.

'Hello, Colin? It's Tim – I need someone to help me adapt a bath to go across the Channel.'

'The bath's not made of paper is it?'

'Not this time.'

'Have you heard of Mark Edwards? He's your man – he once reconstructed a 17th-century Dutch submarine design using a couple of Thames skiffs and some wax.'

'So you think he might help?'

'I think he's the only one who might help. I'll find you the number . . .'

I made repeated attempts to phone Mark and finally, after leaving the phone to ring for what must have been close to a world record, a thick London accent answered.

'Hello?'

'Hi, I'd like to speak to Mark please.'

'Oh . . .'

The phone hit something and I heard the same voice disappear off into the distance shouting, 'Mark!' I held. Eventually a lighter voice with a slight West Country twang came on the line.

'Hello, this is Mark.'

'Hi, Colin at Waterman's Hall gave me your number and suggested I call, I need a bit of help . . .'

I arranged to see Mark for a beer one night after he'd finished work. I thought it might be best to explain the bath project to him face to face. As it happened Douglas was in town that night so said he'd come along too. I arrived in Richmond, got out of the car and was just about to pay the meter in the car park on Friars Lane. A voice behind me shouted, 'You don't have to pay that now, it's after time.' Douglas was early.

'Hi mate, thanks for coming.'

'Thought it might be useful if I was here. We can talk about it in boatie terms.'

We walked down Water Lane and passed the White Cross pub on our left. Ahead of us was the bridge and in front of it a floating restaurant.

'Stunning isn't it.'

My mind was fixed on how to get Mark to convert the bath for as little money as possible. It was only when Douglas mentioned it that I became aware of how beautiful Richmond looked in the warm evening light. We walked down the river's edge past a few slipways towards the floating restaurant. On the towpath, running parallel to the river, were a series of boathouses. Most of the doors were shut but out of the remaining open one came a man, about 5' 8", with shortish brown hair and a bounce in his step.

'So you're going to try and row the Channel then,' he smiled, wryly.

It was true; Watermen did know everything[6].

'How did you know?'

'I was speaking to Colin the other day. Fancy a beer or a glass of something?'

Douglas, Mark and I sat at a picnic table outside the boathouse in the setting sun and talked things through. Mark is the latest in a 300-year-old line of craftsmen operating in the original boat maker's workshop under Richmond Bridge. The workshop is partly under the arches and was built with the bridge.

Mark was in full flood. 'The story goes that to encourage business, the bridge company gave a free or low fixed rent concession to the original occupant of the boathouse. He was a Waterman, see, and they're always clever, so this first boat maker registered his rent-free concession in the name of his young grandson. So, to the great annoyance of the bridge-building company, the boat-making business thrived on the same low rent for the lifetime of three generations of the family until the original grandson died.'

---

[6] I discovered later that officially, Mark had not been sworn in as a Waterman for some reason or other, but in a day-to-day sense he's very much a waterman through and through.

'How old was he?'

'Oh, a ripe old age . . . over 70. Then his son took it on.'

Mark chuckled. He was a Cornishman who came up to the Thames as an apprentice, fell in love with the river and had stayed there ever since. After a long evening together and many laughs, he agreed to help make the bath float.

Douglas and I left the boathouse and walked back along the towpath.

'I think he'll do a great job for you.'

I looked back to see Mark sitting under the arches outside his boathouse sewing something or possibly doing a bit of ropework and knew Douglas was right. Boat makers had sat doing rope work and sewing cushions there for over 300 years before going up the hill. Mark was as much a part of Richmond as the bridge he sat under. I felt comfortable with him. There was total serenity in the scene.

'Yes. I think he will.'

I'd been stretched for weeks. Tiredness at my brutal regime was beginning to affect both my training and job. Finding Mark was the camel that broke me. Mark was located in Richmond, I was training in Hertfordshire and my temp job was in Whitehall. I couldn't pin down my job, keep up 10,000-metre Ergos, weights, running, see Mark and undertake the huge organisational backlog that was building up all at once. I took out an overdraft, stopped the job and started spending time at the boatyard.

As arranged, within days of our first meeting I arrived back at the boathouse. Richmond by the river was just as serene and stunning as before. I walked along the towpath to the boathouses and was met by a paint-addled youth wiping his nose on his hand.

'Hi, is Mark about?'

What to the untrained ear would constitute a cockney accent, but perhaps not the same one that originally picked up the phone, emanated from somewhere beneath the paint, 'Think he's some-where in there . . .'

He wafted a hand vaguely over his shoulder and wandered off in the direction of what had once been a boat. I walked over to one of the arches and entered. This time the boathouse was the antithesis of serenity. This was foreign, chaotic and confusing. In every nook and cranny, there were similar paint-, grease- and sawdust-ridden young lads pawing over bits of boat in various stages of repair. Not one of the boats in their capable hands looked like it would float.

I shouted above the din of various tools scraping and loud music blaring out of an old stereo, 'Has anyone seen Mark?'

The eyes of several youths darted up to view me suspiciously. One raised his head. 'Think he went out . . .'

I nodded sagely. 'If he comes back, tell him I'm in the teashop.'

I left for the teashop under another of the arches and ordered a cup of tea.

'Milk and sugar?'

'No thanks, I'll have it black.'

'Are you sure?'

This had been happening a lot.

'Yes, thank you for asking.'

'Really?'

'Yes please.'

Time went by. I made a few calls and read a bit before going back to the boathouse. Again, there was a loud din of combined humming, scraping and discord as now there were two stereos tuned to competing radio stations.

'Has anyone seen Mark?'

The same youth raised his head.

'Think he's in his office.'

'Thank you . . .'

I stood motionless.

'. . . Where's his office?'

One of the youths, who was covered in wood shavings, smiled and put down the scrapey thing he was using. 'I'll show you.'

We went further into the bowels of the boathouse arch and turned left through a door kept shut by a large fishing weight rigged up as a counter balance.

'Hi Mark, when did you get back?'

'I've been here all the time. You're late.'

The wood-shaving lad smiled. 'I think the lads have been playing tricks on him.'

He left the office and Mark laughed. Over the coming days I

tried to understand the boathouse. It seemed to comprise the master boat maker, a couple of carpenters (one of them a master carpenter) and myriad apprentices who may or may not turn up on any given day. It's not a company in the modern corporate sense of the word, more a loose collective of interwoven friendships and interest groups. To an outsider it was hard to believe that this still existed in modern London. This was an ancient world that had continued rampant and unchecked since at least the 1700s. Since then they've used the same tools, sat on the same seats and drunk the same tea. This gives the place a feeling of solid familiarity, confidence and over three centuries of washing up.

All the invoices were still written by Mark in beautiful copper-plate handwriting. It was like walking into *Oliver Twist*. The apprentices always seemed to be borrowing from, and lending money to, each other and to their various girlfriends who hung around outside the boatyard. When they'd finished that game for the day, they'd borrow money from Mark against their wages. One had seemingly advanced his wages well into the next year. Yet Mark still lent him money if he asked. Tolerance like this doesn't exist anywhere else except in the most exclusive city banks. There was such a complex matrix of who owed money to whom that I became certain there was a fiver that had never actually left the boathouse but had simply been passed around between them to cancel out one debit or incur another.

It wasn't easy fitting into such a closely knit world. I floundered, attempting to fetch numerous glass hammers, left-handed spirit levels, and waited for the kettle to boil at plug sockets that had long been disconnected. Many of the apprentices thought the entire project of rowing the Channel in a bath was an enormous wind up. They seemed to think I was some sort of trickster who would eventually reveal that the entire thing was arranged just to make them look silly.

Things turned round in a single day. A very big man wandered up the riverbank towards where I was working with the apprentices. He'd either got back from a day's work on one of the freight ships downriver, or seven years in prison. From looking at him, it was hard to tell. I'd heard the apprentices talking about him earlier, they respected him – he was hard. I felt nervous as he heaved his way towards us. There was a noticeable awed hush in the workshop. My first thought was to look for the nearest exit. In any kind of confrontation, this man would win.

'So, are you Tim?' he said with a gruffness that suggested aggression.

'Yes,' I said, although finding the fine line between 'said' and 'whimpered'.

For a big man he moved fast. I saw a blur in the fading light of the workshop. The next thing I knew I'd been engulfed in a handshake that drew me into a mighty hug that even a bear might think twice about. I stood back shocked.

'I read all about the paper boat, I've even got the paper cuttings in my cab [the cabin of the freight boat]. As a Waterman apprentice, you've made us proud – well done.'

The apprentices were almost as shocked as me.

He turned to them. 'You know he's a Waterman?'

The apprentices were now *as* shocked as me. I hadn't mentioned my Freedom of the Company to them but it had obviously been in the paper. One of them wiped his hand across his face.

'Really?'

The big man replied, 'Yes. And it's rare that is . . . an honour . . .'

I knew it was fairly rare but it seemed it was rarer than that. With one handshake and a bear hug I never looked back in the boatyard. They seemed to have accepted me. Now I got to ask newer apprentices to fetch the glass hammer. They even let me in on the tricks they were planning for Mark. It was a great time. I got to see the medieval craft of the boat maker up close; an old world that just manages to co-exist with the new one. I think some of them still thought the entire bath plan was a ruse to make them look silly but now it seemed they felt they were in on the gag.

I was now commuting between my parents' house in Hertfordshire, where Betty the avenging angel was living, and the boatyard in Richmond. Less than ideal, as Richmond was on the other side of London. Short of moving to Richmond or finding somewhere else to be able to train for free I had no choice. Hertfordshire was shrouded in a quiet tension between my mother and me. Normally, Mum and I get on really well. She's wonderful in my eyes; I've loved her since I remember anything. When I was small, she used to take out a guitar and sing to me beneath the trees – I loved that, real Julie Andrews-style mothering. Just great. I have a very special mum but I'd noticed there was a tension in the air. I didn't understand it. What was causing it?

I'd come up with another plan to raise cash for a charity. She'd loved the last one and was pleased at the amount of money that had been raised. I'd discovered a new sport and was getting good at that. Mum was a great rower in her day so it couldn't be that which was causing the tension. I was on the Thames every day. Mum rowed on the Thames and loved the river, so it couldn't be that. The plans were moving ahead really fast, which had to be good. There were problems but they were all being sorted. The bath plan was irrevocably in motion and nothing, it seemed, could stop me from actually having a chance of completing it. With all these positives, she should be happy. I was really puzzled. Bearing in mind the open, brilliant relationship I have with my mum, I asked Dad.

'I think it's something to do with your Uncle Tony . . .'

Uh-oh. That was a big problem. How had I forgotten it? For someone who is normally quite thoughtful, this was a staggering lapse. It wasn't even that I'd forgotten him; I just hadn't thought through the impact on my family of my current decisions in relation to him.

Uncle Tony or Great-Uncle Anthony to give him his full name was my grandma's older brother. Handsome, strong, clever and a crack shot. Like many men of his generation, when World War II started he joined the Royal Air Force. His plane was shot down over occupied France but in a stroke of luck, uncharacteristic in the family, he was able to land it safely and get his crew out.

I am from the famously blond-haired looks-a-little-like-Gonzo-from-the-Muppets side of the family. Great-Uncle Tony was from the ravishingly good-looking, dark-haired, dark-eyed side of the family. Also unlike me, he spoke fluent French. Before the war he'd always had some gorgeous European lady to escort somewhere and this helped his skills as a linguist greatly. So finding himself trapped in occupied France he impersonated a Frenchman. Disguised by his dark hair, tanned skin, fluent French and with a twinkle in his eye, he managed, remarkably, to get his crew (none of whom spoke French) across occupied France with a mixture of cunning and charm. Arriving at the coast he put them in a boat and, being a schoolboy rowing champion, he decided to row back to England.

It's always made me feel very small when I hear stories like that: the incredible courage and bravery of very ordinary people. He rowed the Channel to escape from the Nazis. With exhausted relief, when he saw the white cliffs he shouted to his crew, 'I'll swim the rest of the way . . . race you . . .' Then he jumped overboard. This was typical of the man, a sense of fun even during danger. His crew made it back to the UK and all went on to become top-ranking officers in the RAF. They've all talked of his extraordinary bravery and courage in getting them out of the situation. Uncle Tony, having saved them, was never seen again.

A couple of months later there was a break-in at my grandma's family house and his things, including almost every photo of him, were stolen. It may have been a coincidence that his were the only things taken but if it was, it's always struck me as being a very incredible one.

It was particularly hard on my grandma who was then left to wonder if he was perhaps still alive. Many attempts were made to find him, involving everyone from Winston Churchill to the French Resistance. All had their twists and turns and all sadly ended fruitlessly. Mystery continued to shroud my heroic pilot great-uncle and he was finally added to the memorial at Runnymede as being still missing in action 65 years on. He would have liked Runnymede as it overlooks the Thames, a river on which he too rowed as a schoolboy with some success.

Realising I was now attempting to row the very stretch of water where Great-Uncle Tony was last sighted hit me hard. The family story of his disappearance, the one picture of him I'd seen when I was small, the expression on my grandma's face as she looked at the image of the brother she'd lost, all ran through my head.

My family had already lost someone they loved to the Channel. How had I been dimmer than a candle in a sock? I sat in Hertfordshire alone, with thoughts of cancelling the project. Running it through my mind, I realised I couldn't. Things had already gone too far.

I sat thinking of things I might be able to say to try to console Mum. None of them were any good and most of them didn't even make sense. 'Don't worry, Mum, I'm a better athlete than him . . .' That wouldn't work. 'Don't worry, Mum, I've got a better boat than him . . .' If the first one wouldn't work, this one was just pie in the sky.

It was no good. There was only one course of action left to me. I must get on with beating the Channel and make very sure I made it back. In the moment of my new resolve I felt oddly very close to a man I'd never known.

Arriving back at my desk I was again hit by the nagging feeling that there was someone important I'd forgotten to talk to about my plan. I phoned Dom.

'Is there anyone I should have spoken to that I've missed?'

'I don't think so, you've checked it with the French Navy and the English Coastguard . . .'

'Bother. I knew it.'

I picked up the phone and checked they were in before speeding off down to Dover. I'd forgotten to talk to the English Coastguard and it was vital to get their support. I was not sure of the legal position. Could they legally stop me from going? This meeting was going to be tense.

Before leaving I'd glanced furtively at their website. Their catch-phrase is 'Safer lives, safer ships, cleaner seas.' Nowhere on the website were baths mentioned. But what shipping could possibly be cleaner than a bath?

I waited in reception. Very promptly a man in a smart cap and epaulettes arrived. He spoke as punctually as he clearly kept time, 'Merryweather.'

'Is it?'

'Droll. I get that a lot being in this line of work. Now what is it you wanted?'

For a meeting that I knew would be tense I'd not started well. My opening gag had gone down like the LZ 129 Hindenburg. I followed him up a staircase into a room with a stunning view.

'Wow, you can see the whole Channel from up here.'

'You should see the view from the other side. Shall we sit down?'

The conversation continued going badly until suddenly, there was a single beam of light. He'd read about the paper-boat trip.

'If you can make it that far in a paper boat, you must be able to skipper almost anything.'

I had a chance.

'Funny you should say that Mr Merryweather . . . have a look at these plans.'

As he scrutinised the Douglas plan, he explained the situation in this country. It was somewhat different to the one in France. In the UK it turns out that legally the Coastguard (or the MCA, as they now like to be called) cannot actually forbid you from rowing the Channel. However, they can stop you if they find you're being a danger to other shipping, yourself or infringing maritime law. I really wanted the Coastguard to back the bath project. As I knew nothing about the sea, I felt it would be good to have them in my corner.

The meeting finished with the words, 'My official advice is that you do not row the Channel, but if you ignore that advice I suggest you get the help of the Channel Crossing Association.'

There was an association for crossing the Channel? Why had I not known about this before? This is the downside of embarking on totally tangential adventures with no experience. I could have got right to the water's edge, crossed the Channel and at no point even heard of the Channel Crossing Association. Wiser men, even other comics, would have put 'Channel crossing' into Internet search engines and come up trumps. Using complex prediction systems at my birth, both the Shaman and Sibyls were fairly unanimous that I was never destined to be defined as a 'wiser men'. I stared at him blankly.

'Channel Crossing Association?'

'Yes, they're the experts. Sure you've been speaking to them already but just thought I'd mention it. Do you fancy a tour of the station?'

Touring the MCA station at Dover, amid all the very high-tech radar systems and computer equipment that keeps that Channel safe, I realised that this would be a very difficult challenge indeed.

'The Channel is the busiest shipping lane in the world.'

'So I see . . .'

'Some of these tankers have a stopping distance of over 25 miles.'

'Imagine taking a driving test in that in Stevenage . . .'

Again I heard faint cries of 'Brace! Brace!' as the Hindenburg went to crash but this time Mr Merryweather cracked a smile. Further into our time together I felt able to tell him my full plan.

'Ideally, I'd like to make it round the coast and up to Tower Bridge.'

'That's a heck of a trip. I wouldn't make it but good luck to you.

I'll wave when you come past Dover. In fact if you make it to here, I'll even come down to the shore myself and shake you by the hand.'

I left the Coastguard in Dover and drove back up from Kent to Hertfordshire. As soon as I got through the door, pausing only to fire up my laptop, I typed 'Channel crossing' into Google. Sure enough, up popped the website for the Channel Crossing Association.

I picked up the phone and in a brief conversation established they were based in Kent, near Dover. I left the house, turned the car round and drove straight back to Kent. Driving back there, I made a note to move to Kent.

I drove through a wood, out the other side and down an implausibly small rack[7] (could have been a toad) with pasture on either side. 'This is a stunning part of Kent,' I thought as I missed the turning I wanted. After the world's first 57-point turn in the narrow rack I went back down to the turning I'd missed.

I went up the drive to find a house, built in the late 70s with a conservatory on one side, a garage and in the field next door, two llamas nonchalantly chewing in a barn. I knocked on the door and heard a muffled, 'Come in.' I found myself in a hallway. A stocky frame of between 5'8" and 5'10" (let's call it 5'9") with an off-white grey beard, hair and very wide shoulders approached. Duncan Taylor threw out a hand. My first impression of him was one of strength; he looked stoic and solid, but above all strong.

'You must be Tim, do come in. Tea?'

His words came in the lovely undulating, lyrical accent of that part of Kent. I nodded nervously and we went to the kitchen. I was nervous, because even a brief look at their website had convinced me that the chances of getting a serious organisation like the Channel Crossing Association to back the very silly plan of rowing their precious Channel in a piece of plumbing were slim. To me, Duncan had the aura of a man on the verge of using phrases involving the devil, intemperate weather and ice skates.

'Actually could I have mine black?'

'Are you sure?'

---

[7] A thing that's not quite big enough to be a road but just too sophisticated to be a track.

'Yes, thank you, it's quite nice when you get used to it . . .'

While the tea brewed, I filled him in on the paper-boat journey, stressing the safety aspects of it and leaving out the bits about getting trapped in locks, near-death experiences and almost drowning. He nodded, smiled and laughed but with the air of a man who thought that the most important thing in the story was the safety. I mentioned the llamas.

'Yes . . . I'm only head of the Channel Crossing Association some of the time. In winter I fish and for the rest of the time farm llamas. They're great, I'll take you out to meet them later.'

We took our cups and went into the next room.

'Now, how can I help?'

I pulled out all my bits of paper, including the Douglas plan, maps that I'd made out of photocopies of the road atlas and names of people I'd talked to.

'I really want to row the Channel for a charity called Sport Relief. Then I'd like to row round Kent and up to Tower Bridge. I think that by being on the water for longer I might make more money for them.'

I didn't mention the bet with Kenny to win a beer. I wasn't sure I knew Duncan well enough yet to let him into that part of the plan. He looked through all the pieces of paper and sat back in his chair.

'This seems like a great plan. I'd love to be involved. In fact I've never been that far up the Thames before so it'll be quite an adventure for me, too.'

He smiled and stood up.

'I'll go and find some proper charts.'

Then there was an awkward pause. Not just a pregnant one but the kind that takes days in labour to sire and leads the mother of this pause to curse the day her husband got her tipsy and suggested an early night.

'There's just one more thing . . . I'd like to try and row it in a bath.'

Even the midwife of the mother of the pause, paused. The entire room shifted. Duncan turned looking half puzzled, half cross. All the joy had vanished.

'What!?'

'I thought it might be a problem.'

Duncan sat straight back down.

'I think we'd better have a very full and frank discussion, Tim. Taking a bathtub across the busiest shipping lane in the world is a very reckless, stupid thing to do. With the way the current works you basically would be very hard-pressed to make it across anyway even if it wasn't such a bad plan. At the Channel Crossing Association we're primarily concerned with the safety of all, what we call, unorthodox crossings.'

'I can see the bath is pretty unorthodox.'

'By unorthodox I mean crossings of the Channel that have to be supported. It's a term we use for this type of crossing. What did the Coastguard say?'

'He said I should talk to you . . .'

'Well, I'm glad you did. This plan simply will not work. I can't see it happening. It's incredibly dangerous.'

Somewhere in hell, Satan reached for his ice skates.

The conversation continued for several very painful hours; me constantly looking on the bright side, thinking how much money we could raise for charity and how much fun the whole project would be. Duncan constantly looking on the practical side, thinking how much the court cases would cost and how much chaos the whole project would cause. The conversation was not going well and as the Coastguard had made very clear, I needed Duncan to be able to go ahead.

Eventually, he put down one of the various bits of paper or shipping guidelines he'd been reading and, looking at me oddly, said, 'You're really serious about this.'

'Yes.'

'It won't work.'

'I'm not saying it will. I'm just asking you to give me the best possible chance to try.'

He paused.

'Good. I just had to check. It's a terrible plan and you're bound to fail but I'd rather I was there to try to make sure you don't get killed. Let's go to the pub for a celebratory meal.'

'What?' My words came out feebly.

'I'm in! Let's go and celebrate.'

'What?'

'We're going to get you across that Channel in that bath and up to Tower Bridge – or at least be there when you fail. I'm in.'

With that, we left for the pub down the rack, pausing only to say hello to the llamas and tell them the good news.

I was in a state of shock and awe. Not even burning the top of my mouth on the pub's own brand 'mild' mustard or catching a glimpse of my own nostrils caused by a second helping of 'the mild' was able to shake me out of it. I had got the serious and efficient Channel Crossing Association to back me in an attempt to cross the Channel in plumbing. I was stunned.

We had a great lunch plotting all aspects of the bath plan and especially ways to try and make it as safe as possible. After coffee, we walked back up the toad to the car. Duncan hugged me goodbye.

'Great to meet you. I'm really looking forward to this. We'll speak soon.'

I drove off down the rack towards the wood. I felt so dazed I was a hazard to other road users. Pulling over, I parked the car, got out and slumped down on a nearby picnic table.

I'd done it. I thought getting Duncan on side would be simply impossible and now I'd not only got him to back the project but also found a kindred spirit.

Over the next few weeks Duncan and I set to work phoning the French, the Coastguard in Dover, rifling through paper work and discussing charts. Sometimes we'd work together as the sun poured into his study window in Kent. Other times we'd work apart. The project was now gloriously moving forward on every front: Duncan in Kent, Mark and the lads up in Richmond and me flitting between the two.

Duncan spoke fluent French, so I could leave the brilliant Liza to give birth, which was the main thing on her to-do list that month.

This was a golden time in the project. There were no obstacles; everything was running faster than a racehorse with ginger beneath its tail. The French Navy and her officers, far from being true to their petty, bureaucratic stereotype, were being as kind and helpful as it was possible to be. As Duncan was the first to point out it was difficult to tell if this tremendous bonhomie was due to an exhibition of Gallic *fraternité* rarely seen by English eyes, or the case of port we sent them as a present.

One morning I arrived to see Duncan for one of our plotting sessions; he looked drawn. 'We're in trouble, Tim.'

'What?'

'The French have changed their minds.'

'What?'

'They've updated the shipping guidelines.'

'What?'

'Have a look at this . . .'

There on the paper in front of me was devastating news. The representative of the French Navy had kindly sent us an update on the shipping laws and guidelines of France. In front of me in black and white, plain to even my limited understanding of French: no bathtub rowing in French waters more than a mile and a half off the French coast.

'In light of my plan, this is a bit of a blow.'

'It's more than that, Tim. It means it's over.'

'Can we phone them?'

'We can give it a go . . .'

Duncan sprang to the phone. His repeated negotiations were turned down flat. The French position was very clear. If I attempted to row a bath more than a mile and a half from the French coastline, I would be arrested by the French Navy and tried under martial law. This could lead to a lengthy stay in a French naval prison without the slightest need to trouble civil lawyers or justice. It seemed a very harsh position to take. The French Navy had invoked emergency powers and gone from being totally supportive to totally obstructive.

Later that day, my phone flashed into life. It was Liza.

'How's it all going?'

'Not the best this end, how's being pregnant?'

'Still going. What's up?'

I explained the situation, the Navy, the total *volte-face* and big legal hurdle we now faced.

'Tell you what, I'll give them a buzz if you like, just to check it all.'

Brilliant. Perhaps it was all a mistake. Perhaps Duncan's French was not as good as Liza's. Perhaps the French Navy would respond better to the soothing purring of an expectant mother than the working French of a Kentish fisherman.

I spent an agonising half a day while Liza tried to get hold of the French Navy. I didn't know what to do. Should I stop the work on the bath in Richmond and accept defeat or assume that Liza would win through and carry on with planning my dream? It was an afternoon of total ambiguity and the thing about being totally ambiguous is, practically, you don't get a lot done.

Finally, Liza phoned back. 'They really have got a bee in their bonnets about this. They're just not going to budge. I really tried but they're sticking to it. I'm really so sorry.'

So there it was, even the glimmer of hope had been snuffed out by an industrial-sized wind fan. The law was in place. The French Navy planned to defend its shores to the silt. The bath project was over.

Some would say my celebration of the 100th anniversary of the Entente Cordiale was perfect. It had hit the wall: unable to continue due to two totally opposing national viewpoints on sanitaryware. It was finished.

Somewhere in a quiet moment in Hertfordshire, my mother breathed a big sigh of relief.

CHAPTER FOUR

RING A RING O' ROSES,
A POCKET FULL OF RED TAPE

*'A common mistake people make, when trying to design
something completely foolproof, is to underestimate
the ingenuity of complete fools.'*

Douglas Adams

The challenge was off. I refused the main course of depression but
nibbled gloomily at the starter of being less than buoyant with lashings of melancholy on the side. I sat at home in my village in
Hertfordshire, deep in thought. I'd spent months of time, effort and
money planning the trip with the total knowledge and support of the
French Navy only to have them change their minds. The old enemy
had reared its ugly two-faced head. Foolishly, I'd believed the original happy face before being confronted with the cold sneer of the
real one. I felt like Henry V clutching at tennis balls. Game, set and
match to the French. I was totally beaten. The bath project was over.

Like Henry, I raged in private and damned the French for their
lack of truth and honesty. Like many Britons before me I'd expected
too much of our Gallic brothers and found them lacking. It would

be too easy to fall in with the stereotype of the French as the nation of inconsistent, wine-swilling, cheese-eating surrender monkeys but when you're confronted with the side of their character that had been shown to me, it's hard to find fault with the analysis. I'd believed in the Entente Cordiale and the European ideal of a brotherhood bound by a common purpose. This had failed. My faith in Europe was smashed. The entire European Union seemed less a united team, more a warring extended family squashed together, shouting and screaming on a long car journey. The total *volte-face* made no sense. France had proved herself to me as a nation totally lacking logic.

After half an hour of seething about the French Navy's lack of logic, I smiled wryly. There's not a great deal of logic in attempting to row the world's busiest shipping lane in a bath. Still, I felt as I looked, like a black Labrador during the days immediately after being spayed. I'd not just wasted my own time but had drawn an entire team into this complete nonsense.

I sat motionless, devastated: another victim of the perfidious French. Planning and working to a ridiculous goal is the thing I love the most. Taking apart those plans is the thing I hate the most. With a hand made of lead, I telephoned Mark and asked him and the apprentices to stop work on the bath. The next phone call was to Kenny.

'You sound a bit down, what's up?'

'It's all off . . . the whole bath thing. The French have changed their minds and there's simply nothing I can do.'

'Damn! They've just changed their minds . . . just like that?'

'Yes – I can't take on a whole other national government and expect to win.'

'I'm sure you've tried everything.'

'Yes . . . Look, I know there are costs and stuff and I'll pay for as much of it as I can. It's not fair for you to have a bill for this complete nonsense, especially as it's not now going to go ahead.'

'Don't worry, we can sort all that out later. The main thing is, not to get too down. Why don't we go for a beer in a few days to celebrate the idea that got away . . .'

'Thanks, mate.'

A similar call to Simon; later I phoned Douglas and Dom, both of whom were as down as me about it. After a few more phone calls I'd totally dismantled the team and the project was finished.

Many of the people involved said the words 'British', 'Grit' and 'Spirit' and suggested doing it anyway. Many phrases starting with 'The French be damned . . .' or similar drifted into my increasingly downcast ear.

It is 26 August 1346. Somewhere on a hillock in France, people shout and scream, a chaotic melee scrambles around trying to make sense of what is around it. Following a bet with his brother to win a pint of beer, one man avoids the volleys of arrows, runs forward and throws down a glove. He shouts something medieval about crushing France before charging at them.

I'm descended from that man (pint bets obviously run in the family), he fought with the Earl of Northampton (who basically seemed to own him), survived the battle of Crecy and true to his word, the French were crushed that day. He was there on the day the then Prince of Wales won his feathers.

This was uppermost in my mind as I listened on the phone. There's obviously something deep within me that is designed to tease the French: a gene reaching back nearly 700 years.

The downcast team had tapped into some part of me designed to test French resolve. Yet, forcing the French hand would not just endanger me but other members of the team. I'd probably be arrested, but so too would the members of the support crew. If my stupid risk hurt others, it's not a risk that should be considered. At the bottom line, the bath was just a project to raise some cash for a charity; it was never meant to escalate to this level.

To a symphony of 700-year-old bones turning disapprovingly in their graves, I phoned Duncan to thank him for all his work.

Laughing, he said, 'Just a shame the bath isn't a registered British Shipping Vessel, then you could row it where you like.'

That was the only line of the conversation I remember, which shows how hard it hit me. I put down the phone to Duncan and my brain started whirring.

Ever since I first saw the piece of paper it seemed bizarre that an entire country would alter their law just to stop me trying to complete a charity project. I couldn't believe that a sovereign power would specifically victimise me in this way to try to stop me from raising money for a really good cause. As a nation, to deny the right of a citizen to attempt something to help others is as far from

the ideals of Rousseau and Voltaire as it was possible to be. *Liberté,
égalité* and *fraternité* it certainly was not. I resolved to take this up
with the French President if I ever met him.

However, that one line from Duncan led me to think that perhaps
I'd got it all wrong. Perhaps the French were testing my resolve.
Maybe they were saying, 'Tim if you're really serious about this
stupid bath plan – prove it!' except obviously they'd have said it
in French. A strong possibility arose in my head that they were just
playing the time-honoured Gallic game of 'Red Tape'.

Whenever I see red tape something makes me reach for the scissors.

To look at what Duncan had said another way, if I could get the
UK Ministry of Transport to include the bath on the shipping register
I could row the Channel and no one could stop me.

Somewhere in the civil service a telephone rang.

'Hello, sorry to disturb you, I'm sure you're very busy but I need
to talk to someone about shipping licences . . .'

'I'll put you through.'

I waited. This could be crucial.

'Hello . . .'

'Hello, I need to try and register for a shipping licence.'

'Have you checked our website?'

'Yes, but this is something of a special case.'

She sighed, bored. Clearly legions of the self-important trying to
get onto the small ships register had created scepticism.

She sighed again, in case I'd misinterpreted the first one. 'Why?'

'It's a bath.'

There was a pause.

'Go on . . .'

Very carefully I explained the situation with the bath and the
French Navy. I also explained that it was a charity project and that
the Channel Crossing Association and the Coastguard had been
consulted and as far as anyone could see we were doing our best
to ensure the safety of the whole scheme. There was another pause.

'Are you serious? Or is this one of those wind-up things?'

'No, I'm very serious.'

'Send me some pictures.'

She hung up without committing either way. As it was a choice
between sitting at home feasting on a diet of self-doubt or going

out and taking pictures I picked up my camera and headed off to the boatyard in Richmond. Mark came out.

'How do you want to take her?'

'I think the more nautical we can make her look the better. What about putting her in the water and taking the front end of the bath?'

'The one with the taps?'

'No, the other end. We'll take that and if we shoot from the ground up it'll look a bit like one of those early P&O posters.'

I sent off the pictures. The bath didn't quite look like the leading ship in the P&O fleet but as much like a realistic ocean-going vessel as we could make her appear. This was my only chance to get the bath project back on. Would they grant her a shipping licence? I spent two days thinking of nothing else. In an office somewhere in the civil service a phone rang again.

'Hello. We spoke a few days ago, it's about the bath and the Channel.'

'I've got your pictures. I've made some calls.'

Would she grant the licence? She still sounded bored. Perhaps that was just a character trait? But she hadn't put the phone down; it seemed a good sign.

'We'd need to insist on a few modifications to grant the shipping licence. It's just if anything went wrong, we'd look very stupid – we're prepared to look a little silly as it's in a good cause but we can't cut all the corners. Have you got a pen?'

Originally they asked for a total change of plan, effectively turning the bath into a boat. I objected and suggested another tack. They changed that and sent it back. This was classic old-school horse-trading. A Grand National of phone calls took place between us.

'We'd need to insist on some sort of buoyancy aids, like on a catamaran, in order to give it an outboard and more stability.'

'Great – I'll have a Victorian black-and-white tiled bathroom floor.'

'Erm . . . right . . .'

Or, 'We're going to have to insist on a masthead.'

'Right, I'll make it a showerhead and have it plumbed in, would that count?'

'Erm . . . yes, I suppose it would.'

And, 'You're going to have to have a waterproof enclosed area for the electrics for the lighting you must have.'

'Super, I'll have a washstand built. That'll store them and I could have taps plumbed in on top of it and a shelf for shampoo . . .'

More sighing. At every turn I'd think of a way of trying to stay true to the original bath plan whilst still acceding to their requests.

'You've got to fly the Red Ensign flag – don't tell me you'll make a bath towel out of it?'

'Absolutely not. Who'd make a bath towel out of a Red Ensign? Outrageous!'

'Oh and you're going to need an anchor.'

'Great.'

The anchor would add weight but it might come in useful. The compromise we agreed was the closest to my original intention they would allow. It would enrage bath purists in that it was more a bathroom than a bath but on the plus side it was a bathroom that was a registered British Shipping Vessel with an SSR Number.

I was in Kent with Duncan. With joy we telephoned the French to tell them I'd passed their red-tape initiative test, the bath was a ship and the challenge was back on. Somehow, they didn't seem as pleased as I thought they might, but accepted that legally I could now row it across the Channel.

The bath challenge had come back from the brink.

'Celebratory lunch at the pub? The bangers and mash is lovely, they make their own mustard you know.'

My eyes and nose watered at the mere mention of the famous locally made 'mild'.

'I should probably make some calls . . .'

I hit the phone again and Mark got to work on the raft of changes to the bath. Kenny and Simon smiled, Dom got out the charts for more planning and Douglas sank a beer in delight. The team were back together.

With all these changes to make, my place seemed firmly to be at the boatyard. It was hard work but a lot of good fun. Each day after working on the bath I'd get to take out a skiff and row as far as I could up river and back again. The boats were all moored on a pontoon next to the floating restaurant and were looked after by a swarthy, strong-looking apprentice called Luke. I've never been more impressed by anyone else on the water. Luke seemed semi-amphibious. He wandered along boat tenders, leaped between skiffs and punted and rowed as though he had been born in the water. Mark was an impressive oarsman but Luke had the magical poise and effortless balance of a swan. He seemed more at home on the riverbank than an otter – it might just have been me but he looked a bit like one too.

'Mark says you can take out that boat . . .' He pointed to an old Thames skiff.

Another paint-stained apprentice called down from the towpath, 'Nah, Luke, Mark said to send him out in that one . . .'

He pointed down at a thinner boat, shaped more like a racing scull.

Luke laughed and turned to me. 'You wouldn't make it back in that . . .'

I must have looked down as he quickly added, 'I mean, with this tide. Here, take this . . .'

The Thames skiff is a totally bombproof boat. Not that it could actually withstand a bomb but in that they're almost impossible to capsize. Whether they'd hold up in the hands of a professional rowing submariner like me was a different issue. I cast off from the pontoon and spent many happy hours rowing in circles near Richmond Bridge.

The incredible thing was that I didn't capsize once. I fell in lots, especially getting into and out of the boats. In fact there was a week where Luke made a few quid betting people that I'd fall every time. He won. Once I even managed to fall in simply by trying to stand on the pontoon.

I was thrilled, wet but thrilled; I'd improved from capsizing to falling in. It's a slim distinction but a promotion nevertheless. Up to this point, my training to row the Channel had been entirely land based. Now, finally, half a year in, I was training in boats. Over weeks, I graduated from circles to ovals, then to ellipses and finally to a wobbly line.

My first wobbly line was a huge success. I remember Luke standing on the pontoon looking shocked. I was so pleased that I carried on, pulling upriver of the bridge. This was uncharted territory for me. Hours later I returned to Luke at the pontoon.

'You must have been miles. How far up did you get? Teddington? Hampton?'

'Erm . . . actually, just around the bend up there, then I got a bit stuck. I freed myself then got caught in a fishing line from the bank and it took ages to get out of that . . . then I tried pulling against the tide but couldn't and it took me further away so I had to wait for it to turn before I could make it back.'

Luke and the other apprentices laughed and teased me affectionately before we tied up the boats and went home for the night.

My wobbly lines turned to straight ones and, eventually, I managed to make it up to Teddington and back. Finally, progress. Gin-soaked fast launches passed me on the way, their captains slurring hoards of abuse, less than clearly believing that anyone as inept as me must be drunker than them, or stupid. Someone should invent L-plates for the river.

Improvement came fast now and very soon I was rowing up to Teddington and back several times a day. I couldn't believe I'd ever found it hard. I even took Mark's racing skiff out a few times and even that didn't capsize me.

I began to see a pattern. With unerring planning and the enthusiasm of an extremist, every time I went out rowing, a blue-and-white speedboat would appear. Like Nelson and de Villeneuve we fought: him for maritime supremacy and me for the ability to stay upright. He laughed as I floundered in his wake and a couple of times turned impressively to pass again and finish me off. Each time I bobbed, wove, lost the oars, banged my knees and did everything I could to capsize but amazingly didn't go under. He smirked as he turned away from our daily skirmish, swilling lager from a can and leaving me to locate the kneecaps I'd lost. I wonder if de Villeneuve drank lager?

During one of these skirmishes my phone rang in the violently rocking skiff.

'Hi, Kenny.'

'How's the training going?'

'Erm . . . pretty well . . . well, sort of OK.'

'Someone in the office lives in Richmond you know.'

'OK, it's a disaster really but I'm getting a bit better.'

'Is the bath in any kind of shape yet?'

'It's coming together, just there were a lot of things to change but we're getting there. It's not done yet but I think it would float.'

'Can you get it to Berkshire tomorrow? Only I think I've found a couple of rowing coaches who might be able to help.'

'I'll sort it.'

I needed all the help I could get. I rowed back to the pontoon. Mark, the apprentices and I carefully modified one of the boat trailers using a sledgehammer. Following this precision engineering, we manhandled the unfinished bath off the trestles. Getting the bath onto the trailer, even on the towpath, took much longer than expected and an hour and a half more than planned. In darkness I left Richmond and set off back to Hertfordshire. I slept violently and the next morning woke early. Following instructions I set off towards Berkshire.

On the way I phoned Mark. 'Is it going to be all right putting her in the water?'

'She'll be fine. All the structural stuff is done so she's going to float. We've got a long way to go, see, but she's going to be great. I gave her a polish last night while you were out rowing.'

'Thanks. Speak later.'

The sun was shining, there was a wind in the air and white tops to the choppy peaks of water on the lake at Eton Dorney. Just two months after my first non-capsize rowing outing, I stood on the banks of the country's leading rowing facility. The massive project to create the Eton College rowing lake was finally finished. The College has created a top stretch of water for rowing.

The road leading up to the lake undulates gently. Either the man who designed this loved hillocks or even the road had been engineered specifically to reduce the bounce you get with a boat trailer. I pulled the car to a stop and surveyed the scene. It was like seeing the future and in the middle of it stood the massive frame of Sir Matthew Pinsent. Of course he was just Matthew Pinsent then but his frame was still massive. Standing beside him were the rest of the legendary Great Britain Men's Olympic First Four: James Cracknell, Steve Williams and Alex Partridge.

To a man who had only learnt to row two months before, this was an awesome sight. This was serious; Kenny had obviously got me some pretty amazing coaches if they were sharing a lake with the GB Squad.

A man walked over. 'You must be Tim – I can tell by the bath. I'm Shane.'

'Hi . . . are you going to be coaching me?'

'Did Kenny not say?'

'No.'

'You'll be with the guys.'

'What?'

I stood stunned and realised my mouth was open. If there had been crops around me, they would all have been safe from crows.

'Come on over and meet them.'

I followed in silence to meet the Great Britain Men's Olympic First Four. We faced each other divided only by a vast chasm of experience. Matt was the first to shake me by the hand. I'd met both Matt and James before, in fact we almost collided with each other when I was coming down the Thames in the paper boat but I'm very forgettable and they've got a lot on their plates so they didn't remember it. When I reminded them, they immediately cracked a smile.

'So you're at it again,' said Matt.

'You nutter,' added James.

I nodded, smiled and met the others. If it's possible to be *very* speechless, I was. I'd only managed to keep a scull upright for the first time two months before and here I was with the greatest rowers in the world. It was a surreal situation. I'd just walked into a very tight unit. Matt seemed to be the most focused man in the world. His entire mind seemed already on the finish line at the Athens Olympic just two short months away.

James was enthusiastic about everything. He asked me lots of questions about how it all worked and before I fully figured out how to answer, he'd said, 'Want to go out on the lake?'

'Do you want to come too?'

'Absolutely.'

The bath needed special oars, as the original ones were now not long enough due to the new tiled floor adaptation. Mark and I had only just roughly made them the evening before.

I'd never rowed in the bath before. I was about to take my first strokes with an Olympic champion standing quietly on the bathroom floor, leaning on the roll top and quite genuinely looking over my shoulder.

I looked at James, he smiled. 'Let's see how she performs.'

I took a deep breath. After a lot of debate Mark had caved in and installed a sliding seat on the bath. I slid up to the top of the stroke, squared the blades, dipped the oars in and pulled back. I was so very nervous. Luckily, I didn't catch a crab[8]. With huge relief I took a couple more strokes. We were making headway up the lake.

Nervously, I turned to James, 'What do you think?'

'You've got a good action.'

Hooray: something for my gravestone.

'But the bath is such an awkward shape and it seems really heavy – is it heavy? It looks like it's making you finish quite high too.'

It had felt to me like I was finishing high compared to the skiffs and sculls, but I didn't know what I was talking about so it was great to hear it from him. Sharing a bath in the middle of the lake, James and I were getting on really well. He's such an approachable character. I felt very at ease in his company, as we joked, laughed and splashed about. It was as though he was the older brother of someone I'd known for ages. There was something that had been troubling me for a bit and I thought James was the man to trust with it so I asked him.

'It's a bit personal this, and erm . . . sorry, but I've got no one else to ask. But, um . . . how do you cope with the chaffing down below?'

'Well, what clothes are you wearing to row in, as it could be that?'

'Mostly, an old college rowing lycra and a jumper.' The lycra is like an all-in-one bathing costume that rowers and other sportsmen wear, made famous by starring in the 1988 Olympics with Linford Christie's lunchbox.

'Anything else?'

'Just my boxer shorts, shoes and socks.'

He smiled benevolently like an older brother, then paused. 'Maybe don't wear the boxer shorts.'

With what I know now about rowing I can only guess just how hard James very kindly suppressed his laughter. Boxer shorts are worse than useless for rowing. All they do is add an extra layer of fabric, get wet and rub against your skin. The best thing to wear for rowing is nothing at all. Wearing boxer shorts to row, all you get is increased chaffing, pain and a less-than-happy girlfriend.

---

[8]'Catching a crab' is what they call it when you miss a stroke. I was so confused the first time I heard someone say it to a bloke, I asked how his girlfriend was coping with the news.

A crowd had gathered on the landing stage. There was a television camera there and some people from the newspapers. I carried on rowing and asking James more questions. He was the most experienced rower I'd met and I wanted to get as much advice as possible from him. There was a whistle from the landing stage and a shout. We looked over. Matt was signalling for us to come over. I pulled on the oars and rowed us back in to where Matt, Steve and Alex were giving interviews to the newspaper people and television camera.

As we pulled into the landing stage, I heard Matt say, 'Let's put a stop to these ideas now, I will not do anything that mad for Sport Relief or any other charity.'

'What piece of equipment do you most recommend for Tim?'

'A straitjacket!' Matt never misses a beat.

Next, they spoke to James who replied, 'You wouldn't catch me doing anything like that.'

To underline this, six months later, James crossed the Channel on a surfboard before rowing the Atlantic.

Steve Williams was next up. 'We've just met him and he's clearly a little bit loopy . . . but good on him.'

Being rowers they were all aware of the challenge that lay ahead of me and gave me tips, advice, training ideas and a rubber duck.

Matt really hit home. 'What length Ergos are you doing?'

I puffed out my chest. '10,000 metres.'

'That's about six miles. If you're going to make it across, you want to look to up that to 25-mile ones. In fact you should really be looking to do 25 miles at least every other day.'

It may sound harsh but I could see he was right. He gestured to the lake, smiled and continued, 'Off you go then. Get a few miles in now.'

They all shook me by the hand. Matt was the last of them. 'Good luck, we'll be thinking of you . . . you loony.'

I wished him luck in the Olympics.

They wandered round to the sleek-hulled four that sat moored to the landing stage next to the one we'd been on with the bath. I sat on the other landing stage with the bath watching them. They got into the four and put their oars in the gates. With a snap I realised this could be the race of a lifetime and got into the bath.

They pulled off a little way from the landing stage, went up to the top of their slides, squaring the blades ready for the start. I pulled level with them and did the same. For once five minds, not four, imagined they were at the start line of the Athens Olympics; four in a racing boat and one in ablution equipment. There was silence on the bank but you could tell there was tension amongst the spectating grass. The turf held its breath, someone shouted and we were off. The GB First Four got off to quite a start but in the early stroke the bath held them. As we powered up the lake at Eton Dorney conditions were choppy – that had to favour the bath. The bath came back at the GB First Four but within ten metres of the start the First Four had pulled into a commanding lead. On the bank, turf accountants tore up betting slips.

I was still going up the lake as they passed me going back the other way. As I was still sweating on my second length, the GB First Four had already finished, got out, stored the boat, cracked open the golf clubs and were walking off to pitch and putt as a reward. It had been a tense race and at the start line was quite close, but by the way they were walking off to play golf I could tell the bath had lost.

I grimaced to myself, cursed the fact I'd not been rowing since I was an embryo and carried on sculling in the bath. Rowing the Channel was going to be tough. There'd be no pitch and putt for me till the Channel had been vanquished. This had been great training for the Olympics: if the Committee ever listened to my requests and took bathtub rowing into the Olympiad I'd be ready. If only the boys could leave the rest of the world as dead in the water as they'd left the bath.

Some days later, I was very sad to hear that Alex Partridge had punctured his lung and could no longer compete at the Olympics. Alex seemed a very good man to me. It's a proper measure of respect that the rest of the crew named the boat they raced in at Athens after him. Alex's injury was a very stark reminder of just how tough rowing is on your body.

I drove back from Berkshire with the sense that things were possible but harder than I thought they might be. People refer to sculling the Channel as 'the pinnacle of single-seat rowing'. Before meeting the GB Squad these words meant nothing real to me. Having seen people at the pinnacle of the sport I realised there was a mountain to climb.

The only problem, other than my fitness mountain, was the weather. The English summer is famous for its rain. Rain was fine for me to row in. Like a man who's just eaten locally sourced 'mild' mustard in a pub in Kent, wind was my main enemy.

June brought two possible 'weather windows'. These are days when the conditions are good enough to contemplate the trip. During those, the bath sat on trestles at the boatyard as Mark, his apprentices and I worked round the clock to try to get the changes completed. It was deeply frustrating to have great weather and spend it, dry in a bath on dry land. Now, all I wanted was to get out to sea and finally attack the Channel.

Leaving Mark to carry on, every other day I'd get out and complete 30 miles, either on the river or on the Ergo. These training sessions were as much about the mental challenge as the physical one.

On the plus side, while working on the bath and training hard, I did have time to deal with one vital question: what to call her? To get the final licence, the bath had to have a name. For the majority who don't know the ins and outs of the paper-boat trip I'll try and explain this bit quickly. Anyone who has read about the paper boat, flip a couple of paragraphs.

In 2003, I set off to break the world's oldest existing maritime record in a paper boat. The record was set in 1619 by a Royal Waterman so I decided to follow the 400-year-old etiquette of writing to Her Majesty the Queen to ask for Her permission to attempt to break the record.

To my total amazement Her Private Secretary wrote back. I think he was shocked that anyone could be bothered to follow pre-decimal etiquette. Also, it seemed the Palace were pleased that someone was trying to do something positive and raise a bit of money for a charity. King James the VI or I (still not taking sides on the issue) had chosen the name of the first paper boat. In my letter I'd rather cheekily asked if Her Majesty would like to choose the name for the new one. After various letters going back and forth and the Machiavellian antics of the then Lord Chancellor, too off track to go into here, the name 'Lilibet' was decided upon. This was the name given to the Queen by Her father when she was a child. It brilliantly summed up the whole childish nature of the paper-boat trip.

I now wrote to the Palace again and after various letters, the name 'Lilibet II' was approved for the bath. Again the name perfectly captured the childish nature of the quest. It summed up the total unawareness of failure you have when you're five years old and the indomitable belief in right and truth that comes from being able to spend time under a blanket with your favourite soft toy if things go wrong. It also made the bath feel like a sister to the paper boat, and having had such a good time in that boat, this was a good omen.

With the changes to the bath completed, my licence from the Ministry arrived just in time for the weather to turn really bad.

Like a small child or neurotic girlfriend at Christmas, I ripped the envelope apart. There it was, my entry into the world of the serious mariner. In black and white with a Royal Crest at the top: 'Certificate of British Registry', registered under the 'Merchant Shipping Act of 1995 and Merchant Shipping (Registration of Ships) Regulations of 1993, as amended'. Her small shipping registration number was SSR111694 and her Hull ID was ME034. But, more than all of this, *Lilibet II* was a bathtub.

What I liked most about the whole licence was that, although *Lilibet II* was a third-of-a-tonne Thomas Crapper bath, she had been put down in the paper work as, and forever in the eyes of Whitehall would remain, a 'sports boat'. Who says civil servants don't have a sense of humour? A member of the legendary Whitehall 'Joined Up Drinking' club had obviously filled in that part of the licence. There was a covering note. In it the thoughtful men and women at the Ministry wrote that they expected the French Navy might wish to see the licence so suggested I keep it with me at all times, even and especially, at sea. To help me, they'd made sure that my licence was waterproof. This genial five-carat gold, laminated civil service foresight is what made Britain great.

The bath was finally ready to hit the water. Mark and I decided that since she was now a ship, we should follow the launch procedures for pagan vessels. I emailed a deluge of druids to find out how pagans launched them. The druids mainly seemed to be in America and were all very accommodating on the email from their wooden laptops. However, the sounds of mahogany keys tapping away across the Atlantic failed to produce one conclusive ceremony but a host of ideas for them. To bring some order to the druidic chaos, I decided to combine their suggestions with the recognised procedures for launching large ocean-going vessels in the late 1800s, namely: put the vessel on the slipway, find someone religious to say prayers, get someone in a big hat, smash champagne over the hull and watch the ship gently glide into the sea.

I invited the druids to come and do the religious bit. They said they were very keen to come so we picked a date they could all make. Brilliant: the religious part was sorted.

As a boy growing up in Derbyshire I lived near the lovable, idiosyncratic small market town of Wirksworth. My mind flitted back to running around the hills outside the town with various other boys and girls, one of whom was called Thomas Crapper. He had a brother called Alan. I'd not seen Tom since we were very small but I was always struck with how calmly he bore the stigma of such a comedy name. He was a few years

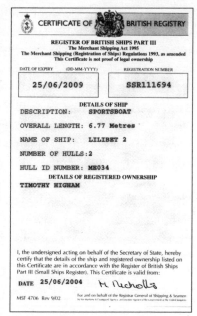

older than me but had been one of my great friends when I was small. If I could find him now, perhaps he could launch the bath.

Unsurprisingly, Simon at Thomas Crapper & Co didn't have a number for him. Bother. I remembered he'd gone into the Army but I wasn't sure which regiment. Again, bother. I thought he was based somewhere near Bath (surely a sign) but couldn't remember the address. I phoned a few friends from that time whose numbers I still had but no one was in touch with him. My options for finding him were getting slim. After a few days of trying the Army, Bath and the 'old friends' route I was stumped.

Then my mother suggested, 'Why don't you just phone his mum?'

Why didn't I think of that? Another example of sack-smothered candle-like dimness. The mother grapevine never ceases to amaze me. Like mighty animals calling across the savannah, mothers never lose touch with each other.

'Hello, Mrs Crapper?'

Within minutes I was on the phone to Tom. He'd love to come and launch the bath. Could he bring his fiancée? Turns out I was right; Tom was in the Army and is now a Major.

After a few nights where, like a small child, I was too excited to sleep, the day of the great bath launch arrived. I jumped out of bed with the drive of a toddler. My beloved girlfriend opted to stay gently snoring in bed; there was no shifting her. At the time I thought it was because she was a heavy sleeper but on reflection it could be that for the previous few evenings she'd had to deal with something like a cross between Tigger and Zebedee and had wisely had a stiff whiskey or three before turning in. Alone, I raced to the river at Richmond. Mark was there, making sure everything was ready: the apprentices ran around seemingly as excited as me about getting *Lilibet II* to the slipway.

The first hitch of the day occurred when the druids phoned on their timber mobiles to say they would not be turning up. Some had woken up late, some had not realised you needed to turn up for flights and some seemed to still be out from the night before. This lack of druidical organisation and planning may explain why Christianity got the upper hand in the race of religions.

With sadness, I thought we might have to skip the religious part of the ceremony.

'Hey man, what happening?'

A lanky Rastafarian lumbered towards us, his dreadlocks shoved up into his multi-coloured knitted hat.

'We're launching a bath.'

'Cool man, cool, irie man, I stay. Irie.'

He lit a form of Rastafarian incense, took a long drag and stood swaying at the top of the slipway. He'd probably just left the group of druids still out from the night before. He leant on one of the guide ropes to steady himself in prayer, the bath juddered on the slipway and Mark trapped his hand under it. The Rastafarian prayed in the medium of gravity and fell over; Mark screamed in Anglo-Saxon and at that moment the unmistakable form of Major Crapper bounded out of the early morning mist.

'Hello Tim. Your plans seem to be going as well as ever.'

I don't remember ever being surrounded by excitable apprentices, upside-down Rastafarians or swearing Royal Bargemakers in any of my early vintage Derbyshire plans but Tom's memory of that time is probably better than mine.

'You haven't changed a bit.'

In fairness, neither had he. Wearing an eye patch, I could have picked him out of a line up at 500 yards. Together we extracted Mark from under the third-of-a-tonne bath and prevented him from evangelical behaviour towards the Rastafarian using the medium of his fist.

From beneath the dreadlocks, 'Peace man, irie . . .'

Mark reached for a boat hook; I got there first. I don't think Mark is cut out to be a Rastafarian. The Rasta, who as it turned out was called Kenroy, seemed placidly unaware of any problem. He got up and examined his incense stick. It had become bent into an L-shape in the fall. He quietly sucked on air to himself, re-lit it and continued to sway gently. The smell of his incense was soon joined by the smell of his steadily burning beard.

'What's the best thing about being in the Army, Tom?'

'Well there's lots but I suppose being able to pick up the phone and say, "Hello, Major Crapper" and no one can laugh . . .'

After a lifetime of people laughing at your name I could sense the triumph.

'. . . unless they're a General.'

I could sense that from triumph, occasionally, a merry General would command defeat. As we were talking I pulled out a bottle of champagne and gave it to Tom. Suddenly, Mark came to life. His years of launching boats on the river leapt forward unchecked.

'She can't be launched by a man, that's bad luck.'

Thank goodness Tom had the foresight to have a fiancée.

'Would you do me the honour?'

She sprayed champagne over the taps of the bath brilliantly. The bath started to roll down the slipway.

Extinguishing his beard, Kenroy began to sing: 'Iron, like a lion in Zion . . .'

He swayed, bobbed and moved to his own beat as the bath entered the water. We all shared the rest of the champagne in mugs before Mark suddenly and solemnly tossed one of the cups out into the river.

'It's for the gods of the river, to give you good luck when you get back up to the Thames. We always must feed the river god otherwise he gets angry.'

One apprentice turned to another. 'Ah, that's why we're always short of mugs . . .'

They'd obviously never searched for them in the Eiger of mugs in the sink. Major Tom and I spent the rest of the morning messing about in the bath. It was the biggest relief of the project to date. Despite all the problems, setbacks and near failures, the bath was finally having her morning in the sun.

Nothing could stop me now.

Chapter Five

HE MARCHED THEM DOWN AGAIN

'I like to give my inhibitions a bath now and then.'

Oliver Reed

The bath launch had left me feeling totally invigorated. I arrived home to find a roughly shaped package held together with lashings of parcel tape.

I was doing the bath thing to try to raise money for the charity Sport Relief[9]. The Sport Relief gimmick that year was to give each fundraiser one sock at the start of your event (with 'Doing it!' printed on it) and the second one (its pair) when you finished the event (which said 'Done it!'). Sir Ranulph Fiennes had suggested that a pair of good, thick socks was the key to most endurance challenges and this worried me. If I only wore the Sport Relief sock (given to me for starting) while doing my event, I'd have one bare foot and that surely couldn't be good. I'd written to Ranulph and asked him what he suggested.

---

[9]Sport Relief is Comic Relief's younger, fitter sister charity, they alternate years. I had completed the paper-boat challenge for Comic Relief the year before and the bath started as a Sport Relief project. This seemed appropriate as there was a serious sporting part to the rowing.

I slit open the parcel in front of me and a note fell out.

> Dear Tim,
> All the very best with your challenge. Wishing you success, good fundraising and not too many blisters!

It was signed simply 'Ran'. He'd added, with a modesty that made me smile, '(Fiennes)' – the brackets are his.

Enclosed with the note was a good, thick sock for my other foot: a typically brilliant, practical and thoughtful response. Other people found out about this and soon I had a small washing line of socks. Ran's good, thick sock nestled next to Dave Gorman's old football sock, a short sporty number from James Cracknell, a boxing sock from Ben Fogle, socks from Ingrid and Chris Tarrant, and flapping on the end, a shocking tie from Richard Whiteley.

Ingrid kindly also sent me a rubber duck, which I named Bernadette[10] and took with me on all my training exercises. I was shocked by how people had kindly thought of fun ways to show their support for what I was trying to achieve. I felt really encouraged before my big trip to the bathroom.

There were still some practical things to be sorted as well as getting the vital 'weather windows'. We still had to find a seaside base of operations. It was all well and good having the bath on the river at Richmond but if the weather improved we'd waste up to six hours, getting her out of the water, loading her on a trailer, driving to the sea and unloading. Duncan Taylor suggested using Folkestone; Dom wasn't sure as Dover seemed a better bet to him; I simply didn't have a clue. Duncan was our cross-Channel expert, so Dominic politely caved in and I agreed to use Folkestone.

Using Folkestone created one added complication. Unlike Dover, Folkestone's harbour is tidal, which means it only has water in it twice a day. The rest of the time it's not a harbour, more a malodorous mud flat with stranded ships balanced on it waiting for the water to come back and make them float again. With Folkestone, you could only get the bath and support boat out to sea in those two

---

[10]Bernard was the rubber duck I'd had since I was small and Ingrid and I thought it would be nice if he had a girlfriend.

daily windows of opportunity. With the way the tide works, one of those daily windows is normally at night. Dom realised this and had I known more about the sea, I'd have seen this could be potentially very important. However, I knew nothing about the sea, so was blissfully unaware. I'm not sure this was Duncan's best piece of advice. It was not the end of the world, but would make things difficult or impossible if we needed to get out to sea fast.

My staggering lack of knowledge and understanding of the sea had played its first crucial part. I knew about tides, I'd seen them on the river and understood how they worked in twice-daily cycles. I even knew about tides at sea. I'd lost my shoes to one once when I was six. But I didn't have the experience or knowledge to understand how the tides might impact on a boat, harbour or bathtub. I'd never seen or heard of the concept of a tidal harbour. For once I'm not going blame my dimness, just a total lack of experience. Many cross-Channel rowers start from Dover for precisely this reason.

The English Coastguard had suggested it and the Channel Crossing Association and French administration insisted on it: *Lilibet II* must undertake and pass a 10 km sea trial.

I'd been watching the weather. Trying to learn as much as possible from Dom about how it all worked. High-pressure ridges seemed to be important. I'm still not sure exactly how, but the normally sanguine Dom seemed to experience a lot of high-pressure ridges as he manfully tried to explain remedial weather to me. Weeks went by without any suitable weather windows. All this time I carried on training on the river at Richmond, getting more despondent as the days went by.

In my understanding of the weather, it seemed, if it was sunny in Richmond, it was bad on the coast. If it was raining in Richmond, it was bad on the coast. If it was windy in Richmond, it was bad on the coast and if it was bad weather in Richmond, it was bad on the coast . . . unless it was good weather at the coast. The main thing I learnt about weather was that to try to predict it is like trying to herd amoeba.

Finally mid-June arrived and with it a phone call from Duncan. 'I think we can give the sea trial a go tomorrow. Can you get the bath down here in time?'

That's the thing with weather. Like a master card player, it always seems to declare itself at the last minute.

I turned a romantic night in into a frowning feminine face and a peck on the cheek goodbye as I sped off to Richmond.

The scramble to load the bath was even more hectic and chaotic than it had been before the modifications. Trying to get a third-of-a-tonne piece of plumbing to behave long enough to trap her into coming onto the sledgehammer-modified boat trailer taught me how primary- and prep-school teachers must feel every day of their lives.

Just when I'd got one bit of the bath under control another bit tried to escape off downriver. As I dived to try and render that bit governable a third bit led the first bit off to another area of mischief. Thinking my best plan was to deal with the bit I'd got acquiescent first, then the two naughty bits later, I tried looping a foot round the fixed point of the trailer. This great plan led to a splosh and me, upside down, wearing the muddy riverbed as a hat. Finally, the apprentices and I tamed the unruly bath but it had taken the better part of an hour and a half. During this debacle, the tide had risen and the car, standing solid as a carthorse attached to the boat trailer, had water running in and out of her exhaust. The car didn't respond to the many polite requests I made to start her. So now we had the bath on the trailer, the trailer attached to the car and a car that wouldn't start due to water in her pipes.

Rallying a few people on the bank we tied a rope to the front of the car and the scratch tug-of-war team pulled the car, bath and trailer out of the river. Although time was short I thought it might be best to leave it for a moment to drain. I went back to checking ropes on the trailer and packing wadding round the bottom bits of the bath where it touched the ropes so it didn't crack. After a moment of deep prayer I turned the key in the ignition, the car started first time. Brilliant. Only an hour and a quarter later than the time I'd planned to leave.

Early the next morning I arrived on the outskirts of Folkestone. After a swearing bedecked tussle with a one-way system designed by Satan himself and several quizzical phone calls to Duncan, I missed the turning I should have taken for the fifth time. Finally I discovered the tiny arch through which I was meant to drive to find the slipway. Driving under this holy grail of traffic features I arrived at the harbour. I stepped out and felt the cool of the sea breeze on my face. In a Hollywood film this would be a romantic, inspiring scene, as they'd leave out the multitude of lost cars tooting in unredeemable damnation, stench of the harbour and swearing native pedestrians.

Before going to find Duncan I took a moment to look out at the sea. Finally, I could see it, the English Channel. Of course I'd seen it before, I'd even crossed it before, a couple of times by ferry, but this was my first sight from Folkestone of my nemesis.

'Something of a false alarm I'm afraid.'

'What?'

'I've just been talking to some mates out at sea and there's a howler coming in, we're not going to get the sea trial in before it hits.'

Brilliant: a totally wasted day. Trying to be buoyant and not take my unbelievable feelings of frustration out on him, I had a drink with Duncan. Predictably, we chatted about the unpredictability of the sea. Then I attempted to turn the car and boat trailer round and set out back to Richmond. I made such a mess of it that I managed to totally block up Folkestone Harbour. Luckily, Duncan hadn't left.

'Do you want me to have a go for you? It's a bit awkward.'

After un-sticking the trailer from the various shops and cars of Folkestone I set off for Richmond. Arriving late, Mark, the apprentices and I unloaded the trailer and floated the errant bath back on the river. As we were walking back to the boathouse my phone flashed.

'I think we can give the sea trial a go tomorrow. Can you get the bath down here in time?'

Mark growled. I sighed, 'Leave it to me . . .'

For the second time in 24 hours the car got flooded and, diving hopelessly at a line, I had another fitting with the muddy riverbed hatter. As dusk fell on Richmond, we left the bath half tied to the boat trailer and, wiping mud from my eyes, Mark and I went up the cobbled street for a pint in the Waterman's Arms.

'Same again tomorrow?'

'I hope not.'

Of course Mark was right. After manhandling the bath into place, speeding off down to Folkestone, feeling the sea breeze on my cheeks and hearing the melodic sounds of local swearing in my ears, a rather sheepish Duncan said, 'Nope, it's not going to happen again today, you see those little white peaks on top of the waves?'

'Yes.'

'We call those galloping white horses, it means there's a storm coming.'

Again I arrived back at Richmond totally exhausted. I knew I must look tired as Mark said, 'Don't worry about the bath, me and the lads'll stick her back in the water, you go off home to bed.'

Very sound advice.

I was woken early the next morning by my phone. 'Tim, it's Duncan, this time I really think we've got a chance. Can you get the bath down here in time?'

It's true; fishermen really do get up unbearably early in the morning. I dredged myself out of bed and reached for my trousers and rowing lycra. I wasn't even sure Mark would be at the boat-yard when I got there, that's how early it was, but I thought if I could just find a couple of early-morning fitness enthusiasts on the river I could load the bath and leave a note for Mark.

I arrived to find Mark opening up the doors of the boatyard under the arches. I'd never been there early enough to see this before.

'I've got a weather window for the trial today. I'm so sorry, can we get the bath out of the water . . . I know it's a pain but I've really got to get this done . . .' Not sure why I was breathless, but I was.

'That's lucky.'

'What?'

'I thought this might happen.' Mark flashed the cheery and slightly mischievous smile I'd come to enjoy from him. Behind him was the bath, still loaded on the trailer from the night before. I was exhausted already that day but so relieved to realise that I didn't have to go through the great irritant of having to load her again. I actually remember smiling, something I hadn't done for the last few days.

We hitched the trailer to the un-waterlogged car and I sped off to Folkestone. I'd like to write, 'It was a sunny day', but it wasn't, it was overcast, with not much wind in the air and the sea state I was told was two. I didn't know what this meant but guessed it meant two out of ten, ten being the worst possible sea state and one being the best.

I miraculously found the Elysian arch after only one miss but then failed to reverse the boat trailer down the slipway. I got out of the car and Duncan kindly had a go at it. The slipway at Folkestone is really tricky (that's a polite way of putting it). It's not designed for boat trailers. It's a makeshift slipway that probably had its roots in launching small craft that could be carried by hand.

There is a much better inner slipway but that doesn't get the water till very high tide and to reverse down that one you have to block the one-way system. Blocking the one-way system in Folkestone is not recommended unless you're a prizefighter or a lemming suffering from vertigo and needing an alternative to jumping.

My only choice was the narrow, outer slipway. Duncan had the knack. He politely asked the early-morning drinkers at the pub next door to the slipway to stand up from their tables. He then cleared their tables away, moving them a safe distance down the street. I would never have thought of asking them to move, and if I had thought of it, I would have got an insurance quote first. They seemed quite used to it, like it was the normal way of launching boats. They were so drunk at that time in the morning that even the bath seemed normal to their addled eyes. Duncan then talked to the fishermen at the café opposite before moving the piles of what looked like lobster pots that were stacked up on the slipway. He was good at this. He'd done it before. I looked on with the impressed awe that Luke Skywalker levelled at Obi Wan Kenobi.

Then he got back in the car, reversed the boat trailer down the slipway and into the carefully stacked pile of lobster pots, while hitting a befuddled pub patron gently with the front of the car. A ranting exchange later, he pulled the car back up to the top of the ramp, lined it up and reversed again. This time, he made it perfectly, conquering the world's most difficult boat trailer reverse.

We unloaded the bath onto the water and tied her off to the slipway. This was the first time the bath had sat in the sea. I drove the car and trailer back up the ramp, parked and paid the extortion money to the meter. We re-situated the tables and straightened out the lobster pots before I bought a drink for the couple of inconvenienced pub patrons. Using her slipway instantly explained why it's rare to meet a serious mariner who has ever set sail from Folkestone.

Duncan started up his boat. It was a very old-fashioned craft and has the only clinker-built hull still left in Folkestone Harbour. He was justifiably proud of this, and with the amount of money he spent keeping this treasure above the waterline, he had a right to be. I jumped down into the bath and got everything ready. I remembered I'd forgotten the oars. In all the excitement of putting the bath in the water, I'd forgotten the oars. This was a very significant oversight. True to my own form I'd have left them in Richmond;

today I'd only left them strapped to the car at the top of the ramp. This was a sign; today would go well. As Duncan brought his boat round I ran up the ramp, collected the oars, checked I'd paid the meter and ran back to the bath.

Duncan shouted over, 'Let's get this started!'

The sea trial was vital. The bath and I had to complete 10 km out at sea. This is just under 6.5 land miles or just over 8.5 sea miles. To satisfy the French Navy, I had to complete it in kilometres, miles would not count. Normally, they make cross-Channel rowers do this to check they are actually fit enough to row the distance. In my case it had been made very clear to me that it was not just to see if I could make the distance but to check how this most unorthodox of unorthodox crafts would cope at sea. If the bath failed, Duncan would not risk the Channel Crossing Association in a battle with the French and would withdraw his support boat. Even as a Registered British Shipping Vessel with no engine, legally, I needed a support boat to cross the Channel. Without it I was stuck. Also the English Coastguard had made it very clear that without the knowledge, experience and support of the Channel Crossing Association they too would take a very dim view of my crossing. Essentially, for the legal reasons I've paraphrased above, without passing this sea trial, the bath project was off. The stakes were high.

Duncan increased the throttle on his engine, I gripped hard on the oars and we were off.

My first time rowing out at sea was a totally pivotal moment in the plan. It was every bit as important as the first time I managed to row without capsizing – an epoch. And just like the first time I managed to row without capsizing – an epoch I'd left until very late in this plan. What if I couldn't do it?

As I struck off towards the harbour arm at Folkestone, my action was nervous, jerky and very inefficient. All my senses worked way too hard, I overreached at the catch, went up the slide too fast, or too slow, and all in all felt very self-conscious. The sea didn't help. It kept moving down when I wanted it to stay flat and up when I thought it would stay down.

I've only experienced the gut-wrenching awed and confused feelings I felt on my first day rowing at sea once before. That time, I was sitting on a bench under the clearest starlit sky. It was a cold night; snow shone on the ground and reflected off the frozen lake. The girl sitting next to me bathed me in her dark effervescent eyes and stuck her tongue into my mouth. The agonising first few seconds of that moment, as I tried to work out the rules of that new game and at the same time take in and deal with those startling, wonderful feelings were exactly the same as my emotions as I swerved hopelessly around the water at Folkestone and proficiently crashed into the harbour arm. Rowing now, as kissing then, I was engulfed with sentiments that normally only enter the mind of a man newly departed an aeroplane one parachute short of a successful landing.

You'd think that rowing at sea would be like rowing on a river, but it's not. The sea consistently moves in three dimensions. It's like chasing a frog around a waterbed. When you're rowing on the river or a lake, it's a relatively flat surface. There might be a bit of current on the river or some chop on the lake but basically it's flat. You come up and down the sliding seat, pop your oars in at the top of the stroke and pull back, rolling the seat backward, horizontally to power yourself forward. Rowing is the only high-speed sport where you strain every sinew to power forwards as fast as you can, not looking where you're going and facing backwards. The entire power movement in rowing is horizontal. At sea, there's no horizontal. It shifts constantly. This makes it impossible to get any kind of decent strokes together: the enforced rhythmlessness of a hippo playing maracas overtakes you.

The sea allowed me strokes when it wanted me to take strokes. It moved itself when it didn't want me to take strokes. It somehow contrived to put air where the water used to be midway through strokes and generally conspired to make me catch crabs with one or both oars almost every stroke. I saw Duncan's face. He looked on from the support boat, powerless to assist me, with deep concern etched into every furrow. He didn't say a word but it was obvious he was thinking: He's not going to make it across the harbour let alone the Channel.

With this added pressure and the sea playing with me, things were bad. I should have hated the sea with every stroke I took. Every bit of my being should have wanted to get off the water and away from this embarrassment. The thing was, I loved it. Like a battered spouse, the more the sea threw at me, the more I loved her for it. I wanted to learn. Every time the sea moved the water away from me I adjusted the oar to meet the challenge and very slowly began to feel like I was riding the sea. The sea was a particularly frisky horse with ginger up its nethers, but it was one that I was learning how to tame. By constant concentration and watching every second where the water was going on both sides and repeatedly altering my hand heights to match the sea's peaks and troughs I was getting control. Even when the water rose on one side and my hand lowered to counter that, I still had the upper hand. I even began to glimpse rhythms in the sea's contrariness. Somewhere in the Nile Delta a hippo led a conga line to the strains of '*La Cucaracha*'.

Every moment I spent out at sea was a joy. I was there: a speck in an ocean, constantly battling to stay in control and every second I managed it was a triumph. It was wonderful out there surrounded by beauty. Somehow, now I'd got my bearings I felt part of it. Duncan looked relieved.

'You're getting the hang of it now,' he shouted through the wind.

Now I knew he thought I could do it. I had to row 5 km out and 5 km back to complete the ten. I was not very clear on what a kilometre was, but I knew it was less than a mile and thought we must be about 5 km out by now. We'd been out there for a while when the wind picked up.

'That's good. Let's turn her round and head back.'

Great. Going back never seems as far as going somewhere. I turned the bath round and made for Folkestone. This gave me a stunning view. Now there was no Folkestone to see. All I could see in front of me as I rowed to Folkestone, facing away from it, was the sea. It stretched out before me until it blurred with the mist and became the sky. All that faced me was cold blue of different shades with the odd plume of white: the beauty was breathtaking. There's no past or future at sea. That day, there was just me and the sea locked in the present with each other for company.

Concentrating hard, I made it back to Folkestone, tied off the bath, got the car and messed up reversing it down the ramp. Duncan tied off and arrived at my side. We moved the now-horizontal patrons of the bar and their tables, shifted the lobster pots again and Duncan reversed down the slipway. With obscene difficulty, the two of us managed to float the bath onto the trailer. The tide helped as little as possible, as she wanted to get out of Folkestone as much as I did. We managed it. I'd never manoeuvred the bath onto the trailer with only one other person before. This was quite an achievement. I made a mental note of what we'd done. Finally, we tied her down and I drove the car up the ramp.

At the top I parked the car near Holy Grail Arch and the loading the bath symphony for two men, a trailer, car and tub concluded to the slurred clapping of the patrons of the pub, one of whom even shouted, 'Encore.' Actually, on reflection, he might have shouted 'wanker': difficult to tell with the slurring. I broke into a jog back to Duncan as a bottle whistled past my ear.

'I thought we were going to have to call the whole thing off at the start but you really got the hang of it. Well done.'

'Thank you.'

My eyes shone with the awed enthusiasm of a child given its first helium-filled balloon. I rolled the words mellifluously round my mouth before I let them out.

'My first 10 km at sea . . .'

'We actually only managed 6 km.'

'What!'

Somewhere a helium-filled balloon burst.

'Now, there's a few things we need to say about the bath . . .'

This sounded less than ideal.

'. . . She can't turn well enough; if we get stuck in an emergency I can't tow her; the fastenings holding the ropes are fine on the river but . . .'

'Let me get a pen and paper.'

I was trying to give myself a chance to think, to find something positive.

'So there's the turning, towing and fastenings issues . . . anything else?'

'I'm not sure that the prow will stand up under duress at sea; she's not stable enough . . .'

The list went on and on to depressing infinity and beyond, finally finishing with, 'Look, Tim, why don't we just get you a normal boat, and you row the Channel in that? You've clearly got a good chance with the skill you showed today. But in that thing, you've not got a hope. Tim, this is a failed safety test, and even if you hadn't failed it – rowing the Channel in that is just not possible.'

Personally, I'd been passed as fit on the safety test but the bath had totally failed. I think Duncan wanted me to know just how hard it would be to row the thing out at sea, and it was, but now I'd had a taste of it, I wanted more. I met his eyes firmly with mine, they locked on to each other; there was a pause while I thought of what to say.

'It may not be possible to row it in the bath, but all the same, I'm going to try. Let me get a pen and we can write these safety failings down and sort them out.'

I got the bath back up to Richmond and Mark was woeful. He looked through my list, 'How can they fail her? Why do they want that? This seems like a really bad plan to me . . .'

Now we began even more tweaking to the bath to get it to stand a chance of passing the next safety test. Many of the things we'd been forced to change to get the shipping licence were the cause of the problems we now faced but we just had to adapt our plans to include them and yet still modify the bath for safety.

We added stronger fixings for the rope work. We strengthened the prow by adding more struts and braces to the inside of them. This made the whole thing even heavier but again it seemed I was being left with little choice. We made massive, strong lines to enable us to tow the bath better and created a rudder system to help with the steering.

Mark looked up, 'Monkey's fists.'

'What?'

'She needs monkey's fists.'

He left me bemused and headed into the boathouse. I watched with amazement as Mark proceeded to twist and turn the rope around the front of the prows. He created two massive intricate balls of rope.

'They look like the cufflinks you get in posh shirt shops.'

'Nope, those are Turk's Head knots, these are Monkey's Fists.'

It takes a black belt in knot tying to tell the difference but apparently it would make towing the bath behind another boat safer. We worked hard for days and days on the modifications. All this time the sun shone down and glorious weather reigned supreme as the bath sat in bits on the riverbank.

Late one night, following a golden Oriental sunset, Mark and I finished the bath. Finally the modifications were completed. With this amazing weather, getting a new date for the sea trial quickly was going to be easy.

We looked down in the increasing dark at the bath on the bank: the two buoyancy aids resting on the trestles; the black-and-white tiles above that with the various bits of rope work coiled neatly. Just below a Monkey's Fist on one of the buoyancy aids Mark had proudly painted *Lilibet II*. Sitting in the middle of the tiled floor, the copper of the Victorian slipper bath glimmered in the lingering light. Like the back of a racing leopard, the rim curved from the low end with the taps, up to a beautiful arch at the head end. Behind that in the slight breeze, the Red Ensign flag tried to puff itself away from the small mast. Rising up from all of this, and glinting in the light from the newly turned on street lamp, was the showerhead. Like two gleeful five year olds Mark and I looked at each other.

'Get a bucket of water and let's test the plumbing.'

We put a bucket beneath the floor where we had installed a small pump to suck water up from the river and into the showerhead plumbing system. We looked at each other and Mark flicked the switch to turn the pump on.

'It works!'

A few short showers and much laughter later, both wet, we went up the hill to the Waterman's Arms.

Dominic had always maintained the success of the whole plan hinged on good weather. The bath was completed just in time for the worst July weather on record since World War II. Storms lashed the South Coast and more than 13,000 homes lost electrical power. Churchill achieved his aim with weather like that from a bath, but his was fixed to the floor of Number Ten Downing Street. The storms continued. Lashing the country as a whole. Even homes as far away as Wales lost power. The gods conspired against me. Perhaps I shouldn't have had a Rastafarian at the launch but opted for the more traditional Church of England cleric.

After weeks of weather so bad I couldn't even train on the river, I got a phone call from Duncan Taylor.

'I think there's a real chance we can give the second sea trial a go tomorrow. Can you get the bath down here in time?'

I shuddered. I'd heard this before. Mark, his apprentices and I loaded the bath in the pouring rain onto the bath trailer. I sped down to Folkestone as rain bounced off the windscreen in drops the size and weight of hailstones.

I arrived in Folkestone and started with a chat from Duncan. 'I'm really sorry Tim, I know how you feel about this but if the bath doesn't pass this one, that's it. We have to look at you rowing in a normal boat or not at all.'

We began a movement of the unloading the bath symphony with an especially enlarged grunting, sweating and swearing section. The only person whose spirits were lower than mine was the pub patron whose drink I spilt. I re-parked the car, paid the hush money, ran back down the slipway and tripped over a lobster pot. I picked myself up long enough to jump on to the bath, slip and fall in the water. On the plus side, the sheet rain had stopped and just as Duncan predicted, the sun poked round the wisp of a dark cloud. The dark cloud and the sun had a momentary battle of wits before the cloud retreated and the rain was no more. I pulled myself out of the mephitic water, soaking wet. Although the rain had stopped, the net result was the same. I was wet.

'Stop messing about Tim, we're up against it, let's get out there.'

On the last sea trial I had triumphantly conquered the sea. Now I was a natural. It came as a bit of shock to find that I was still as awkward and terrible at rowing on the sea as I had been the last time. Sailors talk about 'getting their sea legs'. I'd never understood what it meant but I certainly didn't have mine. The bath and I did a brilliant impersonation of a rabid drunk trying to walk the line as we zigzagged out of Folkestone. Various fishermen looked on and laughed. I couldn't tell if they were laughing because I was rowing a bath or because I was terrible at rowing a bath. I consoled myself that this confusion was a similar problem to that which dogged Spike Milligan and swerved violently into the harbour arm. Looking to see if Duncan noticed, at least now I knew what they were laughing at.

The one positive thing I found was that it took me less time to get used to rowing at sea this time. Last time I only got it after about an hour or even an hour and a half. This time, after a devastating first half-hour, I'd got it under control.

After five nerve-racking kilometres Duncan shouted, 'Right, that's it, let's go in and have a chat!'

What did he mean? Had it passed or hadn't it? Could I finish this project or not? The words seemed to hang in the air. He gave them no qualifying statement.

I turned and made for the harbour arm. I tied up the bath, moved patrons, their tables, spilt more drinks, got the car, fought the tide to load the bath, nearly flooded the car (again), spilt lobster pots, reset tables, settled patrons and bought more replacement drinks with my heart tied in knots. Had the bath passed? Still no word from Duncan: he scribbled furiously on his sheet of paper and said nothing. I finished paying for the replacement spilt drinks at the pub. It was amazing how custom appeared to have picked up in that place. Whereas the first time I bought replacement drinks, there were only three drunks, now there were between 15 and 20. Somewhere in the dark recesses of my mind, a penny rolled a tiny bit closer to the cliff.

Duncan still said nothing.

'Well?' My nervousness was horrible.

'She's passed. Not with flying colours but she's passed. Well done. I feel I've got to say she's still not going to make it across the Channel and I think you're mad for trying but if you want to try – I'll back you.'

I could have hugged him. On reflection I wish I had. *Lilibet II* had passed her second sea trial. She's a third-of-a-tonne, un-aqua-dynamic piece of ablution equipment. She was never going to pass with flying colours but a pass was a pass and that was all I needed.

'Shall we check the weather forecasts for tomorrow?'

We got into the cabin of his boat and checked the weather. I so wanted it to be good. I finally had a bath that had passed, I was fit, I was even in Folkestone and ready to go; all I needed now was a weather window. Yes, it was British summer time and the weather had been stoically awful to celebrate but surely I was owed just one good day of weather. Just one chance to try to finish this and get across the Channel.

I didn't understand a word of the weather forecast. Dom had spent days trying to teach me whether a Dogger was worse than a German Bight or explain why a Viking never met FitzRoy at Trafalgar without the slightest success. Yet, thanks to Dom I could now make the right approving noises, I just thought of sampling jam and purred. Duncan looked up from writing things down in a book.

'We've got a weather window tomorrow. If you want to try it, let's go then. I'll complete the final checks on my boat.'

'I'll give you a hand if you like before I go and complete the final checks on my bath.'

'Polish the taps you mean?'

'Check the plug is in!'

There was a jovial sense in the air as we started the final checks on Duncan's boat. Finally, after months of planning, setbacks and disasters I was just one night-time away from attempting the plan I'd tried so hard to create.

I phoned Kenny, Simon, Comic Relief, Dom, Douglas, the Admiral, Mark, my girlfriend, family and the rest of the team to let them know we were on final standby to attempt to go with the weather window the next day. Everyone was as excited as me about it. Dom prepared to plot the course. Kenny prepared a journalist and photographer to come down. The others raised their glasses and sat back in their chairs. The bath Channel plan was on.

As I was doing this, Duncan made calls, too. He phoned the various people he knew he must: the Coastguard, Harbourmaster, French Navy and the others at the Channel Crossing Association to let them know about it. When we'd both hung up from our respective calls we popped the hatch and started work on the final checks to his boat's engine. There was a huge sense of excitement and the kind of childish enthusiasm that strangely makes you feel slightly nervous. I knew Duncan felt it too as he slipped and dropped his screwdriver into the running engine. It made a noise like a cow caught in a fence, shuddered and stopped.

'Is that bad?' I'm not an engineer.

'It's going to mean a complete new engine.'

'Before tomorrow?'

'No. Tomorrow is off.'

Finally the bath had passed her safety tests, I'd got a perfect and near-impossible-to-find weather window, I'd beaten every obstacle that had been thrown at me including circumnavigating the labyrinthine web of French bureaucracy: and one slip of the fingers had scuppered my support boat. I could not attempt the Channel without one.

The entire venture was up in the air again.

CHAPTER SIX

GLOWERING LIKE THE MOON

'The English Channel is a ditch and will be crossed
as soon as someone has the courage to attempt it.'

Napoleon Bonaparte

What I know about engines wouldn't fill the back of a stamp, but even I knew this was disastrous. Duncan reached for his mobile.

'Hi. My engine won't start . . .' He wouldn't admit the mishap to his fisherman mates. 'Are you and your boat free tomorrow?'

There was an agonising pause. Without a support boat I couldn't take advantage of the good weather we'd got after two long months.

Duncan put his hand over the phone. 'He's just checking his diary, Tim . . .' The diary checking took a disturbingly long time. How many giddy social engagements could one fisherman have? Duncan broke into my thoughts. 'He says he's got a bunch of bankers to take fishing.'

'Shouldn't that be a wunch of . . . ?'

Duncan looked blank and returned to his phone. 'Can you get out of it?'

Another pause. Duncan turned to me. 'He says how much, Tim?'

I had my new support-boat skipper.

Duncan Taylor had seen me through my troubles with the French government, helped rejig the bath's design and been the one skipper I'd found who believed the entire project was feasible. He seemed genuinely sad about not coming with me.

The following morning I woke far too early. Obsessed with getting to the quayside in plenty of time I'd arrived with hours to spare. I paced up and down running through final checks. Bananas? Check. Toothbrush? Check. Why had I packed a toothbrush? I was interrupted by a shout and glanced up to see a burly stereotype of how a fisherman should look lumbering towards me.

'I'm Andy. It really is a bath!'

A plate-sized hand was thrown out. Andy's handshake felt like a bear hugging an ant. He retracted his paw. My new support-boat skipper was a man boasting language so rare and raw it would make the Chairman of the Selection Committee for Undiscovered Words at the Oxford English Dictionary dive for his notepad. I'd no idea about his seamanship but took confidence from his salty demeanour. Just from the grease on his overalls I was sure this man knew the Channel brilliantly and would help me get across.

'I'll fetch my boat.'

Andy crashed away and another new member of the team arrived. Gavin Trevan is a friend from home. He'd finished his exams and was in that one Elysian summer we get of having nothing to do. He'd decided he'd come along on the support boat. Kenny had sent a reporter and photographer who now fetched up as well. The reporter pulled out his pad and pen.

'Can I have a interview before you set off? This new record you're about to set. Has it ever been set before?'

I suppressed a smile, mumbled, 'Err . . . no,' and carried on mixing the vile energy drink I'd invented using cranberry juice, sugar, salt and various other bits and bobs.

The plan was that I'd be towed across to France from Folkestone as this was the harbour in which Duncan had suggested I base the bath. Arriving there, the bath would be detached from the support boat and I'd row it back to Dover as this was a fair few miles further north-east up the coast from Folkestone and would mean I was closer to London. This would help when setting off on the round Kent leg of the journey. It had been cleared with the French authorities, the English Coastguard and Channel Crossing Association. Everyone was happy.

My phone rang. It was the French Navy, I assumed calling to wish me *bon chance*. The officer on the line informed me that, on that specific day, it was now totally illegal to row anything from the French coast to England. It sounds fantastic and implausible – I'm still questioning it – but it was exactly what happened. This is the crucial difference between having a Coastguard who act inside civil law (England) and having the Navy to look after the coast (France). Their Navy can immediately invoke emergency powers and they'd done just that. It didn't matter if *Lilibet II* was a bath or Registered British Shipping Vessel; the new powers counteracted both. I coolly observed it was a remarkable coincidence that these powers had come into play today. He made no reply. I tried to reason with him, making everything much worse. Due to an act of bureaucratic malice I couldn't understand, my entire plan appeared to be in ruins.

'But Monsieur, how can it be illegal to row from France to Dover when it is not illegal to row from Dover to France?'

'By saying "not illegal" do you mean legal?' This from a man who just six months before had professed not to speak or understand a word of English.

'Exactly, Monsieur . . .'

'*Alors*, Tim. It does not seem *logique*,' he confessed. 'I will call you back.'

We all waited for *logique* to triumph.

My phone rang again.

'You are right. It is *illogique* to say you can't row from France to Dover but you can row from Dover to France. So now it's illegal in France to attempt to row from Dover to France. *Je suis desolé*.'

A slim possibility flashed through my mind.

'So it's not illegal to row from *Folkestone* to France?'

'*Non*.'

'Then I'll do that.'

Hammered by black-belt extreme logic the French Navy caved in. Realising the position they'd taken was at best untenable, when I'd offered them Folkestone they'd taken it. This was the opposite way across the Channel to the one I'd planned but I'd still have rowed it. Due to protracted negotiations with the French I was now hours late starting out but if the weather held it wouldn't matter.

My brass Victorian showerhead gleamed as I rowed out from

Folkestone Harbour in the early morning light. Plumbed in, I could take showers on the briny. I looked up at it fondly only to see it snap off on the low swing bridge of the inner harbour. Damn. I dived into the water and passed it back to Andy for storage. I would have to do without the en suite.

Rowing hard, I inched my way beyond Folkestone's harbour wall. The buildings on the shore became smaller and less distinct. I was at sea, a lone engine of industry amid a mass of calm. It was a beautiful experience. As I looked round me that sunny morning I'd never felt happier. All the troubles and crises that had plagued me evaporated as I pulled towards my goal. Finally, I understood the call of the sea. I looked over at my support crew, a body of men handpicked for their intimate knowledge of the Channel and brilliance at sea. One of them leant over the side of the boat, waved cheerily and vomited violently into the calm blue. The reporter joined him. Andy waved sheepishly.

Two-fifths of my crack team were blowing chunks into the ocean. I tutted to Bernard my rubber duck. He gave me his usual glazed look back, but I thought I saw my disappointment with the support crew reflected in the shiny, enamelled paint finish of his googley eyes.

I checked my watch. After several hours of rowing it was still ten to seven in the morning. It had failed due to the salt water. Having a concept of time was vital to rowing the Channel. All the complex navigation theorems (including the key Speed versus Time equations that Dominic and I had slaved over) were now going to be impossible. But one of the support crew came to my rescue. I'd begun to notice that he was vomiting regularly and each time he threw up I shouted for the time. He was chundering roughly every half-hour. As a unit of measuring time at sea I'm not sure the Royal Navy would have been thrilled, but it was good enough for me.

The English Channel is the busiest shipping lane in the world. More ships and tankers plough their furrows up and down this stretch of water than anywhere else. To avoid crashes, and make life easier for the French and English authorities, it's divided into two lanes – a bit like a massive dual carriageway with a central reservation in the middle marked by large red and white buoys. I wished I'd known just how busy it was and cursed myself as I pulled into the first lane.

You can read statistics about the sheer enormity of tankers but it doesn't necessarily mean anything. Seeing these leviathans for the first time is something else. They are absolutely enormous – up to a mile and a half long. Many have stopping distances of 20 miles, so on land if you put the brake on at Nelson's Column you'd come to rest in Hatfield. Practically speaking, it means that by the time they've got close enough to see you and applied the brakes, they have passed through where you were and someone from the shipping line is phoning the undertaker. Some tankers have turning circles of 25 miles, which means if they want to do a U-turn in the English Channel they can't. I was crossing the world's busiest shipping lanes at right angles to the traffic flow in a piece of copper plumbing. It was like playing 'chicken' on the M1 riding a snail.

I mention this because around midday my worst nightmare happened. A tiny blue dot on the horizon turned out to be a mile-long behemoth bearing down on me really fast. Would the tanker follow theoretical naval law and give me right of way? Or would it smash me to smithereens? Trapped in my comic conceit, was I about to die chasing a punchline? Maniacally I increased my stroke rate; effectively I was a slightly arthritic worm trying to outrun a cheetah.

My mind, however, raced much faster: where had I put it? My hands shook slightly with the adrenaline. I opened the washstand and rifled through it. Nestling in the bottom, next to the shampoo was my early warning device. All captains must have one. Mine was red and shaped like a large party hooter. This was bound to save me. Sucking in air, I paused before blowing it as hard as I could.

No effect at all. I blew it again: zero impression. There was nothing I could do to get out of the way. I prepared for death. All was lost.

With one last throw of the dice, the following frantic conversation took place over the radio: 'I'm in a *bath*! Back down! BACK DOWN!! Over?'

Total silence.

A throaty, Dutch-sounding voice eventually came back: 'Are you alone?'

What was he offering? To soap my back?

To my amazement, and for the first time in maritime history, a tanker backed down for a piece of plumbing on the high seas, creating the 'FitzHigham Precedent'.

With huge relief I noted the massive bow waves – previously equal on both sides – suddenly became unequal. That meant she was turning to avoid me. The tanker passed within half a nautical mile. When dealing with something that size at sea, this had been a very close shave. Baths are cunningly designed to keep water in and the wash from the hull engulfed me. Soaking wet and bailing like a dervish, I couldn't find it within me to complain. I'd narrowly avoided being killed and cursed myself again for not installing a toilet on the bath. Smell the fear? I was sitting in it.

The water was now less choppy and my strokes easier. Soon it was like rowing on a lake again. I'd made it to the 'central reservation' dividing the shipping lanes. The support crew threw up in celebration. I shouted across for the time, they called back between chunders. I'd made it halfway across the Channel in about the same time as it had taken the female record holder to complete the crossing. Her boat had weighed the equivalent of three bags of sugar, my bath weighed a third of a tonne. This was going well. I was ahead of the schedule Dom and I had worked out. As I punched the air in triumph, my watch flew off my wrist and sank. In the depths of the Channel there's a small area where it's always ten to seven.

I'd now lost even the semblance of time. I looked down at my state-of-the-art compass. The shop told me it had glow-in-the-dark directions and even worked upside down. I now discovered that the one thing this expensive piece could not do was find magnetic north. I gazed at the uselessly spinning needle. It could be that the copper was confusing it. Or simply that it was total rubbish. I grudgingly accepted that my compass had also failed. I now had no method of telling direction or time. I had a vomit-festooned support crew. I'd narrowly avoided being scuttled by a tanker. My rubber duck was nervous and my showerhead had snapped off. These things were less than ideal; but, very much on the plus side, I could now see France. I hadn't noticed her at first. She slowly rose up behind me with all the cunning subtlety of a Parisian whore. I looked over my shoulder. There it was: the clear, defiant, beautiful Gallic coastline was beckoning me in. Nothing could come between us now.

The storm started slowly at first. Spots of rain, turning to drizzle, the sun haring off behind clouds, wind getting worse. Bernard turned to me and said, 'I'm just going out and may be some time.'

I steadied him and carried on pulling through the increasingly deteriorating weather.

'Will you give up?' yelled the reporter through the spray.

'Giving in is not an option,' I yelled back.

He made to write it down, slipped and vomited.

Things were becoming quite tough. I'd now been rowing for over six hours and my body was in crisis. My hands had lost a lot of skin and my nethers were deplorable. The least said about my buttocks the better. I was very tired. In good weather I was sure I could have driven myself on, forcing my battered frame up and down the sliding seat, but my physical problems got worse with the storm and my spirits were getting low. Andy screamed over the spume that he thought it was time to call off the attempt. I repeated my mantra about never giving in, pulling through what had now become a brisk Force 4 and would soon leap to a full-scale Force 6.

The indispensable *Reed's Nautical Almanac* describes the various sea states. At the time, I had read no explanations of sea states above a Force 3 or 4, as those were the very worst I'd been told to expect. A Force 3 suggests winds of 7–10 knots (defined as a 'gentle breeze') with wave heights of 0.4 metres. Force 4 suggests winds of 11–16 knots (defined as a 'moderate breeze') and wave heights of one metre. Even a one-metre wave is challenging in an ocean-going bath. What I now found myself in was a Force 6 described as winds of 22–27 knots with wave heights of up to three metres. But definitions in a book are useless when confronting nature face to face. The wind now pivoted to go not with the tide but against it, driving the sea into an army of vicious white-topped waves. In froth-tipped choppy short waves like that, getting any kind of oar purchase is impossible. I was seeing Duncan's galloping white horses up close. The storm was deploying all its troops and had just unleashed the cavalry.

Mist surrounded the bath and now I lost sight of my support crew. The waves responded by getting much bigger and crashing down on the bath. I bailed frantically. In the now dense fog, my perception sharpened. Things were not going according to plan. One particular wave was so violent it ripped the copper off the roll top exposing a nasty, serrated edge.

A massive wave threatened to tip me over. As the bath lurched to my left, I dived to the right to keep it stable. The bath paused, before slamming back down onto an even keel. My relief was short lived. The moisture on my shoulder was warmer than the water. I looked down. I'd cut my shoulder quite badly on the serrated edge. Blood seeped through the lycra sweater. When you're drenched with water blood doesn't stay long on your skin, but it was coming out thick and fast. The arm began not to respond properly. This could have been the shock or the cold chill of the wind but I began to suspect it was something to do with the cut. Obsessed, I carried on pulling with my remaining good arm towards where I had last seen the French coast.

There was a horrible clunk below, a sound like a muffled gunshot, and a rip. The bath juddered in the water. All I knew at the time was that it felt like we were getting lower on my left-hand side. Something – a log? – had hit the bottom and ripped a hole in one of the two pontoons designed to keep the bathroom floor afloat. This was serious. I'd seen Errol Flynn movies as a boy. What Flynn did in these situations was light a cigarette and toss things overboard. With my good arm I hurled the tool kit, First Aid box and the crappy tracking system overboard. The bath was now leaning well down to the left. I grabbed an oar with my right hand and continued rowing for France. I'll be fine, I thought. I can make this. I'm British. When I look back on this it was insane.

The rudder cables became useless and I lost my ability to steer. I was helpless amid the swirling maritime mass of industry. The sea had turned malevolently dark. What had once seemed friendly was now a violent monster trying to kill me. Three-metre-high waves crashed down on top of me.

I wasn't terrified or even scared. I didn't have the luxury of time. To be scared you have to realise that you're in danger and dwell on how things might end. That takes time. I spent every second I was out there making constant adjustments to my seating position. When not doing that, I'd be concentrating on how my hand would drive the oar through the water. Most of all I'd focus on what I could do to try and keep the bath up in the water.

Wave after wave rained down. I screamed at God. If he answered, I couldn't hear him over the ocean's noise. Facing the terrifying walls of water punching down on me, I realised that I'd soon be another member of my family lost in the Channel. More than anything else that realisation spurred me on. I found some last reserves and pulled to where I thought France must be. There was a gap in the fog and waves, and a moment of calm. I think, bizarrely, the sun even shone briefly. I heard voices: not the siren voices I'd been hearing in the spray, but very human, very alarmed, voices.

'Bloody hell! There he is! Bloody, bloody hell!'

The support boat had sighted me through the mist. Later Andy told me the reason he'd been able to find me at all was that with one arm and a sinking bath I'd been rowing in a giant circle.

Andy threw a line. I dived to get it and missed. Everything was now happening in three vivid dimensions. One moment Andy and the support boat were below me down a watery slope. The next they were way above, then hurtling down at me. Many times I watched them powerless in a trough or threatening to crash on top of me. Boat and bath were swilled round, forced above and below each other, battling the sea.

Trying to catch a line in this situation with one good arm is not easy. Eventually I got it. Straining hard they dragged me beside the support boat, mystified why I was so heavy. In my defence I'd lost a lot of blood and wasn't thinking clearly which might, in some way, explain what happened next. It turned out that the reason I seemed so heavy was that I had storm-lashed myself to the bath, dementedly prepared to go down with my vessel. They had pulled alongside the support boat not just me, but a third of a tonne of sinking sanitaryware.

Andy held my good arm, slashing through the cords which bound me to the bath. Both of us were totally focused on what needed to be done, rather than speculating on the mess we were in. He pulled me up and over the side rail of the support boat, landing me on the deck like a stunned mullet. Now the pain hit me like a fist, but I knew if we were not very careful we'd lose the bath altogether. Nursing my wounds was not an option.

I ran to the side and caught hold of one of lines attached to the bath and clung on to it. It was the only thing holding the bath to the support boat. Without my weight to keep it upright in the water, it had gently flipped over. Desperately, I looped the rope in my hand to the rail and Andy got hold of the other one. The bath's flag floated away from our grasp. A desperate lunge with the boat hook and I'd caught it. Losing the flag was unthinkable. The waves whipped up again, the spray cutting into my cheeks, and the bath finally rolled beneath the waves. Just one pontoon was now still visible, the rest lay below water. Through biting spray I saw Bernard sinking out of sight and leant out to where I'd last seen him, clawing the sea. Andy grabbed me as the boat lurched again, hurling me back on deck. Without him I'd have followed Bernard to a watery grave. With my one good arm Andy and I attached the bath to the side of the support boat as the wind, rain and waves lashed us from all sides. At this point both of us firmly believed that the sea would claim not only the bath but support boat as well.

It turned out we were in French waters, four tantalising miles from finishing the trip. Any decisions about what we should now do had to involve the French authorities. Reaching Calais wasn't an option. Due to the delay at the start caused by all the negotiating with the French on what was – and wasn't – legal on that day of the year, I'd missed the weather window. It is very fair to say that, being only four miles from completing the challenge, we probably would have finished before the storm hit. Without the negotiating, we'd now have all been tucked up, safe and warm, in a nice French port waiting out the storm with a Croque Monsieur, a bottle of red and the words 'good job we're not out in that' ringing comfortingly in our ears.

We made contact with the French. Their attitude was 'I told you so . . .' Ironically, it was the very time taken earlier that day, by the same French administrator, telling me that if it went wrong he would be saying 'I told you so . . .' that had led to the fact that it had gone wrong, and which now gave him the chance to say 'I told you so . . .' However cross I felt at his sneering delivery, I suppressed my anger and dealt with him with sunny courtesy. Even under immense strain, politeness is vital. In the true spirit of liberty and fraternity the French then refused us permission to land at Boulogne, before suggesting that their solution to this was to put explosive charges on the bath and blow it out of the water. They claimed the bath was a danger to all other shipping, a questionable assertion given we were now out of shipping lanes. When I pressed them they maintained blowing up the bath would deal finally with the bath question. They even offered to provide the detonative charges.

With a badly injured arm and the whole situation in chaos and confusion the storm lashed in again. Things were unclear and worrying. Phone calls and radio conversations went back and forth between us, the French and Duncan in Kent.

Andy had been mostly silent since I arrived on the support boat. He looked at me, 'I've not seen a rowing effort that bloody gutsy in the bloody Channel before. You sort this and I'll make sure that damned bath gets back to the UK.'

I wasn't thinking clearly, but went back on the radio[11] to the French Navy man, 'Just to remind you, Monsieur, that the sinking of a Registered British Shipping Vessel without the permission of the Captain will be taken as a bit of an act of war . . .'

Pin-drop silence on all frequencies in the English Channel followed. Back in Dover you could just hear the Coastguard saying, 'Could you come here a moment sir, there might be a problem.'

Supremely exhausted, blissfully unaware of the ramifications of what I'd just said I stood motionless in the cabin of Andy's boat.

I flicked the switch on the radio, '. . . Over?'

Silence reigned until the Frenchman finally came back on the radio. Under maritime law I was right. He gathered himself and said, 'You are the Captain, may we have your permission to sink her?'

'Absolutely not.'

We may have been stuck in the Channel in a hideous storm with a disabled bath hanging off the stern, but now we were having fun.

Andy broke into a grin. 'Right. Let's get this crapping Crapper back to Folkestone. Go and check that that bloody thing's still tied on. This is going to be *fucking* rough . . .'

The crew of the support boat were now in a terrible way and I felt for them. Were it not for me and my foolhardy plans they never would have been in this terrible situation. However the problems with the French authorities had turned any ill feeling within the boat towards those outside it. We worked hard in our common goal of getting the bath back to Blighty.

Ships then came from the other Channel nations to help us. It was very moving and proved that it's not just Britain but all the other nations along the Channel's shore that don't like the French.

---

[11] For clarity I've made this a single radio conversation as there were lots of simultaneous conversations flying back and forth on several mobiles and using various different radio frequencies making it very hard to be sure which part of which conversation occurred on what apparatus.

The sea continued to batter us. One moment the bath was tied up behind Andy's boat, the next it had slipped a line and was broadside across the bows, flying towards the cabin at warp speed. It was a horrid crossing back.

The storm was now Force 7 or 8. When you're in the middle of them it's difficult to measure these things accurately, but it seemed very bad to everyone on that boat. I don't get seasick, so Andy kept turning to me to do things. My competence at sea was being radicalised by this terrible punishment and a real rapport developed between us. Although we'd only known each other less than a day, Andy and I had bonded. He could see how difficult things were becoming for me and suggested that I went below and as the weather was now easing slightly, I agreed. I slumped onto the bed below deck and immediately jumped up again. There was no skin left on my buttocks. I lay on my front, nursing my shoulder as it hung over the edge of the hard, thin, foam mattress. It was a nasty throbbing mess. I passed out. Coming round, I found my scrotum bleeding, joining my shoulder and hands. This was the lowest point of my journey so far. Whichever way you looked at it, whatever gloss I put on it, at a very basic level I'd failed to do what I had set out to achieve. I sat below deck and tried to text the people I loved, but my swollen fingers weren't able to frame words on the tiny keypad. I finally managed to construct something approximating a message and clicked 'send'. There was no reception.

The support boat lurched down in the water; I hit my shoulder and passed out again. Coming round, I found myself in a strange world with no smiles. A world that didn't have the colour yellow. A world that never heard laughter. A world totally of my own making. As well as failing I'd almost lost the bath and narrowly avoided declaring war on France. I couldn't begin to think how I could come back from this. There was no money to stage a second attempt. My body was going to need some serious medical attention before I'd even be able to sit on a chair with ease let alone attempt the Channel again. The bath had a great hole in her side and the roll top had been ripped off. She was a complete mess. All my training, planning, thoughts and determination had led to utter failure. My charity fundraising plan had gone seriously wrong.

I reflected bitterly on my successful paper-boat voyage down the Thames and the depths of despair I now felt. The support boat was carrying me home but I didn't want to see anyone I knew. I had failed. Peering out of the tiny porthole I saw Folkestone bathed in light, the weather beautiful over Kent.

Bernard had sunk down into the depths. My life and priorities became very warped as I sat below the deck and wept for a rubber bath toy. I'm not a superstitious man but at that moment I realised it was 13 July.

Bugger.

Chapter Seven

A MONSTROUS CROW

'If not actually disgruntled, he was far from being gruntled.'

P.G. Wodehouse

Getting the bath out of the water was going to be impossible. She had turtled under and was clinging on to the support boat by just one line. Upside down and water heavy we'd need a crane to lift her out. We were about a mile off Folkestone Harbour when a gaggle of Dutch voices cut the air. People were gathering on the deck of a massive salvage boat floating outside the harbour arm.

A Dutch voice shouted over, 'Is that the bath we've all heard so much about?'

Very soon the salvage crane on board whirred into action. Kindly, they plucked the bath from the water like a bedraggled sock and plonked it on their deck. She was a mess. Water poured out of the hole in the flotation tank. The rim of the copper bath had been viciously ripped off and much of the bath itself was totally bent out of shape. Already having lost her showerhead, *Lilibet II* looked very sorry for herself. She'd be insulted but it was entirely right she'd finished her attempt on a salvage boat.

The Hollanders roughly patched up the flotation tank before lowering her into the water. I reached for one of the spare oars.

'I'll row her back.'

'You're not up to it.'

'I know . . . but it's important.'

Andy relented and I lowered myself gently into the bath. In unbearable pain I pulled towards Folkestone. It was probably only half a mile by now but I felt every inch of it in my back, buttocks, hands, shoulder and plums. I was in agony.

Duncan was waiting on the slipway. I thought he'd have a cross, angry or an irritating I-told-you-so look on his face but the only emotion he showed was a huge sense of relief.

We tied off the bath. It was a sunny day on the quayside in Kent. I stood looking at the total wreck before me. The bath had a huge hole in it. I had a fairly big hole in me and the crew had all decided to take up jobs in landlocked places like Derbyshire.

Although the sun was out, the sea was still angry as we found when trying to put the bath back onto the trailer. With me very disabled, it was tricky but we managed it.

Eventually, we sat down to a pint. It had gone very badly. Duncan was the first to take up the conversation.

'I've said this before. It's just not possible.'

'I was just four-and-a-half miles off. Without the faffing about and the weather problem, I might have made it.'

'I think there's something in that . . .' Andy mused, more to his beer than anyone.

We'd all had a very lucky escape. It was a great bit of captaincy from Andy that had got us through.

We all left the pub after just one pint and Gavin and I made for home. As darkness fell we left Folkestone. As darkness fell further we arrived back in Folkestone. I wailed. The satanic one-way system had deceived us into a two-hour round trip. In darkness Gavin and I left Folkestone again. It was then that the trailer lights chose to break, which seemed to do something to the car's engine. We pulled over and with the engine running I popped the bonnet. It was so dark but in the dimness I could smell fumes and see there was oil and petrol all over the engine.

'Need a light?'

Gavin helpfully leant over with a lighted candle. We both paused for a moment, surveying the petrol, oil, fumes and proximity of the lighted flame to all three.

'Gav . . . I think perhaps we should look for the torch, don't you?'

'Good idea.'

By a flickering torch I attempted to rewire the electrics and patch up the engine. I was so tired and recovering from inadvertently nearly being blown up, I decided to check us into the first hotel we came to and sort out my shoulder and all other problems the next day.

'Do you have a room for two please?'

'No sorry, sir, we're fully booked – let me check the other hotels in the area.'

I must have looked terrifying in that hotel lobby caked in blood, mud and oil. Gavin didn't look too marvellous either. He had the nervous air of a man who'd glimpsed death twice that day and wasn't yet sure he'd genuinely escaped it.

'I can't explain it, sir, but all the hotels between here and the M25 are fully booked tonight.'

'Brilliant, thank you, goodnight.'

'Has it been a long day?'

'You could say that . . .'

I'd failed in the Channel, narrowly avoided war with France, suffered exploding engines and now I couldn't even check into a hotel successfully. I'd had finer days.

Gavin and I struck for home.

The next few nights were horrible. I was so tired I could cry, but each time I shut my eyes, images of storms, waves, blood and the spectre of my Uncle Tony shone out of the darkness at me. I'd tried to use his nemesis for something stupidly comic. Now it consumed my dreams to tell me off.

After getting my shoulder strapped up and more general medical attention for the rest of me, there was lots of thinking to do. Where was I supposed to go from here? Was there enough money to pay for another attempt? Would the team want to be involved in another attempt? Could we fix the bath? Could I get fit for it? Had I just proved what Duncan had feared all along, that rowing the Channel wasn't possible in a tub? It basically all boiled down to one question: should I try again or throw in the bath towel?

I'm not good at giving in. For as long as I can remember, I've never given in, and hate watching others do so. My determination verges on the insane. Yet my determination was sorely tested now.

Spending time away from the bath was nice. I got to spend time with my friends, the girl I loved and my family. What was the point of it all? Sport Relief didn't seem remotely bothered at the failure of the bath trip. I'm not sure they thought it was possible anyway. I was still badly bashed up and was enjoying having time to rest. My body enjoyed not training so hard that it took up every second of my day. Now it was focusing on dealing with the pain caused by basic day-to-day issues like sitting down.

When I was small I fell off my skateboard coming down a hill and ripped all the skin off my backside. I had to sit on a cushion for weeks. This was worse. The pain caused by the lack of skin on my buttocks was excruciating. I found any excuse possible not to sit down in company. The few times I went out to dinner in this period always led to the inevitable moment: 'Shall we sit down?' I came up with a variety of excuses, none of which really worked. 'No thanks, I've just joined that religion where you have to eat standing up during July . . .' 'No thanks, I prefer to eat mine pacing up and down, it's part of a diet thing I'm trying . . .' 'Do you mind if I eat mine kneeling? It's in memory of St Joseph?' You'll no doubt be surprised to learn, none of these worked and I spent evenings almost passing out with pain, and not, for a change, at the conversation.

Kneeling at my study desk, my computer flashed and made an irritating noise. An email. It was from someone I've known almost longer than anyone else and yet now hardly ever get to see. Some friends you don't need to see to feel close to or simply be inspired by. We were tiny together in Derbyshire and in the same class at our little school. We played together at break times and at one point even had shoes that matched. I'm sure they were called 'Pods' and we thought they were great, semi-magical in fact. Everyone else thought they were silly.

We raced up and down the tarmac playground together. In summer we were let out into the field to run around and in our final year we were even allowed near the school pond to watch the water boatmen. When I was small she was my close friend. I still remember waking up in the morning, pulling on my socks and looking forward to going to school, not for the lessons, but because I knew we'd get to play together in the breaks.

Now she's a professional sailor and her determination is legendary. The email inspired me and made me curse my lack of determination. The writer of the email: Ellen MacArthur. I read it, replied and determined to make another attempt.

I phoned Simon to tell him.

'Simon? I want to have another crack across the Channel . . .'

'What? It's an insane plan, you might die properly this time . . . I'm in.'

Somewhere south of Wapping, the phone rang: 'Kenny? I want to try and give it another go . . .'

'How much is it going to cost me this time?'

I'd done a rough budget. I'd learnt from the failed attempt, budgeting was something I simply had to get better at. I could hear Kenny smiling.

'Sure. We'll put the money in place to help you try to kill yourself again . . . gladly.'

With sponsors like these, who needs enemies?

My shoulder healed slightly so I joined Mark and the lads in trying to put the bath back together. It really was a mess.

There was a silver lining to the dark cloud of my failure. Simon phoned from Thomas Crapper & Co.

'Tim, you may have fail . . .' he coughed and began again. 'Tim, you may have . . . not quite made it across the Channel in your bath but don't forget your main aim was to raise money for charity. You can still raise money for charity. In one of the sheds at Thomas Crapper and Co we've still got His Imperial Majesty King George V's travel bath. You could auction that off and raise money for charity that way.'

A masterstroke. I left Mark on the riverbank and drove up to the head office of Thomas Crapper & Co. It was a long journey, as I had to keep pulling over to air my raw buttocks and wipe the seeping goo from the seat of the car. After getting lost and missing the innocuous gate twice again, I turned in and up past the cricket pitch on the left. The sheep went on with the same particularly important piece of eating as before and the stream continued to babble happily on the right. I brought the car to a standstill in the bath park, opened the door and bounded out to weave my way deftly through the bath labyrinth. Not finding the Minotaur, I met

Simon standing in between the massive Victorian urinals (rampant) beaming in his Edwardian beard.

'What stunning urinals you have.'

He smiled, making his moustaches rise at the corners.

'I've been meaning to tell you this for ages and now's the perfect time . . .' He pointed to the design of a bee stunningly inlaid in the porcelain of the urinals. 'This is a Victorian joke, a sort of a pun.'

My brain started to bombinate. I love puns. 'A bee?'

'Think, Tim, what's Latin for bee?'

'Erm . . . flower bee is *Apis floris* . . . oh Apis . . . "A piss" on a urinal – brilliant.'[12]

'Now come and see the travel bath.'

The silver lining to my dark cloud came with solid silver taps.

'The taps, plug and all the plumbing is solid silver. He was a man of style, George V.'

Simon explained that during Britain's first darkest hour – the First World War[13] – the government asked the King to go round the country and rally the people. The King agreed immediately but had one condition. He must have a bathroom installed on the Royal Train. So Thomas Crapper & Co installed the iron masterpiece and all the solid silver plumbing onto the Royal Train. This was paid for by the War Office. Why have more ammunition when you can have plumbing like that? I'm not an expert on the history of sanitaryware but if there is a greater plumbing masterpiece than this, I'd like to see it. When it was removed and a new one put in its place for the current Queen, Crappers couldn't bare to see their great work destroyed, so kept it.

'I'll have it polished up and get the enamel looked at, as it

---

[12] The bee transfer was placed on the urinal as a target – the Victorians knew men liked something to aim at. Cleverly, the bee was even positioned in the ideal place to minimise splash back. Two lesser European bathroom companies have produced a range like this but substituting a fly for the bee (Latin for fly: *Musca Domestica*; not amusing at all) and have put the target in the wrong place, leading to many splashed trousers at hotels in County Cork.

[13] When I was small it was always known at home as the 'First Local Difficulty'. My great-grandfather was the only pacifist my family has ever managed to produce. It says a lot about him that he was a pacifist in World War I who won the Military Medal. This is the 'highest' medal you can win if you're not an officer. Another member of the family (an uncle or cousin, Albert) won the Victoria Cross in the same war. This is the British Army's highest award for gallantry.

would be good if it left here as we intended when it first went out.'

I left Crappers that afternoon and phoned my girlfriend.

'What do you know about charity auctions? I've got a bath . . .'

She had loads of experience at that sort of thing so we worked happily together setting it all up. I went out to the boatyard in the day and worked hard with Mark, then when I'd finished, we'd meet up in the sunshine and plan the auction together. This was a lovely period of my life and of the bath project.

There'd been some press about my failure to cross the Channel. Cynics would suggest that there would have been less press had I made it. One day I got a call from an events company asking if there was anything they could do to help. They'd read about the bath project in the paper and heard that I was going to try again.

I explained that although I was going to try again, I was currently focused on organising an auction to raise money for the charity the trip was in aid of. The man on the end of the phone, Andre, sounded really excited, 'I'd love to help. Where are you at the moment?'

'At the boatyard by the river.'

'I'll come.'

He arrived on the riverbank in a shining open-topped silver Mercedes. The man who stepped out of it would have looked more at home in Monaco or Capri than Richmond. With noticeable incongruity he arrived among the oil-stained overalls of the boatyard. One of London's top party tsars had joined the bath team.

Over the next few days Andre and his team put together all the ingredients of a top night. They found me a huge house to hold the auction in, right in the centre of London. It was stunning, had a huge drawing room, was empty and, better than anything, the owners said we could use it for free.

They opened a charity bank account for the money we hoped to make from the auction. Andre had the great plan of getting a drinks sponsor on board. He thought up ways of lighting the event, staffing the bar, making the place look good and generally did everything that events companies do best. One day he phoned.

'Tim, we can't just auction off the bath thing—'

'It's the Royal travel bath.'

'Yeah . . . we need something more. I can use some contacts and get us some other stuff to go with it. How does that sound?'

'Great.'

He sorted out a Cartier diamond, Rolex wristwatch, some other gems, jewels and even furniture to go with the bath. Brilliant. This was going to be a very special night. It all moved so fast. It's amazing to watch the London party maestros when they get going. They have address books to rival the Delphic Oracle and are not afraid to unleash them.

'I'll sort the press and shall we have some VIP guests too?'

Very soon he'd invited more press than I knew existed. Comic Relief and I couldn't believe the effort that was going into this. He even showed me the RSVP from Tom Cruise's office saying Tom was in town for a movie premiere that week and would love to come and help such a good cause. Things were getting out of hand. My tiny charity auction had taken on massive proportions. The travel bath was so pretty and had obviously generated a huge interest. The whole thing was wonderful. As I continued working hard on *Lilibet II*, I began to look forward to what would be the night of the year.

I forget exactly what it was that made me question him about it, but innocently one day I tried to be helpful. 'If you give me the cheque book I can go and pick up—'

'There's no need . . .' Andre looked stressed, but then he had a lot on his mind.

Eventually he signed one of the cheques from the bank account we'd opened and I went off to pick up whatever it was. It seemed odd to me that I couldn't sign cheques on a charity bank account that had been set up in my name. Not being the brightest bear in the toy box I asked my girlfriend about it.

'I'm sure that's normal, darling . . . He's probably just forgotten to put you on the account.'

'Are you on the account?'

'No sweet-pea but why should I be?'

I looked at the cheque and saw that the bank holding the account was offshore: again, merely slightly unusual but enough to get me thinking. It seemed an awful lot of effort to open an offshore account simply for my charity auction. He'd become a very good friend, particularly with my girlfriend, so I thought I'd just politely ask him about it.

'I see the bank's offshore.'

'Yes, it's the best way of doing these things for tax.'

'Right.'

I don't understand tax so didn't question that, but it led to anther question that then bugged me. 'At the auction, as well as the credit card thing that you've sorted, people often want to give cash – you know in buckets – for the charity . . .'

'Yes.'

'Well, how do we pay that in at the bank?'

He then made a mistake. If he'd thought fast, he could have come up with something better than what he actually said. He might have been tired, or he may have thought I'd support him in it. He looked at me oddly, and a cold tone entered his voice.

'Here's the thing. If we bank it here, we have to pay tax on it, so the best way to deal with it is to put the cash in suitcases and take it over to the offshore bank ourselves.'

'Right . . .'

'That way we don't pay tax . . .' He looked deep into my eyes for a reaction before adding hastily, 'Oh and the charity gets more money out of it.'

I may not understand tax but I knew that being asked to carry suitcase-fulls of cash through airports by conspiratorial-sounding men was a bad plan. I carried on listening to him talking and as I did, realised I didn't know anything about this man at all. I'd met him through the newspaper. I'd checked out his website and it all looked square, but he could have just made it up.

I decided to let him run with things. I didn't have any proof of anything other than that he had a very relaxed attitude to tax. I thought that by giving him more rope, and making him trust me more, if he was up to anything bad, I stood a better chance of seeing what it was. I decided to keep my girlfriend in the dark on what he'd said. I didn't want to worry her. I think perhaps he was gambling on the fact that I'd look very silly if I pulled the event at this late stage so thought I'd join him rather than cancel.

Something happened by chance. An elderly lady sent me a cheque. Not having my address, she posted it to the building the auction was due to be held in. In being re-routed, it somehow missed Andre and ended up on the desk of the man that brokered a deal involving the building. With the cheque was a letter in her spidery handwriting and not knowing what it was, the broker put my surname into Google and phoned me up.

'Why am I sitting here with a cheque for you?'

I explained to him in total innocence about Andre and the events company and the charity auction. The voice that came back was measured and I felt sure could be slightly sinister in the wrong situation.

'I'd be very careful if I were you. Andre has been doing some things recently that have not gone well for him. He's done some things for me in the past, which were good, but I wouldn't touch him now. He's not doing well, if you understand me. Do you know for a fact that he's even still working with that events company?'

Then he said something I could not ignore.

'I thought he'd left the country . . .'

Suddenly the candle burnt a tiny hole in the sack and a chink of light was opened.

'. . . Now, where shall I send this cheque?'

I now know something of the fringes of what I'd become involved in. You may think I'm overpainting the situation. I will try and explain as much as I can. I'm not able to say where I think the broker stood in all this but suffice to say that Andre was a very desperate man indeed. He'd done some 'work' for some people involving very large sums of money – let's call them collectively 'Gangland Inc'. This had gone badly and the money had disappeared. Andre then took up the cutting-edge style of entrepreneurialism pioneered by the Krays, and robbed a few houses to try to make some of the money back.

I didn't want to go to Andre with what I knew. I couldn't produce the paper proofs I'd been shown and my girlfriend was becoming very protective of him.

Finally, a few nights later, she sat in tears on the sofa and told me why. 'He told me not to tell anyone as he's embarrassed about it, so please don't say anything darling, but he's got testicular cancer and may only have a few months left.'

As I wrapped her in my arms and hugged her till she cheered up, I felt awful. What if she was right? What if I was judging a dying man harshly? Feeling two-faced and horrible I began to subtly check on the things he'd set up. My newfound budgeting skill came in useful. I checked with the suppliers on the things he said he'd got us for free due to their generosity: the flowers, lighting, lighting designer, doormen and carpets. The suppliers painted a very different picture. They all expected to be paid: some of them upwards of £10,000.

The budget for the auction was staggering. We couldn't make any money for the charity with such massive expenditure. I poked around further. I hated doing this but felt I'd been left with no choice. The drinks sponsorship turned out to be genuine, and initially I thought this might offset the massive bills he was running up all over London but when it was confirmed that their sponsorship merely came in the form of free alcohol, I realised I was in big trouble. Everything else he'd told me was a tissue of lies.

The house he'd got to hold the auction in was the subject of an ongoing wrangle between a third-world government and some sharp-practising businessmen. The developing nation alleged that the businessmen swindled the house from their country in the late nineties. Whatever the truth of the allegation, to use that building to host a charity auction to raise money for a charity that funds projects in the very country who allege the house was stolen from them is a nonsense.

The offshore bank account was being used to funnel money from three other offshore accounts that were the subject of a fraud investigation. I wasn't even a signatory to my own charity account.

The Cartier diamond, Rolex watch, furniture and other stuff that Andre wanted to auction off under the nose of the entire press corp turned out to be stolen goods: the product of his descent into petty thiefdom. He was intending to use my charity auction as a fence to sell stolen goods to the likes of Tom Cruise.

How had I gone from trying to raise money for a charity to living on the fringes of international celebrity fraud?

Andre, meanwhile, was staying with my girlfriend in a house in the middle of nowhere in Scotland. I had to spend an agonising weekend, knowing that he was at best a crook and fearing that at worst he could be much more. Also he was with the woman I loved in an isolated location.

Standing up to my neck in this horribly murky water, I baited my hook and picked up the phone: 'Andre, hi, the beer delivery is coming in early. I'm away training, shall I send a mate of mine to pick it up?'

There was a pause. I thought I heard dropping spoons in the

background. It was a big gamble, he could have just said 'yes' but I reasoned he was so in need of the cash he'd want to get the beer for himself. Also, as far as he was concerned, the auction was still going ahead so we needed that beer.

'No, I'll come down from Scotland early.'

'That's great, thanks so much . . .' I hung up.

The next half a day I spent in London waiting for my girlfriend to get back to the flat. I didn't want to call her, as I knew she'd realise from the tone of my voice that something was up.

Finally, I couldn't wait any longer. 'Where are you now?'

'On the way back, darling.'

'Is Andre still with you?'

'No, he left before me to get the beer delivery.'

Horrible hours later she arrived through the front door. I pulled her into my arms. 'How was Scotland?'

'Fine, we played cards . . .'

'Did you win much?'

'I won the first few hands but in the end Andre cleaned up.'

'Baby, we need to talk . . .'

I unburdened the whole thing to her. Showed her the paperwork and very gently let her know that a man she'd trusted had let her down.

With good spirit she recovered quickly. 'But he's on his way to get the beer delivery. How will we . . . ?'

'I'm not sure that's a problem.'

At the same time, Andre was eagerly closing the door of his Mercedes to pick up the beer in central London; somewhere in a warehouse in west London, the beer sat safely in crates. As soon as I knew he'd left her alone in Scotland, I cancelled the order.

'If you have any doubt left about any of this, please phone him . . .'

'I'll meet with him.' Still she believed in the fundamental goodness of people.

She left a message; he left the scene. Where he went, I don't know. When the beer delivery didn't arrive he left an abusive message on my phone. It said he hated me for having not joined him in his fraud. Before he hung up he swore vengeance on me, then ran away.

In a couple of hours I'd dismantled the whole auction and saved myself, and more importantly Comic Relief, from a terrible situation. I cancelled all the suppliers across London, who shocked me

Mark Edwards,
(Royal Bargemaker),
Tim FitzHigham and
Major Thomas Crapper

Sunrise on the second attempt: following protracted
legal issues - see chapters 2, 3, 4 and the epilogue -
the actual design of the bath I was permitted to take
to sea, complete with Victorian tiled floor, taps and a
washstand, became more a bathroom than a bath, but
was officially now a Registered British Shipping Vessel

Steve Williams,
Matthew Pinsent,
Alex Partridge, me
and James Cracknell

(*Above left*) Being winched out at the end of the first attempt. A less than ideal result

(*Above right*) Broken in victory. The moment I successfully made it to France

(*Left*) Under the watchful eye of my support-boat skipper, Andy

The Bath and the French naval base at Cap Gris Nez

Kind people

Big tankers

Big cliffs

Eureka... I've made it, says bathtub hero Tim

BY DAVID HARDING

AS BATHS go it is perhaps the most mobile since Archimedes, but last night Tim Fitz-Higham's floating tub took its place in maritime history.

The intrepid adventurer crossed the finishing line at Tower Bridge to become the first man to row a bath up the River Thames.

He was cheered by boats from the Port of London Authority and cheered on by well-wishers from the river banks as he finally pulled the tub on his 250km (160 mile) journey.

He said: 'I can't believe it. I feel on top of the world.' I've made it at last.

Mr FitzHigham then celebrated in the only way possible — he bought home for a bath.

The 28-year-old began his epic voyage supported by Mensa — two months ago. He set off from the French coast at Cap Griz Nez and then heading up the Channel.

On his way up he braved the world's busiest shipping lane and battled against wind and tide – all in a 1.2m bathtub complete with antifouling.

The final stretch of the journey, begun in bright sunshine, was probably the easiest of the task taking, was probably the easiest of the task taking, just over an hour to complete. Mr FitzHigham said.

As well as creating a rowing first, Mr FitzHigham is raising money for Comic Relief. You can donate on www.timrow.com

A man in a bath on the Thames... Tim's back

BY DAVID HARDING

MOVE over Dame Ellen MacArthur, Britain has a new hero of the high seas.

Tim FitzHigham, the man who rowed across the Channel in a bathtub (and travelled the Thames in a paper canoe, lest we forget), has begun the final stage of an epic journey to London.

Setting off from Gravesend yesterday afternoon, Tim powered his 1.5 metre-long bathtub to Erith, 16km up the Thames.

Armed with two bottles of water, ten bananas and a bottle of cranberry juice, the 28-year-old comedian set off at 4.40pm. The journey, which took just under four hours, leaves him just two short rows away from the finishing line at Tower Bridge.

A headwind was his biggest problem. But, cheered on by passing boats and a fly-past by a Spitfire, Tim rowed on. He said: 'It was really hard work at first until the Dartford Bridge but then the wind eased off.'

He began his epic journey, to raise money for Comic Relief, when he set

FROM START TO FINISH – IN A TUB

STAGES 1 & 2
Start: Folkestone
Folkestone to Gravesend
Channel Tunnel
Calais
Gravesend
Whitstable
Sheerness
Ramsgate
Margate
Folkestone
Finisty Cap Griz Nez

STAGE 3
FINISH Tower Bridge
WOOLWICH
LEWISHAM
Greenwich
Erith
DARTFORD
GRAYS
GRAVESEND
2km

Finally, Tower Bridge

(*Above*) Disembarking –
Phil still on camera

(*Right*) With Richard –
City of London Alderman

(*Below left*)
Mum, Dad and me

(*Below right*) Lieutenant-
Commander Dom Hurndall
RN Ret. and Simon Kirby,
MD of Thomas Crapper
& Company

The FitzHigham, finally my family seat

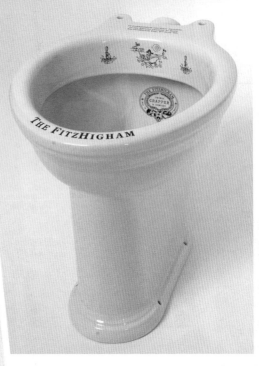

A day off in Cornwall during the
tour of the award-winning show
'In the Bath: Unplugged'

with their kindness. Many even thanked me for having saved them the expense of not being paid. I also had to email all the people who had been invited. I felt terrible about this but, at the time, there was still a chance that Andre might be caught so I agreed not to let people know the real reason why the event had been cancelled. I think I blamed a cold in the end, which was a very lame excuse. I hate any whiff of things that aren't true, and kindly, people didn't push me on it.

The best thing about the situation is that I'd realised what was going on quickly enough to stop everything and no one had lost money. But the silver lining to my dark cloud turned out to be made of lead. My cloud crashed swifter than the Hindenburg and I was left sifting through the wreckage for some debris of hope. The charity auction debacle had really shaken my grip on reality. I'd always thought the world was a generally sunny place but coming across people ready to abuse my optimistic outlook for bad purposes really shocked me to the core.

Subsequently I found out that Andre had been cleverly booking airline tickets on my girlfriend's credit card and had also taken money from her. It was a real lesson to learn: some people can be very cruel. I felt like everything I held close was shifting. Morally, I was a man trying to run up a hill that I'd just found out was made of sand.

I'd failed in the Channel, I'd let down everyone who'd believed in the bath plan and now the sparkling charity auction had turned into a near miss with the fraud squad. My only current hope was that the weather would improve, Mark would get the bath finished and I might be able to make another attempt as soon as possible.

The weather now became awful again. By this point, I'd spent months training, rowing and battling the Channel which meant I'd not been doing anything that made money. I was chronically short of funds, so needed to do something to make some cash.

Leaving university, I'd moved abroad and ended up farming. On my return, I didn't know what I wanted to do. I spent some time with various tutors at RADA before moving on to balance various unsuccessful day jobs with a bit of comedy and acting. Through a series of lovely flukes it was, oddly, comedy that had become the mainstay of my life since I gave up farming. I'd even been nominated for the prestigious Perrier Best Newcomer Award at Edinburgh and since then consistently and joyously failed to live up to my own early promise. With my confidence in the world at an all-time low, I headed for the only place no one would notice a lunatic – the Edinburgh Festival Fringe.

In 2003, I'd turned up at Edinburgh and told the story of the paper-boat trip. I wouldn't call it a stand-up routine, more a story that made people laugh – an enterlecture, or my version of raconteurism. As I'm sure Dr Johnson would have said in later life, trying to define things takes the fun out of them. Whatever that hour of me wittering on was defined as, the show *Paper Boat* became a surprise, if modest, hit of the Festival that year. My tiny venue was totally sold out for three weeks and many of the papers kindly made it their pick of the Festival.

I'd never intended to do a show based on the paper-boat journey, but as a comic, I'd always talked about the things I'd seen and that was just one of them. I thought I'd try a similar hour based on the bath trip to date. Life had got me down, things were not going well and that's often the source of great comedy. While many comics have written well when they've been depressed, I was not one of them. Every time I thought about the bath, the trip, the hilariousness of the ruse – I found myself in bed, lying in a darkened room.

Needless to say, my 2004 bath show was the comic equivalent of a train crash. The audiences, most of whom had come in 2003, were courteous but it was nowhere near my best work. Newspaper critics swarmed in to rip the show and my life to shreds. One reviewer decided that the entire reason the show was rubbish was my choice in shirts.

I'd always tried to take a fairly level-headed view of reviews but already shaken by the total lack of cheerfulness in the bath project, I started to spiral. I was a man swimming hopelessly against a tide of sadness that wanted to engulf me. I gasped brief mouthfuls of hopefulness but in the main, the waves took me. They were relentless.

The only glimpses of light were: my shoulder was better, the bath had been fixed and I might get a weather window in September and finally finish this.

At the end of the first week in September, I got the flu. Long-distance rowing with the flu is not advisable; it also makes your job much harder at sea.

Mid-September, I got a phone call from Duncan. 'Tim, there's a weather window tomorrow . . . I think we can try the crossing again.'

'I'll be there . . .'

'You sound terrible.'

The one good day of September weather coincided directly with the worst day of my illness. I couldn't go: I wasn't the first to be thwarted by it, but man flu had won again.

My last chance to turn things around in 2004 had disappeared. What I'd planned as a hilarious two-week jaunt over the summer would now have to be abandoned or become an obsession that would live on for another year. And for at least another year, at every party, every introduction and most of all, always in my head, I'd be 'the man who failed to row the Channel in a bath'.

I was not in control of my own life. I'd set myself up as a total failure. Just as Dave Gorman predicted[14], my life had become a waking nightmare based on a P.G. Wodehouse plot. Sadly for me there was no Jeeves on hand to pull me out of the onion soup.

There's nothing better when you've had a really tough summer than knowing you have winter ahead, with dark early nights, a roaring fire and the woman you love. My girlfriend and I were getting on like a house on fire, in fact so well it was more like a city on fire. I'd kept a lot of my inner thoughts to myself and concentrated on being there for her. This stopped me thinking too hard about my own gloom and let her know that she was my top priority. Due to work commitments she'd had to move countries, so after missing the last weather window I went to be with her.

Things were going great, although we were living apart. I've always thought that you should never trap the people you love and I felt we were trapping each other by trying to be together while being forced to live apart. Both of our lives found it hard to cope with us taking a week or two off a month to see each other and do nothing much else. That winter, we were away and went to watch a cricket match together. We sat curled up on the boundary,

---

[14]Dave and I had become friends playing in Edinburgh years before. It was during one of those boozy nights he first said, 'Tim, you only exist because P.G. Wodehouse didn't invent you first.' We've been good friends ever since. When he heard about the bath project, he left the same line as a message on my phone. Everyone involved in this book thought it was such a good summary of me that they put it on the cover.

talked, laughed and hugged. She'd been the lantern of my world ever since I first saw her as a girl at college but I felt very clearly now that our relationship was holding her back. We kissed goodbye at the airport and have never seen each other since. Love, like happiness, is an instant, an unforgettable moment in time, and trying to freeze love or keep it in the jar of a relationship kills it.

It was the right decision. At the time it hurt me more than rowing the Channel had done. I stopped swimming against it and gave in to the sea of sorrow. Mentally, I hit the floor.

I'd sunk both my bath and relationship. The charity auction was a farce and I was now trapped in a limbo of bad weather over winter. I was embroiled in a tragedy entirely of my own making. At Edinburgh I'd even died on stage in a bath. My nightmares returned and my sleep became violent again. I spent the winter in a very deep cliché, writing terrible not-quite poetry, drinking more than a bitter, cynical cop in an American B-movie and wondering if I'd make it to spring. I didn't want to see spring. I didn't return calls and did my best to isolate myself from everyone who knew me.

I joined the illustrious list of people who've died in baths to become a downmarket version of Agamemnon: except obviously he was Greek and probably wore a sheet at the time. That winter, all was darkness.

CHAPTER EIGHT

PRUNING THE PLUMS

'Stop dying at once, and when you get up, get your bloody hair cut.'

Lieutenant Colonel A.D. Wintle
to his critically ill batman Cedric Mays, who obeyed the order

My blithe plumbing-based ruse had become an albatross. I was a conceited comic trapped by my own comic conceit; living proof that the English love eccentrics – just not as close friends. Every time I thought about the bath I found myself lying in bed with the curtains closed.

Finally I got myself together. I realised how childish, selfish and whiny I'd become. I'd been under a lot of pressure, things hadn't gone well, but it's how you deal with problems that defines you. Self-pity is something no one in my family had ever done and I couldn't fathom how I'd ended up doing it now. My behaviour was shameful. Finally a line from my grandfather appeared in my head: *'nunquam te confundant illegitimi'* which I think roughly translates as 'never let the bastards grind you down'. My grandfather was Victorian when it came to swear words: swearing is fine as long as it's in Latin. It was like someone shining had just grabbed me by the throat and showed me myself. I stopped moping. Simply (perhaps tritely) put, it's better to have tried and died than never to have tried at all.

By March, I was back to reading books on training. I wanted to ease into things gently, didn't want to pull anything. April saw me actually training. Betty and I undertook gruelling sessions together. My avenging angel battered me again, just as she had the year before. I had to fight consistent battles on that Ergo. When things were hurting and I wanted to pass out from the pain, a new voice appeared in my head and said with a silvery tongue, 'Don't bother finishing it, you won't make it anyway, remember what happened last time . . .' Every time it whispered, I dug deeper, found something extra and kept on rowing.

I made calls and began putting the team back together. It was April and a weather window could happen in May.

I'd been trying to contact Duncan Taylor on his mobile and house phone for most of March with no luck. I couldn't work it out. He was normally so reliable. Perhaps he was away on holiday. He knew we'd need to start planning. Finally, in mid-April, his wife picked up the phone at the house. I was really relieved to hear her voice.

'Tim, thank goodness, I've been trying to get hold of you but didn't have your mobile number . . .'

'Duncan's got it.'

'Tim, Duncan's dead.'

Something had just hit me in the forehead. My head hurt.

'What?'

'I know how close you'd become and I'm sorry. I wanted to let you know sooner. He loved planning with you and was so looking forward to . . .' Her voice trailed off and she cried the tears of a woman who's loved the same man her whole life. It was gut wrenching to hear down the end of the phone, and I felt powerless to help her with her grief.

That winter, Duncan had gone to see his doctor with a pain in his chest. He thought it was just a cold or the flu. It was cancer and he died within weeks. Cruelly snatched from his wife and family who didn't really have time to say goodbye. A huge, strong man, seemingly in the best of health with a tremendous energy and sunny outlook had been snatched from the people he touched. I was one of them and it hit me really hard.

While he was seriously ill, Duncan had instructed his wife to tell

Andy to take me across the Channel. I put down the phone to Mrs Taylor and sat deep in thought. More than anything so far, this made me think about giving the whole project up. Then I thought of Duncan and his belief, even when he was ill, that the bath crossing should go ahead.

I picked up the phone and soon heard, 'I wondered when you'd be calling, trying to get us both killed again . . . you mad, mad . . .' Andy was back in the bath.

April passed in a pained and horrible sweat of swearing at Betty, running for hours and doing weights until my arms burnt.

One evening I was eating a baked potato in a flat in London with a friend of mine called Charlotte. Her flatmate breezed through the door.

'Phil, this is Tim.'

'Hi, Tim. What are you up at the moment?'

'I'm training to row the English Channel in a bath.'

Setting off the top of Phil's very tall, former cavalry officer frame was a look of total bafflement. Charlotte smiled as Phil's lips parted to speak again.

'What?'

I told Phil about the bath trip and how far we'd got. He gave me his card.

'I make travel documentaries. I'm sure there are loads of people interested in this bath trip but if you'd like I could come along to try to record it.'

I liked Phil. He was straightforward and believed in things with a great passion. We talked further over the next few days and agreed he would follow the bath trip and we'd try to make a documentary out of it.

Over a celebratory beer, he smiled and said, 'So where is this bath? Perhaps I'd better go and see it. It would be good to get some film of it.'

That was a good point. While I was concentrating hard on my nervous collapse, Mark had carefully put the bath into storage over winter.

'Hi, Mark, where is she?'

'I've rented you a field near the river. She's there, being looked after.'

Mark, Phil and I arrived in a place called Upper Halliford,

somewhere near the Thames, west of Richmond. I brought the car to a stop outside a white cottage on the road adjoining a large iron gate. Behind it were buildings that looked unmistakably equestrian. Phil jumped out and pushed the gates open. I drove into the stable yard. A man appeared from behind one of the barn doors. Mark got out of the car.

'He's here for the bath.'

The drive snaked round the stables to two more sets of gates. The one on the left went into an empty, overgrown and rambling field of nettles. The one on the right led to a graveyard for dead mechanical stuff. I gasped with shock. If the bath was buried in there, we'd never get it out in one piece. The 'caretaker' opened the one on the right. I looked nervously at Phil.

'Oh my mistake . . . she's in here.'

I let out a sigh. He opened the one on the left.

'But that field is empty.'

'Nah . . . you take this and follow me.'

He handed me a sickle and began chopping his way through nettles with a scythe. After 90 minutes of chopping, slashing and being stung we made it to the familiar black-and-white Victorian tiles of *Lilibet II*. She had been totally safe all winter to everyone except sickle owners, people with dock leaves and the supernatural spectre of Death. Safe she might have been; fixed up and in a state to row she was not. Mark had very crudely patched up the storm damage from the last attempt but she certainly wasn't seaworthy and it appeared, looking at the wreck in the nettle patch, that even if I hadn't been felled with man flu, rowing her the previous September would have been almost impossible. I regarded her battered form and stroked her with an affection I'd only felt before for my dog. Like my dog there was a feeling that the bath had never let me down and had tried her best. For her loyalty I'd rewarded her with languishing in a nettle patch through a really bad winter.

We found several willing villagers and manhandled the bath onto the trailer to take her back to Richmond and the boatyard.

May passed in a welter of more weights, more swearing at Betty the Ergo, more running, and working on the bath to try to fix the problems of the year before.

In London all was total smiling, sunny bliss. In accordance with my earlier thoughts about weather, the weather in the Channel was awful. With a horrible sense of déjà vu, I could see that this year's attempt was going exactly the same way as the one the year before. So it was with some relief I picked up my phone on 8 June.

'Tim, it's Andy. I think we've got a chance tomorrow. Can you get the bath down here?'

I phoned the Admiral (ret.). He'd been away a lot more than I expected but amazingly picked up the phone. I put it to him that I wanted to go tomorrow.

'Don't attempt the Channel again unless it's flatter than the top of my gin.'

'Thank you, sir.'

Mark, the apprentices and I loaded the bath. A wailing penetrated the air.

'One love! One heart! Let's get together and feel all right . . .' Kenroy swayed drunkenly at the top of the ramp.

Gavin, my number two from the first attempt, had moved to Canada during the winter. He'd flown there to avoid the sea and moved to the most landlocked town he could find. This left me slightly stuck. Without a friend to help me run things on the shore, the bath project would basically be untenable.

Luckily one of my oldest friends had decided to quit work for a bit. Unlike my sketchy employment record since college, Chris had held down the same brilliant, corporate, grown-up job since university. He didn't take a gap year or run off to farm pigs and nutmeg in the West Indies like me. He'd been steadily funnelling cash away while working for a big company. My grasp of what his job actually entailed was vague. What I did know was that he'd done it for a long time and so now had decided to take a break to have a think about what he wanted to do next.

'Chris, it's Tim.'

'Hi, mate.'

'You know how you aren't sure what to do next . . .'

'Yes.'

'How about crossing the Channel with me, in the bath support boat?'

'I didn't see that coming . . . but all right I'm in. When?'

'Tomorrow? We'd be going down tonight.'

'I'll pack and be ready.'

Chris Gilmartin had entered the foam. I've known Chris almost as long as I've known Ellen MacArthur. He has an eternally sunny outlook on life. His positive attitude and my relative fear of danger have combined in the past to lead us to attempt some very silly plans. We were at school together for a few years too, during which time we invented some pioneering roof-climbing escapades and fished each other out of trouble most of the time. Now I needed him more than ever.

With the bath on the trailer, I said goodbye to Mark and the apprentices and turned down a very kind offer of some medicinal incense from Kenroy, just as Chris arrived with a rucksack.

'Brilliant. So this is the bath . . . I know I've said this before, but you are a nutter.'

We jumped in the car and sped off.

'How will I communicate with you in the bath?'

Drat. I'd failed to plan a new communication system for the bath. I didn't want to own up to incompetence to Chris this early in the project.

'Semaphore?'

'I'm not sure I know any.'

There was silence then Chris had a master plan. 'Mobile phones?'

'Good idea . . .' I thought it through thoroughly. 'Wait. It's not great as people keep calling my mobile with irrelevant stuff. I don't know that it's irrelevant till I've taken the call and by then I've wasted valuable rowing time.'

Chris thought for a moment. 'Stop the car!'

'What?'

'There's a mobile shop. Let's get you a second mobile that only I'll have the number to. Then if it rings, you know it's me.'

'Brilliant plan.'

The bell rang at the top of the door in the mobile-phone shop in Richmond. The assistant slouched over.

'Yeah?'

Chris kicked off. 'Hi, we'd like a phone.'

'Any sort?'

'We just need it to work for 24 hours, then we're going to throw it away.'

He looked a little startled. People probably normally want them for longer. 'Well there's this one . . .'

I chipped in, 'Nope, doesn't seem sturdy enough for me. It needs to be very tough . . . The sort where it doesn't matter if someone stamps on it.'

'I've got just the thing.' He found us a cheap, brick of a phone. 'This looks like it would survive a gunfight.'

Startled the shop assistant changed into Nervous the shop assistant. 'Do you need it to make outgoing calls or just accept incoming?'

'It's not going to be making any outgoing calls.'

'Unless there's a real disaster.'

We both laughed. Nervous's eyes bulged as he filled out the paperwork.

'Can we pay cash?'

By this time, there was an odd dreamlike quality to Nervous. It could just be that he always floated in this semi-chimerical state. I've known people who've worked in shops who swear that the only way to deal with the boredom is to smoke what Kenroy would term a massive religious experiment. But I got the feeling it might be something else. I signed my name on the paperwork as Nervous summed up.

'One throw-away phone, able to withstand a gunfight, with one outgoing call on credit . . . and you're paying cash.'

'Thank you.'

As we left the shop, Chris was in buoyant mood and, expecting the bath crossing to succeed, he turned to Nervous and said, 'Watch the news tonight.'

Nervous whimpered as the door slammed. It was a very odd reaction. As we drove away I thought about it. Chris was obviously thinking about it too. We sat there thinking in silence: him in his woollen bobble-less hat and dark glasses, and me in dark glasses, a massive coat crammed full of stuff I thought I might need, and cap pulled firmly down over my head.

Chris got there first and turned to me. 'Do you think he thought we were dealing drugs?'

'Yep . . . I think he probably did. Or robbing a bank . . .'

'Oh good . . .'

'Should we turn around and go back to tell him we're not?'

'I'm not sure we've got time.'

Somewhere in Richmond, Nervous reached for the phone, thought about phoning the drug squad, and phoned his best mate instead.

After hitting a top speed of 10 mph on the M25, 17 mph on the M3, taking various side roads, getting lost several times and turning back onto roads we'd just left, we finally arrived in Folkestone. As I missed the Holy Grail Arch for the third time, everywhere in Folkestone phones went off and people began to gather at the pub next to the slipway. When we arrived, I'd never seen it so full. I tried and failed to get the bath trailer down the ramp. Chris had never been part of the unloading the bath symphony for two men, a trailer, car and tub played on the slipway, to an audience of be-fuddled pub patrons and lobster pots before, so he sat cringing, hiding behind his hand.

As he was entering his fifth separate hand puppet of embarrass-ment, he said, 'Do you want me to have a go?'

He made it down the ramp first time. Genius. We unloaded the bath as the shadow of a bear cast down on us from the quayside.

'Right – let's get this sorted this time. No more trying to die on me,' Andy smiled. 'We'll leave with the second tide . . .'

Dom and I had talked about this and I knew I had to be firm. Leaving on the second tide was risky as it meant I'd still be rowing when the day breezes started. The bath didn't perform well above the water in any sort of wind. The day breeze would also make the sea choppier. These two things combined would make things very tricky for me. Leaving on the first tide was even more risky as it meant having to get Andy up early in the morning.

'I think we should leave with the first tide . . .'

'That's at four in the morning!'

'Yes, it's early but . . .'

'It'll still be dark. Are you mad?'

'Yes.'

'I'm really not happy about this.'

A short, sharp conversation later, Chris and I checked into the hotel in Folkestone and booked an alarm call for 3.30 a.m.

'Here's your key, sir. Will you want supper?'

'Yes, please.'

'There's an evening of line dancing going on if you fancy it after supper?'

No gentleman has ever line-danced. We went up to our room to drop off kit. Back downstairs we soldiered through cremated remains in the restaurant. The geriatric cowboys and girls of Kent line-danced across the hallway. Falling prey to the elevator music again we arrived back in our room. My phone rang.

'Hello?'

'Hi, mate, it's Grillo. Just wondering if you're going to make it to my birthday?'

Damn and bother. Another thing I'd forgotten. It was his birthday in a few days.

'Erm . . . I'm not sure how to put this. I'm having another go at crossing the Channel in a bath . . . and I'm not sure how long it's going to take, or if I'll make it this time, or if I'll get sick again, or stuck in another storm, or if I do make it, how long it takes to row to London, or if rowing to London is even possible . . .'

He laughed.

'You're obsessed. No problem. Of all the excuses anyone could have, that's a great one – good luck.'

I put the phone down. Chris looked at me.

'Not nervous are you?'

'A bit.'

It was probably only about 10.30 p.m. when we turned out the lamp and tried to sleep with the gentle strains of nightclub bouncers pounding various heads onto the pavements of Folkestone ringing in our ears.

At 3.30 a.m. Chris started to force-feed me Weetabix. 'You're going to need the fibre.'

'Mate, we don't even have a bowl.'

'I know, that's why I've filled this mug with milk, I thought you could dunk them.'

'How many do you think I should have?'

'As many as you can. You're going to need the fibre.'

With the enthusiasm of a man trying to make another man sick, he dunked 12 Weetabix into the mug, opening and pouring hotel sugar sachets over each of them.

'Go on have one more . . .'

'Mate, if I have one more, I'll throw the lot up.'

'OK, that's probably enough.'

While Chris dunked a further two Weetabix for himself, I went to the bathroom and retched at the mere smell of them. Luckily I managed not to throw up. I used to like Weetabix but now just seeing an advert for them on the TV is enough to trigger the memory of that morning and induce emesis. Even before the happy face at the end of the commercial I'm to be found blowing chunks in an adjoining room. We left the hotel and went down to the water's edge.

The French again invoked emergency powers and decided that on that specific day of the year it was again illegal to row anything from Calais to Dover and Dover to Calais but not to row from Folkestone to Calais. Why this was the case was not clear but I took the chance and at exactly 4 a.m. pulled out of Folkestone Harbour. It was pitch black. Only the searchlights of Andy's boat and the lights along the harbour arm illuminated me.

The harbour we left was deserted except for a few battered drunks swaying gently in the breeze. On the support boat was Andy and his crewmate, Chris, Phil's mate who'd come with a camera, a reporter called Ollie who, following the last attempt, was the only one Kenny could persuade to come on the trip and a photographer called Jamie who'd been in the support boat the last time and had come again to see how it would all turn out.

'Keep an eye on the GPS system.'

I couldn't see anything so would have to rely on the GPS to avoid hitting something in the world's busiest shipping lane. It didn't seem to be working. Great. Things had started well.

As the sun began to break through the early morning sky I pulled hard and tried to keep to my course. The sheer weight and drag of the bath was enormous but the plan of leaving really early was working in that there was currently very little wind. In the emerging sun, the water was beautifully flat. I took full advantage and stroked out of the harbour in a lovely rhythm.

I shouted over to Andy, 'It seems busier than last time!'

'Yes, there's a naval exercise going on.'

Brilliant. Of all the days to choose to hold a naval exercise they had to pick the one day I was rowing. So now, as well as the masses of tankers that loomed out of the dawn light at me, frigates dashed up and down the shipping lanes. This was going to be tricky.

I kept rowing and made calculated guesses, going in front of some tankers and behind others, as I slalomed my way across the Channel. All the time the wind stayed low and the water, although not flat, was certainly nothing like as bad as it had been the last time. I made it across the first shipping channel and into the calm of the central reservation.

Each stroke necessitated a different battle with the sea as she shifted around and tried to avoid the oars. My wrists began to hurt, a dull ache started in my back and I began to notice the odd pain due to broken skin caused by the constant chaffing all over my body. On the plus side, I had an indomitable belief that with each stroke I was a tiny bit closer to finishing the ordeal.

About half an hour later, a tiny row began in my head between this formerly indomitable belief that I could make it and a new legion of doubt plaguing me that I'd fail again.

You can't stop for breaks when you're rowing the Channel as the current takes you off course. This meant there was no time to stop for food. Between strokes, I grabbed the occasional bite of banana and gulped down some of the special mix I'd created involving cranberry juice. Staying hydrated was the key to the whole thing. You're also always at risk from sunburn at sea due to the reflection of the sun on the water. I was sitting in the sea surrounded by a ring of copper. The sun's rays were intense and bounced unflinching off the copper and up at me. I had to work really hard to make sure I kept my fluid levels up. Dehydration would lead to a hopeless loss of direction and inability to function properly. I had to avoid this.

At 10 a.m. I realised I'd been rowing for six hours. Six hours into the journey was when the last attempt failed. This time I was still rowing and the thought that now I was in uncharted waters spurred me on. I was tired though, and my body had started to do strange things. My wrists began to hurt even more: my fingers seemed to respond less well, leading me to suspect that the tendons inside my wrists were starting to swell up. The blisters on my hands had got so big that many of them had burst. The result: my hands bled. Every stroke whipped my back.

My buttocks were becoming horrid. At first it felt like sweat running down onto the floor of the bath. Now, I looked down and realised I was sitting in small pools of my own blood and wet, seeping goo. The skin from my buttocks had gone again.

My mind started to wander. I tried to conjugate foreign and Latin verbs to keep it focused and working. I succeeded for a while but in the end my beleaguered brain packed its bags, hailed a cab, got in with a couple of buxom blondes and went off for a boozy lunch in Soho.

My eyes were fixed on the flagpole, which I was using as a sighter. I realised that if I kept the flagpole and showerhead in line with a fixed point on the horizon and kept the three of them aligned, it meant I was going in a roughly straight line. Very occasionally my eyes darted down to the compass to check this but it was always basically correct. On this attempt the compass seemed to be working; at least for now. I looked back up at the flagpole. Due to my treatment by the French on the last trip, this time I'd refused to fly the French courtesy flag. The Red Ensign hung alone on the flagpole.

At 10.35 a.m. I whimpered. The Red Ensign that had hung so beautifully limp on the flagpole suddenly kicked up and puffed away from it. Instantly I knew what this meant. The wind was coming. A single tear rolled down my face. I was feeling quite physically tired and now had the wind to deal with.

By this stage my wrists were being pulled apart with every stroke. Normally, rowing boats are made as light as possible to avoid this problem but the bath weighed a third of a tonne. This coupled with the very awkward angle that I was forced to use to finish the catch, due to the height of the sides of the bath, meant that they had swollen up and were in a terrible state. I looked down at them and realised that they were the width of my hands at their widest point. The pain was intense. Now the tendons were so swollen, I couldn't straighten my fingers. As I just needed them to curl round the oars, this was not a problem. When the sea was behaving so stunningly I'd just gritted my teeth and pulled on but now the wind was a factor, things would get bad. My morale sank.

Soon, the sea began to be commanded by the wind. First the chop got marginally worse. Then small dancing white horses, more dancing white foals, began to appear on the tops of the chop. I whimpered again. This attempt would end like the first. What would happen to me then?

At this point the current kicked in with a vengeance. I wrapped my bleeding claws around the oars and pulled hard. Somewhere deep within me a dark part of my mind woke up and began to drive me on. With a Herculean effort I rowed for the next 20 minutes only to remain absolutely still. I saw a marker buoy that I had passed a few miles away that, if anything, seemed to get closer, meaning that I was being swept back to England. I increased my pace. Being taken in the grip of the current back towards the UK meant the end of the attempt. As I tried so hard to pull forward, the current succeeded in pushing me back. It was a battle I knew I couldn't win.

I thought hard. I may not have been able to beat the tide in the long run but I could hold off her victory for as long as I could breathe. I kept rowing at between 28 and 30 strokes per minute, which, after six and a half hours rowing, was simply the very best I could manage. Ten more crucial minutes went by and I continued to row at the height of my ability and strength to stay absolutely still. The marker buoy just was not getting any further away.

Andy shouted over from the support boat, 'It's no good, Tim, we're going to have to call this off. We're going nowhere.'

Gasping for air, I couldn't speak but words ripped viscerally from the pit of my stomach.

'No! Ten minutes more!'

I was not going to give in. Either the tide would give in or I would not be coming back. That was the decision I made. I increased my stroke rate and gasped for breath. I was in a lot of trouble.

Chris yelled from the boat, 'Come on, Tim!'

Tears ran down my face. The pain was unbearable. My thighs burnt as, totally exhausted, they powered me up and down the slide. Blood, tears and goo mingled in the bath. I thought bitterly of how hilarious rowing the Channel in a bath had seemed, cursed myself, and kept rowing. Simply put, my body was at breaking point; my heart raced blood and oxygen around my veins, trying to keep my exhausted frame in the race against the tide. My mind became important and cruel. It would not let me stop. Something very frightening was happening. I found the truest expression of mind over matter I've ever known.

Again, Andy's voice cut through the air, 'Come on, Tim, that's over ten more minutes! Let's call this a day.'

'Ten more!'

I pulled as though my life depended on it. I just would not give in: all this gut-wrenching effort to sit totally still. Then through the tears, I realised the buoy that I'd been sighting off appeared to have moved further away. I kept pulling like a maniac and checked again and sure enough, the buoy had moved. I was going forward. The current had given me a chance. I continued to row at the same intense pace, not sure how long the current would give me to get somewhere. I pulled on, got a chance for some rhythm and took it.

Andy leant over the side. 'That's it! You're moving forward now!'

Tears ran down my face into the bath. I looked up to the sky, 'Thank you, God.'

Now I inched forwards. After just over 40 minutes of sitting still, now each stroke took me closer to France.

Beating the tide had exhausted me. It was a peak in the trip I hadn't expected to have to conquer. I hadn't planned for it. I was quite prepared to row for 12 hours if necessary to get the crossing done. I'd trained hard to be able to do that. However, I hadn't factored in this sudden burst of energy that would be needed between the sixth and seventh hours. I'd often seen marathon runners who'd had to run one lap faster than they planned forced to pull out of the race, because they'd exhausted themselves and this was the same result that beating the tide seemed likely to inflict on me.

My body had taken a serious hammering over the last seven hours and that was a factor too. But my brain, or whatever it is within humans that drives us, was fast becoming unstoppable. It sought the coastline of Gaul with the feverish desperation of a drug addict.

'Please let me stop!' I wailed, not at the support boat, or the people on it but at the thing in my head that drove me on. I screamed, I cried, I prayed for death as a blessed relief. The dark place in my mind that forced me on began to conspire with my internal organs. The exterior of my body was shot to pieces. It was in a lot of pain but internally the FitzHigham organs were intent on never stopping. Air came into the lungs. My heart ran like a well-oiled engine. Blood coursed through my veins and out of all the various cuts. I felt like a massive industrial machine. Fuel came in, was converted to energy, and powered me forward. All the lightness in my psyche wailed against the primeval maniac now in control both of my brain and this indomitable factory.

I entered hour eight. I turned round and could finally see France. She had sneaked up on me again like a ninja. My left shoulder, that had been so badly damaged in the last attempt, now began to throb again. I kept going but was in a lot of pain.

Andy shouted over from the support boat, 'Tim, you're rowing back towards England – turn round!'

I checked the compass. He was right. Probably by straining to look at France or due to the pain in my shoulder, I'd somehow managed to turn the boat away from France. I wasn't actually rowing directly back towards England, more in the direction of Portugal. But either of them is the wrong direction when you're aiming for France. I corrected my heading but my left arm was beginning to be a little less than useful.

'Guide Me O Thou Great Jehovah' flooded round my head. I thought I might die to John Wesley. My mind battled itself. My body battled my mind and itself. The church choir singing John Wesley battled with Kurt Cobain and the crashing chords of Nirvana. My head swam: what had started as a mere slight argument in my mind now escalated into a near-schizophrenic war zone. I looked over the side of the bath at the cool of the water and thought, 'I could swim the last bit . . . that would make it all stop.' Suddenly the face in the photos at my grandmother's house flashed out of the water at me. Finally perhaps I understood something more of what had happened that day in the Second World War.

Chris Gilmartin's voice cut through the air and hit my mind like a life preserver. 'Tim, four miles to go – pull hard!'

The current around the point of Cap Gris Nez is very strong. It got up now as the wind got worse. Many people make it this far and still fail. My arm finally gave in. I was left with just one decent functioning arm – my right one. My fingers had become so caked in blood and the tendons so buggered that I couldn't stretch them out. I wrapped the claw on the end of my good arm around the oar on my left and kept pulling. Normally this would have made me go in a massive circle. Luckily for me, the current was so strong in the opposite direction, that by pulling on one oar against it, the net effect was that I was going straight. My head hit the oar and I came round. I realised I'd momentarily passed out.

Gilly's voice cut through the air again. 'Tim – only three miles to go – row like a bastard!'

Something within me snapped. I entered a very dark place. Although the sun was streaming down on me, all I could see were shadows and darkness. I pulled and pulled and pulled. Up to the top of the seat, put the oar in, power back down to the bottom of the seat. The monotony of the action did nothing to numb the pain. Periodically if the current dropped slightly I'd have to swap my good arm to the other oar but for the main I kept with the one blade and used the current instead of the other oar.

I was broken. I felt like a small girl out there on the mighty sea. I thought I could see all the people I saw on my training rows at Richmond floating alongside me out at sea. I waved at them. I looked over my shoulder. There was the watchtower of the Navy base at Cap Gris Nez. Would the Navy come out? I retreated back into the hallucinogenic haze of my thoughts. My body was shattered, I hit my head on an oar and realised I'd briefly passed out again.

Gilly shouted from the boat, 'Two miles to go: keep going!'

The words 'never give in' kept thudding round my head. It was a terrifying place to be in mentally. You realise how people are able to become killers. Nothing seems to matter any more but finding a way to ease your pain. All this for a hilarious plumbing-based ruse.

'Ah! Le bain! Le bain! Bonjour! Bonjour!'

I looked up; again, I may have passed out – it was difficult to tell what was reality. There was a roar of engines and boats around me. Had the French Navy come to arrest me?

I focused on the boat nearest to me. In it was a sturdy French fisherman in a hat with as much oil on him as Andy. Suddenly there was a small flotilla of French fishing vessels around me, who all cheered me on and surrounded me as I rowed towards the coast. The last mile and a half was the moving celebration of the Entente Cordial I always knew was possible. The French government and Navy may have made things impossible for me, but the fishermen of France had come out to show their support.

I rallied. Something ancient in me stirred. Broken I may have been but I would not let the French see that.

The beach at Cap Gris Nez is stony and many ships get wrecked on it. The stony beach shelves nastily. Above it is an incline to a ridge at the top. On this ridge is the naval watchtower. Arriving at the beach I looked around. I thought someone would come and welcome me. I would even have been happy if there'd just been a sailor with a pair of handcuffs (in Soho, that constitutes a good night out). But there was no one on that beach. I was very down. Then I looked up to the ridge at the top. It was lined with little groups of French people, cheering and waving. The true Entente Cordial spirit was at work again, brightening up the barren and rocky headland. These people had broken into their own naval base to come and say well done. It proved one vital thing to me: the people who really hate the French government are the French.

I looked up to the ridge, a tear welling up in my eye, and tried to think of a way to express this love. I thought of my GCSE French and how little it had prepared me to deal with this situation. I looked at the boats floating next to me then faced uphill again. I addressed the crowd.

'*Merci . . . merci . . .*'

There was a huge cheer.

'. . . *Où est la gare?*'

There was silence. I heard muttering. Then laughter: then another huge cheer.

I heard Chris and Andy on the support boat, 'What's he said?'

'He's just asked the way to the station.'

'Looks like he could use a train on the way back!'

The French Navy did not arrive on the beach that afternoon. The French people lining the cliff top and in the small fishing boat flotilla around me had shown the true spirit of their nation: finally, *fraternité* won out in the end.

I had made it. I'd made the first unassisted crossing of the English Channel in a bath. A phone rang.

Chris picked it up. 'Tim, it's Dom . . .'

I rowed out to the support boat. Gilly handed me the phone over the side.

'Dom . . .'

'Chris . . .'

'No, it's me, Tim . . .'

'What . . . has it failed again?'

I burst into tears.

'No, I've made it . . . I've made it . . .'

'Wait . . .' He turned to the people around him. 'He's made it!'

I heard another huge cheer down the phone. I just kept repeating, 'I've made it . . . I've made it.'

Chris leant over the side of the support boat and took the phone back. 'He's a bit tired and emotional . . . Sure, I'll tell him.'

I waved at the French again. I'd made it across the Channel in nine hours and six minutes to join Bleriot, Captain Webb and Dr Blanchard in the history of that illustrious waterway.

Andy appeared on deck. He didn't seem that comfortable with

the enormous display of emotion going on so rubbed his hands on his overalls, looked down and said, 'Well done! I didn't think I'd ever see that! Now, you should probably check the safety hatches.'

I opened up the first one. 'This one is all fine.'

Just the small amount of water in it you'd expect for a boat that had been out at sea for most of the day. I opened the second to see water sloshing everywhere. 'This one is about 80% full!'

Andy appeared back on deck looking shocked. 'What!'

He looked down over my shoulder through the hatch. 'Bloody hell! No wonder she was heavy. With that amount of water in one of them, it's lucky you made it when you did or she would have capsized again! Let's make for home.'

I slumped on the deck of the support boat lying on my front looking out to sea. I looked down at my hands and wrists. My tendons were so swollen it would be two days before I would be able to use a knife and fork again or even curl my fingers round a pen. I couldn't sit down, as my buttocks were lamentable. After over nine hours on a tiny wooden seat, my arse was bleeding. My scrotum was more slit than a pair of 1980s jeans. It was horribly swollen. Men don't normally declare, 'I was gutted my balls had got larger', but I simply couldn't close my legs. I moved more bow-leggedly than John Wayne. I tried to be polite to the journalist and cameraman on the support boat but at the same time, every time the inside of my thigh brushed against one of my swollen raw testicles, I wanted to scream.

I tried to phone the various people who were closest to me. I wanted to let them know what had happened but I was totally unable to use the phone. In the end, Gilly dialled numbers and held the phone to my ear, as it was too small for me to grasp properly.

'Kenny?'

'Yes, Chris. Please say he's not dead.'

'No, it's me – I've made it!'

'You legend! You're a complete nutter but well done!'

Many other conversations like this happened as I shouted into the tiny phone over the roar of Andy's engines. Giving up on yelling as a plan I dictated more texts to Chris.

Somewhere in the Yangtze Valley, China, a phone buzzed. Up to his knees in mud, carrying a camera, Phil Carr punched the air. 'He's made it!' Phil would hopefully be back before I got to London but for now his number two had got the shots.

I went into the cabin. I couldn't hear too well as both of my ears had a combination of chilblains from the wind across the sea and sunburn from the intense sunshine. This had led to pus getting into my ears and causing them to be slightly blocked.

Andy looked round. 'Great job . . . really proud of you . . . oh my knees . . .'

'You should get them looked at, mate . . . and again, thank you. I couldn't have made it without you.'

I went below deck and closed the hatch. I tried to take off the rowing lycra gently but ended up ripping off even more skin. I took the surgical spirit out of my backpack and rubbed it into my inflamed, lacerated scrotum. Having had some small experience of this before, I knew I had exactly two seconds before the unbearable pain hit. I used them to pull the lycra up again. Then pain. The last nine hours were put into their proper context by the agony. I looked at the porthole and passed out.

When I came round we were just outside the harbour arm at Folkestone. The sun was streaming down. Like John Wayne in *The Searchers* I waddled out on deck and looked back across the Channel at where France probably still was. After a really tough year and a half I'd finally laid to rest my Channel ghost. As I looked at the sun bouncing off the water I felt satisfied. If my great-uncle had known I'd made it across – even in such a stupid way – I think he would have smiled. A warm, happy feeling seeped through the pain.

Now there was just the small matter of the 170 miles between Tower Bridge and me.

CHAPTER NINE

HUMPTY DUMPTY HAD
A GREAT FALL

'He'll never sell ice creams going at that speed.'

Eric Morecambe

Andy pulled his boat into Folkestone Harbour as I rowed the battered bath behind. People gathered on the quay shouted out to us, 'What happened?'

Andy looked down at me then shouted up, 'I thought I'd let him make it this time!'

A cheer went up. Many of them I recognised as line dancers. They began to disperse. I'm not sure if they were there to welcome me or if they were just there walking off the effects of the previous night's country-and-western-based overexertion. Either way, it was good to feel they might have turned up to welcome the bath home. The general happiness was mixed with tension. The tide had definitely turned and the water was going out: we had to get the boat and bath moored before we lost the water in the harbour.

We moored the bath at the inner slipway. Andy moored up slightly further out towards the outer harbour, near the low swing bridge that had claimed the showerhead a year before. I went aboard his boat.

'What now? How's the weather for an attempt to make it up to Dover in the morning?'

I could see the shock in Andy's face mirrored in Chris's sunglasses. He took them off and revealed that Andy's shock was nothing compared to his own. They could both see the terrible state my body was in. I knew it too but was buzzing with the fact that I'd achieved what everyone thought was impossible and crossed the Channel.

'Let's have a look at the charts.'

Andy took out the charts of Folkestone and the stretch of the coast up to Dover and then on to Sandwich. I followed the line of the coast northwards.

'Where's London?'

In my head London wasn't that much further than Folkestone by sea. As I looked at the charts it became apparent that London wasn't even on the same charts as Folkestone. London turned out not to be on any of the charts Andy had on the boat. I looked at Andy. 'I'll get the atlas from the car.'

Andy laughed. 'It's not what we normally do at sea, but then we don't normally row baths.'

I knew where London was of course and I knew where Folkestone was, but I think I'd been in denial and wanted them to be closer to each other. By ignoring their positions I think I thought they might move a bit nearer to each other to help me out.

We left the boat and headed to shore. Some of the remaining line dancers went to shake my hand. I smiled and showed them my hands apologetically. They winced, much as I'd have done if they'd shaken my hand. They congratulated me verbally and let me waddle off towards the car.

I overheard one lady turn to the man next to her as they wandered off towards the hotel, 'So he's come from Wales?'

'No, France.'

'Oh, that's all right then – that's much closer than Wales.'

Chris, Andy and I gathered around the atlas on the bonnet of the car. I opened the page at London and Kent. Thinking aloud, I said, 'London really is quite far away . . .'

I'm not sure Chris thought I was serious about the London leg of the journey but he measured things nevertheless. 'It's about 160-odd miles, give or take, especially the way you're going to have to do it.'

'Brilliant.'

Dom and I had come up with a plan and divided the journey round Kent to London up into sections; distances we felt I could row in a day taking into account the important tide and current issues. The next leg on our plan was to have been Dover to Ramsgate. Due to not being able to row from France to Dover, I'd now have to insert a new leg into the plan, which would have to be Folkestone to Dover, then Dover to Ramsgate. Looking down at the atlas the enormity of it all hit me. London was a very long way away.

Why had I said I'd row to Tower Bridge? My body was in a terrible state. All I really wanted to do was sleep. No one had ever gone to these lengths to win one pint of beer before. But I was committed to it and wanted to get started straight away.

Andy's phone rang; he picked it up and listened intently, 'Right . . . Yes, I'll tell him . . .'

He turned, in what was a rapidly fading light. 'The weather's turned again, you'll need to wait at least a day to get up the next bit to Dover. Also I'd suggest you find that leak in the flotation device and fix it . . .'

'Has anyone ever rowed to London from here before?'

Andy thought. 'Not as far as I know. I'm not even sure how possible it is . . . but then I've said that before.'

Fleet Street's Finest, well, more Bermondsey's Finest – Jamie the photographer and Ollie the journalist – had gone to a hotel room to 'file copy'. My phone rang: it was Ollie. 'Tim, I'm up in the room, can you come and just check a couple of things before I send this off?'

I hung up as Andy said, 'I've got to get home. My knees have taken a battering, I've really got to get them sorted out.'

'Thanks, mate, I know it's been tough but we've done it. Keep me posted on the weather and I'll find that leak.'

Chris took me, tired, and in a lot of pain, to the hotel room to see Ollie. Jamie the photographer opened the door.

'I've got some great shots, I've filed and really should leave soon. I've got to photograph some party girls in the West End tonight.'

He must lead a very surreal life. I stood with bleeding buttocks and answered Ollie's questions before he and Jamie left for London having filed the story using a laptop and the hotel's sporadic Internet connection.

As they were leaving, Ollie turned. 'The room's booked all night if you fancy a lie down – I won't be using it from London.' I heard the latch go on the door. Next thing I remember was Chris saying, 'Sorry to have to wake you, mate. We could have a problem.'

I'd been asleep for a few hours. As I'd slept, the tide had gone out of the harbour.

Chris and I stood alone on the pavement outside the hotel, looking down at the bath on a mud flat in the empty harbour.

'Andy wasn't sure the bath should stay in the water with the bad weather tonight but how do we get it out with no way of floating it onto the trailer. There's no water – we definitely can't carry it with just two of us.'

'Hmmm . . . I'm not sure sleep was my best plan.'

'Also, that mud has got really sticky. I'm not sure we're going to be able to stand up in that for long.'

I could see his point. I looked at the bath, the mud flat and the conspicuous lack of water. The bath couldn't stay there, as it might not survive the predicted storm. I needed a plan.

'Right, let's go to the pub and think this one out . . .'

'Uh oh . . . Isn't that how we got into this mess in the first place?'

We pushed open the door and entered one of Folkestone's feistiest pubs, full of very big, loud men. It was the sort of place that even Andy would befriend an undertaker before going into. Chris, who is smaller than me, looked like a lost five-year-old among the hulking masses that surrounded the bar. At just over six foot I might have passed for aged 12. It went dark. We stared up at the grimacing face of the barman. He could have been the landlord and it might have been his attempt at a smile. It was difficult to tell. I became aware I was wearing pink socks.

'What can I do for you?'

Never before have I been more aware of my pink socks. He blew smoke over the bar.

'Funny sort of outfit . . .'

Never before have I been more aware of lycra, which I was still wearing. I may have conquered the Channel but right now could have been just seconds away from death or an entirely new set of sexual choices induced by a misunderstanding over my attire. Chris coughed nervously and his eyes widened. He'd just noticed the pink socks.

I looked the barman directly in the eye, 'I've just rowed the Channel in a bath and I need some help lifting the bath off the mud in the harbour. I'd like to buy a drink for anyone who would like to help, and one for you, landlord.'

The pub went silent. This was dangerous. In my head when Nelson said things like this, people cheered. The silence continued as the words bounced around the inside of the landlord's head. He chewed his cigarette.

'It was you in that bath?'

'Yes, and I've got it stuck on the mud.'

There was a further grim silence. All eyes in the pub (and there were an odd number of eyes I noted) were fixed on a small lycra apparition and his sidekick who might have passed for a football.

'All right, lads, who's going to help this nutter lift his bath out of the water?'

Then there was a cheer. Chris was in total disbelief. Nothing in our various adventures had prepared him for this. We led the pub out into what was now starlight and down the inner harbour slipway. Between 10 to 14 massive men lifted the bath out of the mud and carried it up. We were all caked in mud. If I'd flicked mud at these men in any other context I'd have been dead before it left the spoon. But lifting the bath, they could not have been happier. Chris ran off to get the car and trailer. He arrived back to find the rugby team of men and me, having enjoyed a mud bath, standing smiling at the top of the inner slipway holding aloft the copper one ready to deposit it on the trailer. He pulled the trailer over and we gently loaded the bath. It had never been that easy to load the bath in the whole history of the project so far.

Tightening the last ropes I shouted in triumph, 'To the pub – thank you so much! Drinks are on me!' I sounded more like the Milky Bar Kid than Nelson, but a cheer went up and we went back to the pub. On the way, I went white. Chris noticed.

'What's up, mate? That's gone well.'

'There are no pockets in a rowing lycra.'

'Good job I've got my wallet then.'

In the pub our new friends wanted to know all about the Channel crossing in the bath and we told them the stories. The things we'd seen, the failed attempt. Chris was far better at putting things into words than me. I was still so sore that my focus was more on basic things like not fainting. The landlord brought us both drinks: very kind of him.

I had originally planned to stay in the bath that night but the predicted storm, the problems with the bath's flotation tank and my battered body changed that plan. Chris and I left the pub and walked back to the hotel. Back in the room, I phoned Kenny.

'Well done. That really is super.'

'Thanks, mate – I'm pretty shot to pieces and we're stuck here for at least a day.'

'But you made it. Now we just have to get you round Kent and up to here.'

'Yes, it's a bit further than I . . .'

'Where are you? It's a very odd echo.'

'Erm . . . in the hotel.'

'I know that but . . . are you in the bath?'

'Erm . . . yes.'

'I would have thought you'd had enough of them for one day!'

'I think I'm addicted.'

'Have a great night and well done.'

I sunk back into the bath and let out a scream as the water hit my cuts. Chris shouted through from the next room. 'You all right, mate?'

'Yes, fine thanks.'

And in a way I was. My body was in a very bad way but I'd made it across. With the Channel vanquished my journey could really begin. Finally, after a year of the sponsored bath project, people at last had something to sponsor.

The predicted storm was not as bad as everyone thought it would be. Again, that's the thing with trying to predict weather. The leak, however, was much worse than everyone thought. Mark sent down advice as we worked hard to fix the problem and dry out the bath. My plan to carry straight on with rowing round to London had been immediately thwarted.

Eventually, after trying to fix it near the water in great weather, we had to admit defeat. I found doing anything dextrous almost impossible as the tendons in my wrists were still so swollen I couldn't clench my hands. There was only so much Chris could manage on his own so we took the bath back up to Mark in Richmond to get it sorted. I folded a bath towel and put it on the passenger seat. There was no way I could drive with my hands in the state they were. I bled onto the towel as Chris drove us towards Richmond.

Under cover of darkness Chris and I dropped the bath off in Richmond for Mark. There was no great arrival there. The only person around was the restaurateur who owned the floating restaurant next to the boatyard.

'So you made it across the Channel then?'

'Yes.'

'What now?'

'I'm going to get this fixed and row up to London.'

He looked at me waddling like a hampered crab, smiled and said, 'You make it up to London and there's a bottle of champagne in my restaurant for you.'

We unhitched the bath and trailer at the boatyard and Chris dropped me off in Chelsea. After telling Grillo I wouldn't make it to his birthday I thought it might be nice to surprise him. We stopped off to get a card. Chris wrote in it for me, as I still couldn't hold a pen.

The pub door swung open. Grillo turned. 'What the . . .'

'Hi, I'd shake your hand but it's probably not the best idea. Happy birthday.'

It was a very special night. I basked in the very warm glow of being around my friends and enjoyed them enjoying the fact I'd finally succeeded.

'We're eating in the room upstairs . . .'

We all filed up the stairs behind the birthday boy. My heart sank as we entered the upstairs room, and saw a collection of wooden seats. The landlord had clearly got a job lot of them from a condemned Methodist chapel. I whimpered and grimaced as I sat. It is impossible to get comfortable on a former non-conformist chapel chair when you have no skin on your buttocks. I didn't mention this to anyone. However, there was one thing I couldn't disguise: the state of my hands. Everyone was so kind in not making a fuss. It was the sort of evening that would have been known in

Victorian literature as a hero's welcome. Girls' eyes sparkled and men patted me on the back. It was lovely. But any pompous thoughts of heroism were soon as burst as the blisters on my plums. My hands were still so butchered I couldn't pick up a knife and fork and the kind girl sitting next to me had to cut up my food for me. A man meekly having to be fed by a girl as his buttocks gently bled is not the image of Victorian heroism that would inspire Tennyson.

The next day I spent at the boatyard with Mark. There was very little I could do practically but at least I could tell him the problems I'd faced and how the bath had held up in the water. One thing was uppermost in my mind: how to stop the problems with my wrists that I'd had rowing the Channel. After talking to various people and thinking about the problem, it seemed that it was the angle at which I was pulling through the stroke that was causing the trouble. I left the boatyard that night with the question of how to fix it rattling round my head.

That night I arrived in Pimlico. Gliding down the street towards me was a friend of mine, Laura.

'Darling, I'm so super-proud of you,' she smiled.

We hugged and went off to find some food. I chose the restaurant.

'Are you sure you want to eat here, darling? That one we passed up the street looked much nicer . . .'

My mind was set. Nothing would change it. This one had soft chairs.

Over food, I told her all about the bath trip so far. The other advantage of the place we entered was that it was food you could just about get away with eating with your hands. Phew. At least I'd avoided having to ask her to feed me like the poor girl from the night before. She laughed and smiled as I rolled out the full story of the crossing. The meal passed so fast that had the gentle cough of the proprietor not brought it to our attention, neither of us would have noticed we were the only ones left in the place. At first I thought me eating with my hands had cleared the restaurant but it was late: although I left the proprietor an extra tip just in case.

The next morning the weather was still terrible in Folkestone. I arrived at the boatyard in Richmond to help Mark. Again, there wasn't much I could do but submit to the teasing of the apprentices. They were proud that the bath had made it but still couldn't resist the jokes at the expense of my hands. A knife, fork or normal-sized pen was too small for my battered hands but Mark had an oversized thick pencil. I could hold this in very short bursts before the tendons in my hands and wrists went funny again. I had come up with a thought in the restaurant the night before of how to solve the angle problem. I handed my drawing on an envelope to Mark.

'What's this?'

'I've had an idea for some new oars to help me avoid getting swollen wrists.'

Mark held the envelope in his hand and said nothing. The apprentices stopped. I'd not designed anything since Douglas and I had come up with the bath design over a year before.

Mark sighed. 'I'll see what I can find.'

I went to put the kettle on; at least this was a job that my hands could manage.

Over the next couple of days, Mark managed to get the bath fixed. Finally, the leak seemed under control. We then spent two days, while the weather was still horrible in Folkestone, testing and refining my new ideas for oars. The thing with new blades is that it's all in the gearing. The width of the blades versus the overall length of the oar gives you the difficulty you will experience in pulling it through the water. A very long oar with a very thick blade will be almost impossible to pull through the water. I needed very long oars as this would make the angle I pulled through the stroke at less painful, so we had to take the width of the blade down. However, you don't want to take the blade too thin, as then you can't get the purchase on the water you need to power through it. It's a question of trial and error. How wide could the blade be and still allow me to pull it through the water successfully?

For two days we faffed around trying to get this right. There was nothing else we could have done as the prevailing wind at Folkestone was in totally the wrong direction. Learning to row with totally new oars is like learning to row again. It all feels funny and wrong. Especially if they are as different from the pair you've been used to as my new ones were. I arrived back from one testing row.

Mark looked down from the slipway. 'Who'd have thought when you first started . . .' He turned to someone on the bank. 'Didn't know anything about rowing and now he's designing his own blades . . .'

I got out and peeled the lycra from the still-bleeding cuts on my bottom.

'The oars feel much better. I'd say we're there.'

Silently I wondered if my bottom would ever stop bleeding. My phone flashed in the bath, it was Andy: 'Tim, I've got to see someone about my knees but Eric says he'll be your support boat up to Dover.'

Testing the new blades had been useful. Not only had we tested the new blades but also seen how painful it was for me to row. My body was not holding up well. My buttocks were healing very slowly and I was still walking like John Wayne due to swollen plums. My wrists were also in a very bad way. There was a dull, thudding ache in them. On the plus side, I was now able to use a knife and fork. Mark told the apprentices I was now going to try to make it back to London. They took one look at me and laughed. My ravaged body enabled me to move with the graceful alacrity of a near-dead man of 97. I didn't look like I could make it up to Richmond High Street let alone row the 160 or so miles I was suggesting.

The bath was ready again. Now, the weather in Folkestone turned vile. I waited in Richmond, rubbing cream into cuts and surgical spirit onto my plums.

'Tim, it's Eric, can you get the bath down here? We've got a chance of making it to Dover.'

Mark, the apprentices, Kenroy and I loaded the bath. Chris arrived and we sped off down to Folkestone. Arriving, Chris turned the car to the left.

'What are you doing? It's not here we turn, it's . . .'

My words trailed off. We'd found the Holy Grail Arch on the first attempt. Remarkable!

We unloaded the bath using the third movement of the unloading the bath symphony for two men, a trailer, car and tub on the slipway. By now I was even looking forward to the drum solo played on the tables. I pre-emptively bought drinks for the packed pub as Chris reversed into lobster pots.

We floated the bath and Chris and I met Eric. He was a tanned, grey-haired fisherman with a moustache. He was slightly softer spoken than Andy and seemed slightly older.

'So this is the bath . . .'

'Yes.'

'Right, let's get going to Dover then.'

Chris decided to stay on land that day. We'd realised on the way down that if both of us went on the water, leaving the car in Folkestone, how would we get back from Dover to Folkestone?

Eric took his boat out into the outer harbour. I did up the shoes that are fixed to the footplate in the bath, put the new oars in the gate, fastened the catches and we left.

The weather was stunning, if a little windy, but Dom was right in that the wind had been significantly less than on previous days and was in vaguely the right direction for me to row.

I left the outer harbour arm at Folkestone. It was a relief. The tidal nature of Folkestone had been a constant battle throughout the whole project so far. Dover was not tidal, I'd been told, so I couldn't wait to see it. Only being able to get the bath out of Folkestone in two very specific windows of time each day was something which had made dealing with the weather even trickier. When we'd got a snatch of good weather there had been no water in the harbour and vice versa. It had been a case of incompatibility worse than a flamenco dancer dancing the tango with a man who could only reel to the strains of a band playing the waltz. Yet, with every stroke, as I left her, I began to miss Folkestone. She'd been consistently annoying but I'd grown very fond of her. Without this deep-rooted illogical impulse, divorce lawyers would have much more work.

The first part of the row was very good. The current did what we thought it would and there was very little wind. Always on my right-hand side were the massive white cliffs. They'd seemed impressive when I saw them from halfway across the Channel but now, creeping along the base of them, they were simply awesome. As I looked up at them, their sheer angle seemed implausible and the thought that they might at any moment collapse on top of me gave me an extra boost to go faster. I was focusing in my head when Eric shouted, 'Tim! Look out!'

I looked behind me to see that the white cliffs and I were not running parallel as I thought but that they had crept up behind me to form an impenetrable headland. The sea whipped up. When you get too close to the shore, all the sea wants to do is take you in to the shore and smash you up.

'Come out to sea!'

Eric was yelling for all he was worth. I pulled hard but the current was now very much in control. A frantic 15 minutes ensued. Eric couldn't get me as his boat could not get into that shallow depth of water. I was on my own, facing the white cliffs of Dover. Like David and Goliath, only with less-convincing odds. I diverted all my strength into pulling on one oar. This wouldn't be the most beautiful or efficient bit of rowing but with luck it would save me from being smashed on the rocks.

I looked behind me and saw with relief that I'd managed it. I'd cheated my way out of the clutches of the white cliffs and learnt a very important lesson. If I got too close to the shore, I wasn't really able to fight the current.

An hour later Eric shouted again, 'Stop rowing for a bit, Tim . . .'

'What?'

'We're at Dover, you've made it! We've got to wait for a passenger boat to leave before we can get into the harbour.'

I couldn't quite believe it. I'd made it to Dover. I looked behind me at the mighty harbour and castle perched on top. Somewhere up there was the Coastguard station where I'd had a meeting with Mr Merryweather a year before. I waved, just in case he was looking out of a very powerful telescope. Wash from the wake of the harbour arm or a boat jolted me back into focus. I checked the time and looked at the charts – I say charts, it was actually a photocopy of the road atlas – I was using to navigate. I sat in the bath, thought through what Dom and I had discussed about what he thought the sea, wind and tides might do and measured things on the road atlas. After a few moments Eric shouted over, 'Shall we go into Dover then?'

'I want to have a crack at making it to Ramsgate . . . What do you think?'

'It's not a bad idea while you've got the weather . . . I'm up for it.'

'Great. I'll phone Chris.'

Getting reception is not easy, especially when a massive passenger boat is trying its best to scuttle you, but I managed it.

'Mate, we're going to try for Ramsgate.'

'Is that wise?'

It was a fair question. There's not a suitable harbour between Dover and Ramsgate and if the weather turned, I'd be very stuck. Trying to get to Ramsgate was a very risky business and if I didn't make it, I'd have to turn back and seek shelter in Dover.

'I know the risks and just want to take advantage of the weather.'

'I'll phone Dom and let him know.'

I passed Dover and went on up the coast past St Margaret's Bay. The light wasn't great due to cloud cover and the wind wasn't being very helpful but I'd come up with a plan to deal with it. The good news was that the wind was coming in from an angle behind me. When this happened I'd turn the bath so that the wind came directly behind me and used the wind hitting the roll top of the bath, as you would use a sail. This meant that while I was doing this I was technically rowing in slightly the wrong direction but I had the advantage of being able to use the wind. When the wind changed or I'd rowed so far off course that I had to alter direction, I'd row almost at right angles to the wind. When I was slightly the other side of the course I wanted to be on, I'd turn the bath so that I could use the wind hitting the roll top from behind again and row on. The net effect when seen from above was that I was rowing in a massive zigzag. I'm not sure what made me think of doing this, it just seemed the easiest way of getting further and harnessing the wind.

By Deal, I'd really got this zigzag technique sorted and raced past the pier there at some speed. People waved and I saw a figure that looked suspiciously like Chris racing furtively down the pier towards them but I wasn't close enough to see clearly and it could just have been an elderly man pursued by bees.

I arrived at the southern tip of Sandwich Bay. Dom and I had come up with two plans for this part of the journey. If the weather was bad or the wind was against me I was to hug the coastline and struggle as best I could around the bay. If the weather was with me I could take a risk and go in a straight line across the bay. But if the weather turned or current frisked me the wrong way then it would make everything very difficult. If I got it right it would save me a lot of time.

The other problem was that due to the sandbanks and very shallow water, once my decision was made I couldn't change it. This was one of those times where I was totally responsible for my own choices. I looked across the bay and shouted to Eric, 'What does the weather look like it's going to do in a couple of hours?'

'There's something nasty coming in, in a couple of hours, I think . . . but it's tricky to tell exactly how long.'

This was a gamble. Could I get across the bay in a couple of hours before the weather came in? I thought hard. I've always loved risk. I altered course and headed for the straight line across the bay. None of the hugging the coast nonsense for me, I thought.

As if to vindicate me, the wind changed in my favour. I turned the bath in line with the wind to take full advantage of this. Using my new-found sail technique to help me, it felt we were going along at race speed.

Eric shouted across, 'You're doing eight knots!'

Sandwich Bay is stunning. It's such a gorgeous place that, in order not to make the rest of Kent jealous at its beauty, the government put a massive power station there to attempt to spoil the view. A testament to its loveliness is that even with that monstrosity there, it's still stunning. A Kent councillor told me that, having realised putting an ill-designed power station in such an area of outstanding natural beauty was a mistake, the council passed an emergency resolution to pull it down immediately at a council meeting 15 years ago.

As I pulled hard, glided along at eight knots and basked in the sunshine, I smiled. Bathtub rowing had never been this much fun. This was how the entire trip should have been in my head. This was great. I'd almost got across the bay when the wind turned and I realised the bath was much heavier on one side. The leak was back. I downed oars and pulled gaffer tape out of the washstand. When things go wrong at sea, they do so fast. In and out of the water, I improvised a patch, got back into the sliding seat and rowed hard. We'd need to make it to Ramsgate fast. The water that had again got into one of the flotation tanks kept conspiring with the wind to drag me off course.

The mist started to come in. I'd failed; the weather had got me again. I was crushed; I knew Eric would soon be pushing to tow me back to Dover. I cursed, dug in and pulled harder. I took hundreds of strokes, cursed, swore, corrected for the heavy tank and now unhelpful wind, and gave everything to try and make Ramsgate. I didn't want to have to go back to Dover.

The mist cleared. There was a momentary respite from the wind. I turned. There was the harbour arm: there was the torch at Ramsgate, I felt like a conquering Roman. I'd made it.

I crossed into the main harbour for grown-up ships, then turned starboard (bath right, or my left as I was facing backwards) for the smaller harbour. Chris was waiting for me.

'Well done, mate: from Folkestone to Ramsgate in under five and a half hours. That's better than you thought it would be.'

My old phone (the one that was with Chris as opposed to my new gangsta one that was being hunted down by the constabulary) rang. Chris went to pick it up, then handed it down from the quayside to me. It was Dom.

'Hi, Chris, it's me, how's Tim, where is he now?'

'Dom, it's me, I'm sitting in the bath in Ramsgate.'

'What? What happened? You've not crashed, have you? Did the weather turn? I thought it looked pretty good . . .'

'No, I've made to Ramsgate.'

'That's under five and a half hours!'

'I know. The wind helped. I used the top of the roll top of the bath to channel it.'

I explained the zigzag manoeuvre that I'd come up with. Dom listened, sighed and said, 'In sailing, Tim, we'd call that tacking.'

'It's an official thing?' I couldn't believe anyone had thought of it before.

'Tim, you've just achieved your first sailing manoeuvre. I'm quite proud.'

I handed the phone back up to Chris. Eric shouted over, 'Come on, let's get you moored up.'

The sun came out. This was exactly how the bath trip should be: stunning weather, outstanding times and everyone smiling. I pulled further into the harbour and moored next to a grey boat. A man in uniform appeared on the jetty as I was tying the bath to it.

'Ah, we thought it was you. You're the bath man . . .'

'Er . . . yes . . . I am . . .'

I was a bit shocked. Who was this man who knew all about me? Quickly my brain marshalled my mouth.

'And you are?'

'Oh sorry, I'm the officer commanding this lot.' He gestured vaguely behind him. I realised the grey boat was a Royal Navy vessel, the man in front of me her commanding officer and the flag flapping the breeze the coveted White Ensign.

'Been really hoping we'd come across you. Super effort rowing the Channel. We've been keeping up with your progress on the radio channel.'

We shook hands. It was painful for me but some things are important.

'Fancy a cup of tea? I've just boiled the kettle.'

As you may remember, I have a very strict rule: never refuse a cup of tea. If everyone did this, world peace would be just round the corner. Soon the officer, some of his men and I stood on the jetty and drank tea out of mugs. They all asked questions about the bath and journey so far before the officer said, 'Hope you don't think me rude but it does look such a state . . . Would you mind if we gave the bath a bit of a polish?'

Even staunch critics of the Royal Navy will find it impossible to fault them on politeness. Did I mind? I was over the moon. Before I'd finished my tea, the bath was enjoying several members of Her Majesty's senior service giving her a Rolls-Royce of a polish. The officer, other members of the ship's company and I watched the team expertly buffing the bath. As a taxpayer I'd really got value for money. Eric shouted over, 'Tim, we've got to get some paper-work sorted and find you a smaller mooring.'

I thanked the RN for their great kindness and pulled away from the outer jetty. Eric escorted me and the now-gleaming bath round to the small-boats part of Ramsgate Harbour. Now we'd made it this far up, I'd need another support boat to take me further. Getting Eric to come up from Folkestone every day was not an option I wanted to consider, as it would place me back in the hands of that inconsistent tidal mistress again.

Chris and I waved Eric off and walked up the gangplank to check if we could leave the bath in Ramsgate Harbour overnight. We arrived in the offices of the Royal Harbour of Ramsgate. A man was behind the desk. At first he didn't look up. When he did, I was confronted with two eyes looking in totally different directions. I didn't know which eye to meet so took an average and stared down the middle. This had the net effect that, of the four eyes in the conversation, none of them were looking at each other.

'Hello, I've just arrived from France via Folkestone in a bath . . .'

Perhaps Chris and I had just walked into a Marty Feldman sketch. Without missing a beat he said, 'Of course . . .'

'Here's the paperwork. It's laminated.'

'Of course it is. I'll get you a form . . .' He went over to a filing cabinet at the back of the room in front of a window. 'Bloody hell – there's a bath out there . . .' He turned to me with a face that suggested I'd killed his son.

Apologetically, I offered, 'I did say it was a bath . . .'

'What do you want to do with it?'

'I'd really like to leave it here overnight – I should be gone in the morning – I've got a few repairs to do but then I should be off.'

'Where did you say you'd come from?'

'France.'

'Via Folkestone,' Chris added helpfully.

'Why?'

'I'm trying to raise a bit of money for a charity called Comic Relief . . .'

'Look, leave it here overnight. I'll make a note – we've not got a form for baths, and it's in a good cause. I love that guy who does Comic Relief . . . what's his name?'

Everybody loves Lenny.

'That's it . . . Jonathan Ross.'

Chris and I wandered out and stood beneath the clock at Ramsgate. I looked up at the face.

'That's not the right time is it?'

'It's Ramsgate Mean Time, I've been reading quite a bit today – Ramsgate's in its own time zone.'

I looked at the stunning, sleepy harbour.

'Three hundred years behind Greenwich?'

'It's actually five minutes 41 seconds ahead . . .'

There was a pause then Chris said, 'Tim, I've got to leave too.'

I knew this was coming but I'd really miss having Chris around.

'I've got to catch the train. I really can't miss it.'

'The train to London?'

'Nope. The one to China.'

'Seriously, where are you going?'

Ages ago Chris had booked to go on the Orient Express and it was leaving soon. I'd said goodbye to Eric and now Chris too. This was a day of change in the project. I was sad to lose him from the bath journey but also sad as one of my best friends would be gone for a whole year.

'Send me a postcard. And thanks, mate – I couldn't have got this far without you.'

'Sure you would have done!'

With Chris gone I wandered up the hill to the prestigious Royal Temple Yacht Club. This is a very old club for sailors. The bath is a rowing vessel. Normally there is no love lost between sailors and rowers. They don't get on. The reasons are obvious: one is totally reliant on the whim of the wind, the other faces away from the direction they're going in. Both accuse the other of not looking where they're going. One writes with cheese and the other eats truckles of chalk. This could go very badly for me. I pushed the old timber door into the hall. How would they take to me? I stood daunted in the hall. The Royal Temple is an old-fashioned place, with myriad rules and regulations, many of which are designed to baffle the uniniti- ated and some of which are printed in the front hall. The father of a friend of mine is a member and had suggested I eat there when I was in Ramsgate. As if to emphasise its credentials, the Royal Temple is the yacht club to which Sir Ted Heath used to belong. Unfortunately, he'd died just before I arrived and many of the members had just been to his funeral. It was a sad atmosphere in the club as I entered.

I wandered over to the front desk, gave the name of my friend's father and asked where I could eat.

'Not upstairs.'

The reply came with starch.

'Can I eat in the dining room?'

'You can't eat in the dining room.'

'What about that room there?'

'No.'

'Can I go in the bar?'

He thought for a moment. I could see rules and regulations flashing through his mind.

'Yes.'

'Thank you.'

He watched me go towards the bar door.

'Welcome to the club,' he said without the slightest sense of irony. In his mind, I was honoured to be allowed into the bar. So far the old rumours of sailors and rowers not getting on was holding good. I entered the bar.

'Do you serve food?'

'No.'

Things were not going well.

'Not even crisps?'

'We have crisps. Are you the guest of a member?'

'Yes.'

'Is the member with you as I can't serve you without them being here.'

This was getting silly.

'I've just rowed from France to here via Folkestone in a bath and I just wanted a sandwich . . .'

A man at the bar I'd never seen before smiled across at me and turned to the bar lady.

'He's my guest. I'm sure we can make him some sort of sandwich. Come and sit down . . . How have things been going . . . ?'

'Oh, sorry, I'm Tim.'

'Yes, how have things been going, Tim?' He turned to the lady at the bar. 'This is my old friend Tim.'

This kind sailor explained his boat was stuck in Ramsgate. It seemed it had been stuck there intermittently for many years and he was a regular at the yacht club. As I tucked into a delicious sandwich and a Coke he introduced me to various other people in the bar. We talked for a while before the bath story was introduced. They checked the floating apparition in the harbour with the club telescope before they'd believe a word. Then I went through the story so far and as it ended I thought it might be time to take my leave of them. As I went to leave the bar one of the men who had been laughing at the story waved in my direction.

'Wait, I think I've got something for you. How many committee members are in the room?'

Various people raised their hands.

'I think this lad deserves a burgee, what do you think?'

They all nodded and made the gentle hum of approving noises that occur in well-rehearsed committees. In my head the main question was: what's a burgee? I thought this would be a bad thing to admit to so gently hummed too. Various people in the room raised their hands again.

'Nip and fetch him one, would you?'

The bar lady arrived back with a small triangular flag. It was predictably navy blue and had a gold anchor, white horse and crown on it. The committee man presented it to me as the bar laughed and cheered.

'Well done. It's not every day we meet a bathtub rower. A great effort, good luck on your way round. Remember, wherever you are in the world, if you find another Royal Yacht club, fly this flag and they'll let you in . . . and probably give you a drink. Always fly it from your masthead.'

'Thank you, I'll fly it from my showerhead.'

I left the bar to the sounds of more laughter. As I walked down the hill I thought what a great arrangement this was. In my hand was an internationally recognised sign of reciprocal drinking; in a flash an elite fellowship of cross-boundary liver damage had been opened to me. I'd discovered another truly global peace initiative to go with my rules about accepting tea.

The next morning the weather was again terrible. The bath racketed around her berth in the harbour. This would not help the leak. With help I pulled her out of the water, dried her off and fixed the leak again. The weather continued to be terrible as I popped her back in the water.

The next stretch of the journey was a really nasty one. It would take me around the North Foreland – it's the pointy end of Kent. The currents around it are really difficult and just a slight change in the wind can guarantee you wrecked on the rocks. I spent the bad weather walking around the cliff tops looking at the dangers and taking notes on the wind as well as bailing out the bath. I looked out over the dark brooding clouds, driving rain and smashing waves. Water poured onto my face. I was the only captain of an ablution equipment ever to take on this tricky stretch of inland coastal water; I felt like a sailor nervously watching the mighty breakers, waiting to round Cape Horn.

I returned to the bath and bailed out again. Baths keep water in, no matter what: again this proved a fundamental flaw in my plan. I stumped up to the office of the Royal Harbour of Ramsgate again to check I could leave the bath there for another frustrating day. They had been very kind in letting the bath sit there for the last couple of days while I tried to get some decent weather.

The door opened. This time I was met with four eyes: the two

that faced in opposite directions and a new pair behind some spec-
tacles that stared at me with the perception of a gimlet.

'Hi, I'm not going to be able to get out of the harbour again
today . . .'

The gimlet eyes met mine.

'You're in the bath . . .'

'Yes . . . so sorry it's just that the weather . . .'

'I've been hoping to see you before I have to take things further . . .'

'What?'

'I don't like having your bath here.' Of the many things I would
come to criticise in this man, directness was not one of them. 'And
I understand you're refusing to pay the harbour fees.'

'I was told they'd been waived.'

'There's only two people who can waive your fees – that's me
and him – and we haven't.'

He gestured to the man who had kindly waived my fees. The
man looked back at me pleadingly in two directions. It's a look
that people around Hitler probably saw a lot. I turned back to the
gimlet-eyed Nazi.

'There must have been a misunderstanding.'

'I should say so. So not only do you have to pay the charge for
today, but all charges up until this point and there are a few fines
to pay too, for paying the charges late.'

This was too much. I was happy to defend the clearly weak man
who had obviously suffered years at the hands of Ramsgate's Führer
but this was unjust.

'Who is in charge of the port?'

'Captain White.'

'Where's his office?'

'Right over the other side of the quay – over there – and it closes
in exactly one minute.'

He smiled.

'Right – I'll be back.'

Breathless I bumped into the man pulling the door shut at the
office.

'I'm looking for Captain White.'

'Why?'

'I'm in the bath and they're trying to fine me. It doesn't seem
right . . .'

'I'm Captain White – let's go inside.'

In an immediately relaxing office I explained what had happened and why I was rowing.

'You're the man who came from France. I heard you were up at the yacht club the other night.'

'They gave me a burgee.'

'Are you flying it from your masthead?'

'Showerhead.'

'Of course. Let's sort this out.'

The captain barked orders down the phone. For every evil Führer, there's always a Captain White prepared to save the day. Not only was I granted a free mooring for as long as I needed it but also given a place to park the trailer should I need it. This was very kind of him.

With a sense of justice I returned to the office and picked up the passes from the hand of the Nazi who had earlier refused them. The man with the Marty Feldman eyes smiled at me as though, just for once, something positive had happened in his office.

I was stuck in Ramsgate. The weather turned to murder, my heart turned to stone. I wouldn't stand a chance attempting the North Foreland in this. After spending more days in abysmal weather, waist-deep in harbour water, bailing out the bath, I was fed up with life, the universe and Ramsgate. One night my phone rang. It was an old friend of mine called Ollie.

'How are you getting on?'

'Not good – this is not the weather for bathtub rowing.'

'How do you fancy a game of cricket?'

For years I've played for a side called the Mumblers Cricket Club (it's the less well known of the MCCs and is named after Ollie who used to mumble). We only play once a year, when we host a tournament, but it's one of my favourite days.

'How's the weather on the wicket?'

'Dark, windy but at least there's no rain. Are you in?'

Playing cricket in the midst of terrible adversity is more stereo-typically British than rain at the Grand National. I sighed at the cliché, smiled, reached into the car and pulled out my whites.

'I'll be there.'

Arriving at the hallowed ground, I was greeted with the familiar sights. Tents dotted around the boundary, people standing near the pavilion drinking and laughing, and a general feeling that something epic might occur – today could be the year we won a game.

I turned out on a murky, overcast day to thrash at a small, barely discernible red-leather ball. Swatting hopelessly, I realised that today was the longest time I'd spent away from the bath. When I was in the bath in Ramsgate, I couldn't wait to leave. As the ball almost took out my off-stump for the second time in the over, I realised that the ball was not the only thing I'd missed. I couldn't wait to get back to the bath.

Later, I was fielding. The ball whizzed high to my right. It was uncatchable. I dived towards it, fully waiting to land after a heroic miss. Somehow, totally outstretched and horizontal as I was, I realised that in my hand was the ball. I had caught the uncatchable. I held the ball and fell towards the ground using the medium of gravity. I hit the ground and lost my shoulder. As my arm swung gently by my side I could see that the ball had stayed lodged in my hand. I may have lost my shoulder but the batsman was dismissed: a truly heroic cricketing injury. As I looked at my face in the reflection of the polished leather, I realised the truth of what had occurred. I snapped back from the rose-tinted version of events to the stark truth. The ball had whizzed high to my right. It was indeed an impossible-looking catch; I dived fully outstretched, caught the ball, hit the ground and lost my shoulder – just as I had in my reverie. The batsman was dismissed. All that was true. Also true was that, if the batsman hadn't been dismissed, it was about time for her nap anyway. I had dislocated my shoulder to dismiss a five-year-old girl.

While the Mumblers batted on in the main match, I'd become involved in a side match on the boundary with a toddler. My head was clearly so insanely competitive that I'd broken myself to dismiss her.

My pain thresholds were very messed up by this stage in my life. I'd got very used to pain. With a constantly bleeding set of buttocks and massively oversized plums, a small shoulder injury was nothing. With a click and a crunch I pushed the shoulder. After the click-crunch, it was less floppy and seemed to hurt less. The girl gave up her nap, so I continued playing cricket with her, having got myself out in the main game for a swashbuckling 25.

Other than always accepting tea, I have another cardinal rule in life. If you can't lift a champagne bottle, go to casualty. By the close of play, my shoulder had really swollen up and I couldn't even lift a teacup, which broke my first rule in life. I didn't let on to the members of the team what I'd done and slipped away quietly.

Following my second rule to the letter, I arrived at casualty. Interminable waiting, various exams and an X-ray later I was thrust in front of a less-than-encouraging casualty doctor.

'It's dislocated but is back in place now.' He then went on to explain that I'd stretched either the ligaments or tendons above the shoulder (I forget which, it could have been both, I wasn't paying a massive amount of attention at that point). 'Oh and you've chipped your rotor cuff too.'

'What's that?'

'The shoulder is not a well-engineered joint. At some point it was probably more usefully engineered but since we've left the savannahs of Africa . . .'

I won't record the full explanation here, suffice to say, I'm not a medical man but even I could see that rowing the 130-odd miles left between Tower Bridge and me would not be easy with this. It was the sort of thing that one of my old Phys Ed masters (a man who made us run till we could taste blood) would have called 'challenging'. How had a gentle game of cricket turned out like this? I vowed in future to take up less threatening sports like Cumberlandshire Wrestling.

My descent into Greek tragedy was finally complete. With the first of his mighty tasks achieved, the bearded Hellenic hero had fallen prey to his own fatal flaws: his competitiveness and overly aggressive gamesmanship in the face of five-year-old opposition. I was forced to return home to landlocked Hertfordshire and sit with a strapped-up shoulder. Naturally, the minute the strapping was on, the weather turned really good.

The bath project was as smashed as my rotor cuff. It was over.

CHAPTER TEN

SPOILED HIS NICE NEW RATTLE

'This bowler is like my dog: three short legs and balls that swing each way.'

Brian Johnston

Anyone who has dislocated a shoulder will know the thudding pain that pulses with every beat of your heart. Added to this general pain is a very specific pain that feels like someone has a needle in your shoulder and is pushing it in and out, as though their eternal amusement depends on the grimacing this causes you.

This pain is nothing compared to the unbearable agony of having that shoulder twisted, pummelled and pulled about by a physiotherapist exhibiting more zeal for his task than a religious fanatic. His fake tan parted at the mouth to reveal a whiter than plausible smile.

'Yep. It's been quite badly dislocated.'

He grasped my arm and pushed. Something snapped. I screamed and tried to leave the room. My arm stayed in his firm grip.

'It's really back in now. The X-ray was right, it's quite a bad dislocation and there does seem to be a chip in the rotor cuff. You've also damaged the ligaments and tendons at the top of the shoulder.'

'Can I row?'

'Very funny.'

'Seriously . . . can I row?'

'Not a chance. There are two outcomes if you row. The first is that the shoulder will simply pop out again and the second is that you will do irreparable long-term damage to the shoulder . . . just look at the size of it in the mirror. Can you lift your arm up? Go on, try . . .'

I tried lifting my arm up. I got it up a bit but it wouldn't respond beyond a certain height. I tried rolling my shoulder. That didn't work either.

'See, you're not going to be doing anything with that for a while.'

I left the physio feeling very down. I had scuppered my own chances of success. I'd always thought it would be the weather that would finish off the bath project, not my own stupidity. Now the same stupidity that had started the bath project had finished it.

I stood in Hertfordshire with my arm strapped up like Nelson, looking out of the window over the countryside. My shoulder was very swollen. Finally, if only the local village infant school chose the right play – I was a dead cert for the role of either Quasimodo or Richard the Third – my shot at stardom was at hand. The weather outside was blissful. This would be perfect to row the bath. My phone rang. It was Dom. I'd not owned up to him about the cricketing injury mainly as I felt so very stupid.

'This is great weather, Tim, go, go, go. You'll easily make London in this . . .'

'There's been a slight hitch.'

I'd conquered the Channel and felt invincible. Now, I felt weak, old, battered and frail but mostly very stupid. He listened patiently as I explained the situation.

'Well, that could be the end of it.'

'I've got to see a physio again, but it's quite painful.'

I put down the phone and sat thinking. This was a vital time in the bath challenge. The bath sat bobbing up and down in the sun at Ramsgate Harbour under the watchful eye of Captain White. We had done roughly 60 miles of the challenge and still had roughly 120 left to make it to Tower. I sat broken in Hertfordshire. I knew I had to keep my overall body fitness up. I didn't think it was over and that was the main thing in my favour. But how could I exercise? Time spent on Betty the Ergo was not an option as my shoulder was wrecked.

I balanced on a stool and fetched down my favourite book on Nelson. I held the big tome on my knees and opened the cover with my good arm. What had the great man done when he'd been unable to go out to sea? Long walks. Of course: that was the answer. I thought I'd better check it with the physio. I shuddered as his lascivious tone penetrated my ear.

'I want to go on long country walks to try and keep fit,' I said.

'I'm not sure that's a good plan. If you fall over you might damage the shoulder even more . . .'

'Oh. Thank you for the advice. I'll see you for my appointment.'

I checked the strapping around my arm. Found my coat and deer-stalker hat and put on my wellies. Putting on wellies is not easy with a broken shoulder. An hour later I was outside, striding across the fields of Hertfordshire and feeling much better. I took great care over stiles and through gates so as not to hurt my precious shoulder. I walked at a brisk pace, from my village, through the woods, past the golf course and into the next village. I didn't see Mr Darcy or Elizabeth Bennet but I'm sure they were out having a similar walk somewhere. I crossed through the next village and out the other side into more woods and fields. Damn the medical establishment and their advice. This walk was just what I needed to sort myself out. I caught my foot on a tree root, tripped and fell over.

Instinct is a very clever thing. Somehow I contrived to take the weight of the fall on my left shoulder and arm. My damaged right arm didn't touch the ground. It still hurt as I'd jolted it but it certainly would have hurt more if it had hit the ground.

I got up and cursed myself for cursing the medical establishment. Somewhere in a physiotherapy office a perma-tanned hand put a pin and a small voodoo doll of me back into a cupboard; a mouthful of whiter-than-white teeth let out a nefarious laugh.

I got up, my other shoulder hurting a bit, but I was more shocked than anything. I struck out once more and about an hour later arrived back at home feeling much better.

The days passed in blissful sunshine. I walked, read and cursed myself. On the Wednesday I was to give a speech to the Company of Watermen and Lightermen of the River Thames at their hall in London. It was to have been, for me at least, a celebratory dinner for the finish of the bath project but bad weather and my arm injury put paid to that. However, the meal still went ahead and I arrived with my arm heavily strapped up.

Very kindly, they cut up my food for me and all made jokes about Nelson. I was able to eat the meal with just a fork. I gave the speech on how the bath trip had been so far and that went well. I also had to take an oath of allegiance to the Queen. I was being officially inaugurated as a Freeman of the Company that afternoon too and this was part of the ceremony that dates back hundreds of years. The Master sat on his chair in the stunning courtroom at Waterman's Hall and the massive Company Bible was brought out. I knew there was no way I could hold it. The Clerk smiled.

'You could hold it with your wrong hand.'

I wasn't sure if that was legally dubious so decided not to take any chances.

'Put it in the sling, if that's OK?'

The Bible was balanced in my sling and I entered the Waterman's Company, to laughter and more jokes about Nelson.

Back at home after the dinner I resolved to fight my predicament. I simply had to get my shoulder better quickly.

I drank quite a large glass of whiskey and took my arm out of its strapping. Many years before I'd broken my shoulder falling off a horse and that time a nice Indian doctor had suggested many exercises to help me get better faster than usual. He'd based his plan on his knowledge of medicine and yoga. This routine of stretching I now did obsessively. I also got some tiny weights out and started trying to do repetitions with them. It was a very, very painful process but I knew I had to get back to the bath and finish what I'd started.

I saw the physiotherapist again and also a second one. I lied to both of them and didn't mention the weights or stretching but both were amazed at the progress I was making. I hated lying but thought that the torturous system of weights and stretches I'd created was probably not going to make the medical profession very happy. All the time uppermost in my mind was the drive to get back in the bath.

My phone rang. It was Pimlico Laura.

'Why don't you come down with me for the weekend?'

This was great. Firstly, it would be lovely to see her. Secondly, she lived in Kent and it would take me closer to the bath.

She had stuff to do on the Saturday afternoon so would drop

me off in Margate. I was aiming to get to Margate when the bath was able to leave Ramsgate so thought it might be good to have a wander around the place, make friends and see what the mooring situation was like.

I've always had an ingrained distrust of Margate. It could be stories I overheard my godfather telling of Mods and Rockers clashing on the beaches there or the endemic sadness that hangs over towns that only sparkle for a season. Laura dropped me off. She waved brightly, screeched tyres and as pedestrians dived for safety, yelled, 'I'll pick you up later . . .'

I was shocked. There was a carnival atmosphere in the air. The bunting was out and the streets were crammed with people. I had no idea what was going on but it seemed all my visions of Margate were immediately proved wrong. This was a vibrant place full of colour. I tried not to let people jostle my shoulder as I made my way through the crowd. On the way to the water's edge I spotted a sign that said 'Margate Yacht Club: Members Only'. The door was open. Very welcoming I thought, so I went in. I'd been accepted in the Royal Temple so yacht clubs were my new favourite places in the world. If only I'd brought my new burgee with me.

The Margate Yacht Club was less polished than the Royal Temple. Having said that, there are several regiments of soldiers whose boots are less polished than the Royal Temple. In Margate YC there also seemed to be less people. Those people there were crowded around the windows and looked down on something. A lady with bleached blonde hair turned towards me as I entered and smiled. I smiled back: 'What's going on?'

'It's the Margate Raft Race . . .'

'Oh. Can I have a look?'

'Of course.'

From the window I could see the whole of Margate out and playing. They were all massed around the harbour, watching people row old oil drums strapped together. The start seemed to be over the other side of the bay where I couldn't quite see, but the finish was at the coastal end of the harbour arm just below us. The great train robber Ronnie Biggs said he wanted to 'Come home (from Brazil), see Margate and go to prison.' On a day like today, basked in sunshine with everyone out and having fun, I could really see why. Today Margate was Xanadu. The contents of the yacht club were totally focused on the race so I decided the best thing to do was wander down to the harbour and see if I could buy a programme to tell me what was going on.

After carefully guarding my shoulder through the crowds, I made it to the top of the slipway. I turned to the man next to me.

'What's going on?'

'It's the annual raft race . . . How do you not know that? Are you a visitor?'

Not knowing if this was a good thing I answered tentatively, 'Yes . . .'

'Well you've come to the right place. This is the Town Mayor.'

There's a drill when you meet a Mayor. Luckily, I've met Mayors before. Once when I was on tour, I tried to meet a Mayor in every place I played. I didn't quite manage it (some of them didn't want to play) but in three months I notched up 13 Mayors, three Headmasters, a cathedral Dean and a Duchess.

I rolled out the drill and chatted to the Mayor. He introduced me to the Town Sergeant whose job is to follow the Mayor of Margate around.

'. . . But what does he do?'

'Makes sure no one nicks his chain.'

We all laughed. It was probably important in times gone by but today, with the sun out, this was such a happy place that I couldn't imagine anything like that happening. Then I explained about the bath, the trip, the aims and that I'd like to moor up in Margate when I made it round from Ramsgate. The Mayor said, 'Of course we'll find you a place to moor up. It'll be nice to have you. You can either use the harbour, or, if it's finished, the replacement pier. We lost the last one in a storm a while back but we're re-building it.'

After a lovely couple of hours in Margate, I saw people jumping and nervously clinging to buildings. Laura had arrived in her car. Other than the throbbing pain in my shoulder, this was a very happy day.

'I've finished all my jobs. Shall we go for a walk?'

I uttered a short prayer and we sped off. Laura drives with a recklessness that even the most bloodthirsty Viking would find unnerving. We arrived at her parents' house. She got out to kiss her mum hello and while she wasn't looking, I fell out of the passenger seat and kissed the ground in thanks for my deliverance. For the rest of the afternoon we walked through the cornfields to the south of Margate. I took my arm out of its strapping and ran my hands through the ears at the top of the corn. My hands were not quite healed but this was a divine experience. Like a Roman soldier in the poems of Catullus I'd found the couch I'd longed for. I spent the next hour picking corn ears out of the goo patches that still littered my hands. Catullus never mentions this.

The next day Laura dropped me off back in Hertfordshire. I took my arm out of the strapping and, sweating heavily, went back to doing my weights. The events of yesterday had only made me more determined to get back to the bath. I wanted to get to Margate: playground in the sun. My phone rang. It was Dom.

'Tim, I'm not sure how your shoulder is but I thought you should know, there's a really good weather window coming but after that I don't see a weather window for about eight days. I think if you can, you should try and make it round the Foreland.'

'Right . . . I'll give it a go . . .'

I started to make arrangements. With Eric gone, I needed a new support-boat skipper.

Finding a support-boat skipper was turning up an interlocking medieval-style network of connections. Andy and Eric couldn't help as they were in Folkestone. They knew people in Dover but not Ramsgate. By not stopping in Dover I'd missed out a vital link in the chain. The support-boat skipper is an odd thing. If things go well, you shouldn't need one at all. If things go badly, like on the first attempt, your life can depend on them. All they have to recommend them is the fact that they're still alive. It's tricky finding one in a place where you know no one and when you're rowing a bath. Still, I started with Eric and Andy's list of Dover fishermen to find a list of Ramsgate-based fishermen. Most of my conversations that day consisted of:

'Hello, I need a support-boat skipper . . .'

'Sorry, I don't do that – got to go.'

With some I made it as far as:

'Hello, I need a support-boat skipper . . .'

'Where from?'

'Ramsgate.'

'Sorry, I'm not there at the moment.'

'When will you be back?'

'Not for a week or so . . .'

Finally, I got some really good leads that led to:

'Hello, I need a support-boat skipper . . .'

'Where from?'

'Ramsgate.'

'Right – what are you up to?'

'I'm rowing a bath . . .'

'I've got to go – bye.'

Things were not going well. I was again stumped by how un-available the fishing fraternity could be. I tried another number.

'Hello, I need a support-boat skipper . . .'

'I'm really a cockle fisherman . . . I do fish for other stuff.'

'Good . . . I just need a support-boat skipper to get me and my bath out of Ramsgate . . .'

'You're in a bath?'

'Yes – don't hang up . . .'

'I thought I was seeing things in the harbour – where have you come from?'

'Well France, sort of . . . via Folkestone . . .'

'Now it all makes sense – I heard people talking about you on the radio and in the pub – it's for some charity isn't it?'

'Yes.'

We met on the harbour at Ramsgate one morning. I'm not sure what my image of the traditional Kentish cockle fisherman was, but it was not the beach surfer dude who got out of the silver convertible Mercedes that stood in front of me.

'Hi, I'm Dave.'

Behind me, he saw the bath.

'Ah, there she is – you'll have to do a bit of bailing out before we give this a try. This beats winkles.'

I had realised my place in the world – somewhere slightly higher than a winkle.

Chris had left to catch the train to China. Luckily for me Phillip Carr had just arrived back from China. Obviously China has a strict one-in one-out policy, like all the best Soho nightclubs. Phil stood next to me on the docks as we both looked at Dave. Another man in a T-shirt with 'Whitstable' written on it wandered over.

'What are you up to?'

'I'm trying to row my bath round to Margate.'

'Oh, you're the guy in the bath . . . Mind if I come too – I'm not up to much today.'

Whitstable was one of the places I was trying to get to after Margate so I took his arrival as a sign. I viewed his T-shirt with the same prophetic awe that people applied to John the Baptist and invited him to ride on the support boat.

I stood by the bath making my final preparations. Captain White arrived.

'You're off, are you?'

'Yes. Thank you so much for all your help.'

'I just came to warn you – it's my last day today. I can't stay on any further, I was really meant to leave last week. Lucky you've got the weather as I'm not sure how my successor would react.'

I took from his look that his successor might have been either the Nazi gimlet man or some close member of the Führer's family. It seemed from his tone that he'd stayed on to shield me. I never got to the bottom of this but if he did, it was an even greater act of kindness than I was aware of. I shook his hand firmly, winced and thanked him again before he wandered off to his office.

I got into my bath and locked down the oars. My shoulder was still in a lot of pain. All the advice had been not to row with a broken shoulder. Phil was loading the myriad kit bags containing his camera equipment onto the support boat. He glanced over just as I was taking some of the world's strongest painkillers.

'How is the shoulder?'

'It's either going to pop out immediately, which will mean this is a very short day of rowing, or it'll hold in place.'

'What are those pills?'

'Something they give to horses I think . . .'

'Dave says off you go, he's got to do some final checks – we'll be right behind you.'

'Great. Meet me in Margate and bring a vet.'

'What?'

'I'll need more painkillers.'

Nervously, I put the oars into the water and, so carefully it was like I'd wrapped my shoulder in velvet, took a slow pull through the stroke. My shoulder stayed in. I took another very gentle stroke and again my shoulder stayed in. I rowed off past Dave doing final checks and out towards the outer harbour wall.

I was leaving Ramsgate. It was 18 July, over a month since I'd made it across the Channel. The only danger I now faced for my shoulder was if the sea jerked it out of its socket. Knowing that my row could be a short one if the weather turned I tentatively pulled on past the harbour arm and out into the chop. Ramsgate had held me for much longer than planned and almost been the end of the project but finally it seemed I was free. The legendary theme to *The Great Escape* mingled with the wind and whistled round my ears.

I pulled up through an increasing wind and swelling sea past Broadstairs. I saw a couple of wrecks on the rocks that stuck up through the spray. I decided to row round the point as far out at sea as possible without getting involved in the shipping lanes. This plan did not work as brilliantly as I'd hoped. The current seemed intent on pushing me back in towards the rocks. After much straining and grunting we achieved a draw and I stayed away from the rocks at what I judged to be a safe distance. Through the sound of the waves breaking on the shore Dave shouted desperately, 'Tim! Below you!'

I looked overboard at the jagged rocks just a few inches below the surface. It was horrible. The bath needed a draught of ten inches and just one of those rocks could wreck her. I'd accounted for rocks above the waves but not the more damaging ones below.

I saw an area with no rocks directly to my left. I pulled at right angles to my current position using just one oar and took myself out in a north-north-easterly direction. I had to keep my attention focused on where the rocks were not. This was fine when the water was clear. When the water was too foggy to see rocks, I got my knife, attached it to a bit of string and dropped it overboard. Using this method I navigated my way out through the lethal labyrinth. I'd escaped, but this time it really was a case of only just. Dave's boat was equipped with up-to-date sonar equipment to help him gauge heights; I'd been forced to make do with an improvised system, probably last used by Nelson as a midshipman. The main thing of course is that it had worked.

Out at sea near the tip of North Foreland in a bath, the wind began to get worse and my shoulder was not really on very good form. However, against increased odds I made it to Margate and triumphantly pulled in to lie next to the harbour arm. I moored up, ran up the steps and across the street to the sign saying 'Margate Yacht Club'. Brilliant. This was going well. I may have a shoulder that felt like it was about to be pulled off by wild horses but I'd made it to Margate and there was the familiar oasis of the Yacht Club. I smiled, as this time I'd remembered my burgee from the Royal Temple. Surely having it would ensure me an even warmer welcome. This was going to be great. This time the door wasn't open. I rang the bell on the buzzer. A female voice answered. Even better.

'Yes?'

'Can I come in?'

'No.'

'I've just rowed into the harbour and wondered if you could help me finding moorings?'

'No.'

If I hadn't known better I would have suspected this was an automated message. I really needed their help. I knew no one in Margate except the Mayor.

'I really need some help . . .'

'So?'

This was not going well. Where was the cheery welcome that Kubla Khan gave the visitors to his pleasure dome? This woman was so chilly she was at threat from global warming.

'What do you suggest I do?'

'Go?'

Desperate times called for the desperate and thoroughly un-British measure of using my new-found honour.

'I've got a burgee from the Royal Temple . . .'

'So what?'

'I met a blonde lady in here the other day . . .'

'Really!'

'Could you at least tell me somewhere that might be able to help?'

There was a pause. I may have imagined it but I was sure I heard cruel sniggering.

'The Mayor suggested I . . .'

There was a sigh.

'Try the office across the road.'

I entered the office across the street.

'Hi – I've spoken to the Mayor and he said I could moor the bath on the harbour.'

'I wouldn't do that – it'll stick in the mud and you'll not get it out again.' Great, another tidal harbour: I remembered the fun I'd had at Folkestone. This was the difference between a kind invitation from a Mayor who knew nothing about maritime affairs and the informed word of the experienced harbour staff.

'He mentioned a pier?'

'Oh, that blew up to Clacton in a storm – he probably told you – we're rebuilding it.'

'Yes, where's the rebuilding?'

Perhaps I could have moored there, even though it wasn't totally finished.

'We've not started it yet.'

'When did you lose the last one?'

'1978.'

'So how can I moor here now?'

'You want to moor here now?'

'Yes.'

'That's not going to be possible.'

I sat on the harbour arm not quite knowing what to do. I could leave the bath moored on the outside of it. That was a very risky strategy as, if the weather turned bad, it could get smashed. I could leave the bath moored on the inside of it but the informed advice was that I'd end up stuck in the mud and never be able to get out. Perhaps he wasn't telling the truth. I didn't know whether to believe him or not. My time outside the Yacht Club had tarnished Margate a bit for me.

'What's up?'

I looked up and saw the familiar jovial figure of the Mayor. One of only two cheerful people in Margate as it now turned out.

'I wanted to moor up here.'

'Yes – no – you can't do that . . . I thought you meant next year – what with your arm being in a sling and all that . . .'

I suppose it was fair enough.

'Perhaps I could leave the bath here somehow?'

'I wouldn't leave that here – that copper will be stripped down and sold for scrap before you can say "murder".'

An odd choice of phrase but one I'll never forget.

'By smugglers?'

'No, school kids.'

'Shouldn't they be in school?'

'Nah, this is Margate mate . . .'

For a Mayor to admit the ruination of the entire town education system in this way, things must have been pretty serious. We talked further and a less positive picture of Margate began to appear. A man came running down the harbour arm.

'Here, mate! Don't linger here, you'll get stuck in the mud.'

I didn't seem to have a choice. I made up my mind. Shook hands with the Mayor and thanked him for coming down to see me before shaking the dust of Margate from my feet and pulling out of the 'harbour'.

With no moorings in Margate as promised, if the weather became bad, I was in trouble. The tide was turning, hence the 'harbour' emptying. I came up with a plan. Finally, I'd found a use for my hitherto totally pointless and weighty anchor. I could throw it down and wait the seven or so hours till the tide turned again. When the tide came back in my direction I could catch it westbound, just like a bus, and hop off at the next place I knew I could moor: Whitstable. If the weather turned against me, Margate not having moorings could be fatal.

Margate had become clear. All the surface joy in the place had faded. I looked at the town and her empty streets: a consistent and bitter reminder that once they'd been full. The raft race was exposed simply as a constructive way for the local hoards of delinquent brigands and still resident Mods and Rockers to use up the oil drums they had left over from setting fire to things. I remembered Ronnie Biggs's wish – 'See Margate and go to prison' – and realised this was the town motto. With the hinges off and me in potentially a very tricky situation: 'Gateway to the sea, gateway to health' had been exposed as a lie. Now it all made sense. That was why the Town Sergeant was such a burly man. He'd been the only person not to laugh when he said he was there to stop people nicking the mayoral chain. He meant it. If only I'd got a sergeant to guard the bath.

Evidence would suggest that, with no moorings and an automated door message, members of the Margate Yacht Club outside the annual raft race are rarer than the Yeti. I did not fly their burgee from the showerhead of the bath.

* * *

Weather is the single biggest factor in determining events in history. Would Agincourt have turned out the same in the sunshine on hard ground?

I phoned Dave who, thinking I was safe in Margate, had set off back round to Ramsgate.

'There's been a slight change of plan.'

'What?'

'There's a problem.'

'Good, we've got a slight one here too.' As it turned out, Dave was a master of understatement. 'I'll get Phil to call you in a bit – what's your news?'

'The moorings in Margate don't exist.'

'What about the harbour?'

'It's not possible. Long story but believe me if it was at all possible I would have been there now.'

'Oh dear . . . what are you going to do?'

'Row against the tide for as long as I can then anchor down and wait it out.'

'That might be tricky. There's some weather on the way. I'm coming to get near you. Get in to near the coast until we find each other.'

I don't like it when fishermen use the word 'weather' in that way. They don't say 'bad weather', just 'weather'. Weather is all bad to fishermen. To fishermen, weather is defined as a change from perfect conditions.

I rowed as much as I could against the tide. Luckily I saw a buoy, rowed towards it and phoned Dave. The paintings (numbers, letters, colours and shapes) on it seemed to mean something to Dave. I tied the bath off to it. Drat. I still hadn't got to use my anchor. Luckily the weather was still fair if a little choppy but the tide was beginning to race. I phoned Phil.

'Hi Tim, great you've called . . .' There was something in Phil's voice I couldn't place. 'Let me just put you on to Peter.'

'Peter?'

'Your team mate in the T-shirt . . .' I could hear Phil shouting to Peter. 'You'd better come and tell Tim – he could be in trouble if he doesn't know too . . .'

'Hi, Tim?'

'Yes.'

'It's important that you know this. I'm on the run from the American Secret Service. The President is aware of the situation.'

Oh great. Me and my prophetic hunches.

'How? Why?'

'I can't tell you but this is why it's important that we don't go back to Ramsgate – I've told Dave – I might have to take over the ship . . .'

'Don't panic, Peter – I now understand – Dave understands too and is turning the ship around to get you away from Ramsgate.'

'Good, the FBI will be waiting there.'

'Put me back on to Phil.'

'OK.'

Phil came back on the line.

'Great work, Tim.'

I think he may have been being sarcastic or suppressing a laugh at the whole craziness of the situation but I decided not to press it.

'Thanks, mate. All good. See you when you all get back here.'

You may think I'm making this up. Of all the people I could have picked to accompany Dave and Phil I managed to find a man who genuinely believed he was on the run from the FBI and was prepared to take over my support boat to escape.

One question was uppermost in my mind. In this situation, who supports the support boat? I cursed myself for not booking a support-support boat.

Dave arrived with a very stressed-looking Phil and an increasingly paranoid-seeming Peter. I remembered from my Nelson book that just one paranoid or insane crew member had been known to upset the balance of an entire frigate. In another book I'd read that there was one North-West Passage expedition where one officer ended up howling at the moon. This was a very delicate balance. Then the weather turned nasty. After sitting in a terrible storm off Margate for half a day waiting for the weather to give in and the tide to turn, Dave and I had to accept the inevitable. The electronic devices on his boat did not lie, nor did the shipping forecast, nor did the Met Office. This storm was not going to go away.

After half a day of storm the sky went black. It was night. Concern swept the boat and lashed us even harder than the waves. Dave was increasingly worried about getting back round the lethal North Foreland to Ramsgate in the dark. Peter was increasingly concerned as he said the FBI mainly came out at night. And Phil was concerned about being in a confined environment with Peter after dark. There was always the option that had been raised earlier. I could be towed to Whitstable and released near the harbour. It would seem like I'd heroically made it through the storm in the bath. This was tempting on many levels: first, it got me closer to Tower; second, I'd get to look like a hero; and third, I'd get a warm bed in Whitstable and a safe harbour. On the other side of the argument: it was cheating and that was unthinkable.

There are some points on a journey where you have to take a call that is tough on you personally but good for the team. I went to talk to Dave.

'What do you think?'

'We can't stay out in this.'

'We can't get into Margate.'

'You won't be towed to Whitstable.'

'Can we make it to Ramsgate?'

'It's going to be really hard going round the North Foreland in the dark in this storm and with your bath off the back.'

'What?'

'We can't leave it here, Tim.'

'Good point.'

'The other problem is how to persuade Peter not to do anything silly if we go back to Ramsgate – he's been on about this all day – he's in some kind of programme too for rehabilitation. He really does think if we go back to Ramsgate he's going to face charges in the US.'

Phil appeared in the doorway just long enough to hear the last bit.

'So over to you, Tim.'

This was going to be a tough conversation. If he believed he would be arrested by the FBI in Ramsgate, I just had to believe that too, and all could be fine. The boat jumped up and down in the water violently as I rolled over to Peter and looked him straight in the eye.

'Peter. I've been thinking. The FBI must have seen us leave Ramsgate this morning.'

'Yes, but they wouldn't know where we were going.'

'True but they'll be scouring the coast for you by now and are

sure to have made it to Margate and asked questions. The bath is
not very inconspicuous.'

'What?'

'They'll know I've been to Margate.'

He snapped and got very angry immediately. I understood Phil's
worry. He shouted, 'Damn! They might take my businesses away.'

'Businesses?'

'Oh, I'm a millionaire. I'm a millionaire.'

'Of course. But wait. Them seeing me in Margate might have
helped us.'

'How? How?'

My godfather's wife used to work with people like Peter a lot. I
began to remember how I'd seen her handle them when I was small.

'They will think that I've been through Margate. I told the Mayor
that I was heading to Whitstable.'

'So?'

'Well, you're even wearing a Whitstable T-shirt.'

'So?'

'So they'll think we've gone to Whitstable and go to Whitstable.
Meanwhile we go to Ramsgate and drop you off. You disappear
and don't go to Whitstable for a bit and everything will be fine.'

'Let's go to Ramsgate. How long have you been a spy, been a
spy, too?'

'I've never been a spy.' I winked like I'd just said something in
code. It seemed to do the trick. 'Dave! Turn this boat around!' I
attached the bath to the back and we headed off.

The way back to Ramsgate was a horrid journey in the dark. I
heard Dave on the phone to his wife saying, '. . . we might not
make this, I love you . . .'

That's never an encouraging thing to hear from a skipper. Out on
deck I'd rallied Peter. He could not have been more stoic in the situation. He began to repeat himself a lot more. Possibly as his meds
were wearing off – it was difficult to tell in the dark at sea. However,
despite this, he helped me secure the bath on countless occasions
and often only Peter diving and holding on to a line stopped us from
losing it. Phil meanwhile was filming waves, generally being David
Lean and only on occasion looking nervously at Peter.

This was undoubtedly a very tough and supremely dangerous situation. North Foreland is really dangerous in a storm. Although things

were bad, I'd been through bad storms before, recently with Andy in the Channel, and this didn't seem so terrifying. I think I thought we were safer being close to the shore. If that was the case it wasn't true, as I certainly couldn't have swum the distance in the storm we were in. Oddly, I think I felt safe knowing that I had three good men around me. One may have been focused on filming waves, another ruminating on his own mortality and the one third clinically mad; but together we were a pretty good team as it turned out.

I understand we were the last boat that made it into Ramsgate Harbour that night. A testament to Dave's good seamanship and the general teamwork in keeping together.

I finished the day exactly as I'd started, with a shoulder in agony, bailing out the bath in Ramsgate. I looked up at the storm. Things were not going well and as I sat bailing in the rain was reminded of the words of the prophet Paula Abdul.

Chapter Eleven

FOUR YOUNG OYSTERS HURRIED UP

'Interests in life: balls, riding, dining and making a fool of myself.'

George Francis Lyon RN

The day had not gone well. My phone rang. It was Janette. There's a very fine line between agent and psychiatric nurse but most days Janette errs on the side of agent.

'Look at you, getting letters from the Palace.'

I was shocked. I'd received a letter from Buckingham Palace the week before when I was in Hertfordshire healing my shoulder. It was a very generous and kind letter from the Queen via Her Private Secretary congratulating me on crossing the Channel in the bath. Not wanting to be brash, I'd kept this letter secret from everyone. Even Janette.

'What? How do you know about it?'

'Know what?'

'About my letter.'

'How did *you* know about it?'

'About what?'

I'd had a hard day and like every brilliant nurse in a jim-jam clinic, she sensed this and said, 'Hang on, let's start again shall we?'

'Good.'

'I am talking about a letter you've received from the Palace, what are you talking about?'

'My letter from the Palace . . .'

Eventually, after enough confusing dialogue to fill a moderately successful Jim Carrey movie, one of us (and my money would be on it being Janette) twigged that there were in fact two letters from Buckingham Palace.

The first letter, to me at home, was the letter congratulating me on making it across the Channel in the bath. Like a Shakespearian plot, there was also a second letter from the Palace. This had gone to Janette as my agent.

'Shall I open it?'

Perhaps it was just a copy of the first letter? Or it could be something else. Suddenly, I was really excited.

'Yes please . . .'

'Hang on, let me get the scissors.'

With full gravitas, Janette read out the embossed writing like a great actor reciting a speech. Some Soho agents may get invitations from the Palace daily, but for the two of us, this was a first.

'The Master of the Household has received Her Majesty's command to invite Mr Tim FitzHigham to a Maritime Reception to be given at St James's Palace by the Queen and the Duke of Edinburgh . . .'

That night the Royal Ramsgate Harbour seemed to shine. I may have been as stuck in Ramsgate as I had been in Folkestone but I was going to visit the Palace for rowing the Channel in the bath. Brilliant.

To celebrate I decided to sleep in a hotel that night. As I lay down to shut my eyes I determined I would make it to Buckingham Palace in time to hobble around awkwardly as the Queen moved seamlessly away from me down a line up.

Finally, we got the weather. Again.

This time I left Ramsgate with just Dave and Phil in the support boat. We made it round the rocks at North Foreland to Margate. It turns out that this is a very difficult stretch of water no matter how many times you attempt it.

It's true (also fortuitous in terms of keeping the story moving along) to report that this was a very uneventful leg of the journey.

After the sea had done its best to drown me and smash me on rocks again, I finally drew level with the buoy I'd tied off to the last time. Dave shouted over, 'Right now we can row again! Now we're on a new bit. Will we make Whitstable?'

As I dipped the oars in, I knew that we really had to make it to Whitstable. It was the next safe harbour towards London. The other harbours couldn't shelter the bath if the weather turned bad. In other words, if I didn't make it to Whitstable, I'd end up back in Ramsgate again. For the morale and sanity of the troop in the bath, that was unthinkable.

The other significant factor was the tide. Not only did I have to make it to Whitstable, but also I had to make it to Whitstable before the tide turned. The tide had been a factor in Folkestone as the water disappeared from the harbour twice a day. Now, tidally, I was at the place where the Thames met the Swale. At this point both rivers empty twice daily into the North Sea. So twice a day it would become impossible to row against that tide as it flowed east. There were just two specific time windows per day where I could row west towards London. Each window was about seven hours long. If I didn't make it to Whitstable in this seven-hour chance, I would end up either back Ramsgate, moored next to a shipping buoy in Margate or learning to cook pickled herrings in Reykjavik. The clock was ticking. The stakes were high.

It was an evil row from Margate westwards. I passed lots of houses, which on inspecting my road atlas I could only think was Westgate-on-Sea. The wind that had been so useful earlier in the day now tried to take me back towards Broadstairs. My trick of using the roll top of the bath as a sort of sail was utterly useless as the wind was coming straight at me the wrong way. I hit a sand-bank. Dave and Phil were powerless to get to me. The water was too shallow for the bath so Dave's boat didn't stand a chance. What could I do? This was an entirely new problem. I'd never hit a sand-bank before. The bath gently nestled there as I poked around in the water with the oars trying to free myself.

Eventually, the wind and tide wrenched me off the sandbank. This was the first time since that glorious row from Folkestone to Ramsgate that I could honestly say the weather helped me. I think it only did so by mistake. Cursing its kindness the weather rounded on me with vengeance, making the sea really short and choppy. It was almost impossible to take any sort of strokes at all. The wind wanted me to go back to Ramsgate and was attempting to force the issue. I tried to use another trick I'd learnt: hiding in behind any headland in front of me and using it as a windbreak. I realised there was no headland and became marooned on a second sandbank. This one I shared with a seal.

It was all very frustrating. The seal looked at me. I looked at the seal. We exchanged a few pleasantries. I assume they were pleasant; she (I think she was a she but unfortunately didn't get to know him/her well enough to ask) didn't attack me so that seemed to indicate the native was friendly. My attempts to try and row the bath off the sandbank failed. The wind and waves didn't help this time. Eventually, I attached the oars to the bath and got out onto the sandbank. Knee-deep in the surf I pushed the bath off, jumped back on and rowed away in a wobbly line.

Finally I glimpsed the twin towers of the Roman fortress at Reculver. This threw me deep into thought. This was obviously where the Romans had stopped to deal with the tide of the Thames. If only Roman moorings were still as well built as their fortresses I could have moored up there. As I was thinking this, I heard the familiar gentle swishing sound. I was marooned on another sandbank. Bother.

I'd like to write that things got easier. They didn't. This was a very tough stretch of rowing. A short choppy sea, wind in the wrong direction and a multiplicity of sandbanks all conspired to give me the feeling not of rowing the bath but of dragging her onwards. Eventually I saw houses again and let out a yelp of joy: it must be Whitstable. I checked the atlas. It was Herne Bay: still miles to Whitstable. I let out a yelp (less joyful), dug the oars into the water again and rowed on.

However, just past Herne Bay the wind let up. For the first time that day it stopped going against me. After fighting it for so long I now felt less hampered than the relevant Fortnum's department on Boxing Day. With no resistance, it seemed I could now go superhumanly fast; I whipped along the coast towards Whitstable.

Dave and I had come up with a plan. Whitstable sits on the east side of an estuary. On the west side of it is the Isle of Sheppey. If I arrived at the estuary and the tide had not turned then we thought I should have a go at crossing it to reach the Isle of Sheppey. There's no decent bathroom mooring on the east of Sheppey but if we had the tide I could take a chance and go north round the island to try and reach Queenborough on its west coast by the time the tide turned.

On the other hand, if I arrived at the estuary and the wind or tide was against me, I should take the safer option and pull for Whitstable where I had safe moorings. Earlier in the day when I was marooned and writing poetry with the seals near Reculver neither of these plans looked likely. However now, as I checked the road atlas and confirmed that what I could see was definitely Whitstable, either seemed possible. I called to Dave, 'Mate, we've made it – I didn't see that coming . . .'

'Neither did I. You've got the tide – the wind might get a bit changeable but there's a good chance we can make it round the north of Sheppey . . . What do you want to do?'

'Let's go for Queenborough.'

I've always loved a gamble. I started rowing across the estuary. It was unbearably hard and put my newly healed shoulder to the harshest test. The current of the Swale wanted to take me one way, the Thames was intent on driving me another. All the time both of them seemed to want to take me away from the direction I wanted. Still, I battled on and eventually after much straining, made it to the relative shelter of the north coast of Sheppey. I passed a settlement and glancing at the road atlas judged this to be Leysdown-on-Sea. It could have been Warden – due to the spray of the sea the ink on the photocopied atlas had run a bit at that point.

Then, the wind turned, the chop got noticeably worse and the gangsta phone rang. It was Dave.

'Mate, there's some weather coming in here, it's going to be frisky. What do you want to do?'

'I'll have a go at making it to Queenborough and failing that Sheerness.' (It was moderately closer.)

'OK, but you're going to have to pull hard.'

I hung up, dug in and pulled hard. I'd been rowing all day and was shattered but I knew I could make a significant dent in getting to London if I could make Queenborough. I rowed on and just as I sighted what I judged to be the outskirts of Minster or something between there and Warden (the road atlas was becoming more smudged by the stroke) the mist came in. Then the tide turned to race away from London. The wind changed direction and was trying to push the sea back to London. The result for me was very big waves and a lot of problems. It was like being in an epic painting by Turner. Dave's boat bobbed around me. The bath was simply not able to cope with this sort of weather. Then the light faded as the cloud cover thickened. I'm not sure of the sea state that day but it seemed close to as bad as the one I faced in the Channel on the first attempt. White wave tops crashed down on me in the dark mist as I lurched around and tried to take strokes.

I felt I could have carried on fighting through all the other problems that now faced me except the lack of visibility. Somewhere off the port of Sheerness lies a monster in the form of the SS *Richard Montgomery*. This is a semi-sunken World War II American munitions ship. In August 1944, she dragged her anchor in the shallow water and grounded on a sandbank. Now she lies in two sections and conservative estimates suggest there's in excess of 1,400 tonnes of unexploded ammunition still in her hull. You can see where she is due to a series of buoys that mark the exclusion zone around her. She's 'semi-sunken' as you can clearly see her masts poking out of the water at all states of the tide. However, fighting to get past that danger in very restricted visibility was not the best plan I'd come up with. Dave was afraid too; my phone rang.

'There's that explosive ship not too far from us.'

'I know . . . I'm not sure it's a good idea going near it in this storm.'

'What do you want to do? I'm losing sight of you . . .'

'I'm going to turn and make for Whitstable – we can pick this up in the morning. We're not going to make Sheerness in this.'

'Good choice.'

In some ways it was a good choice. In others it was a very bad one. Just as I'd had to battle the tide to get to my current position I now had to battle even more ferocious conditions to get to Whitstable. I was stuck in a howler of a storm. I battled chop, spray, wind, current in the wrong direction and a road atlas that was now just a mass of soggy papier mâché. I'd taken a gamble and tried to beat the weather: again, it had beaten me. It took me over two hours to complete what should have been a half-hour row to Whitstable.

The cloud cover cleared and the rain stopped. The light got slightly better. It was dusk but not black and misty as it had been out off the north coast of Sheppey. There was still mist but the visibility was much better here. A RIB arrived containing the Vice-Commodore of the Whitstable Yacht Club. She shouted over as she drew circles around me in her powerful boat.

'Wondered when you'd get here. What weather you've brought with you. Amazed you made it.'

'Am I glad to see you . . .'

The Vice-Commodore and I had spoken on the phone lots. She was called Wendy and could not have been more helpful.

'You must be shattered but we saw you through the telescope and there's a few people that want to say hello – can you bear it?'

Being stuck between two ports, not making one and having to pull back to the other was exhausting. It was exhausting battling the storm. However, if people had turned up to say hello, it would be rude not to go and see them.

'Of course.'

I pulled towards the jetty at the yacht club. On the jetty was quite a crowd of people. There were children, members of the yacht club, even a press photographer and a reporter. They were all so kind. Wendy had obviously extended a brilliant hand in organising this. It really cheered me up. They presented me with a Whitstable Yacht Club burgee to fly from the masthead: again, navy blue with a red cross on a white shield. By the end of the day my mood had totally reversed and I was thinking, thank goodness I hadn't made it to Queenborough or I would have missed this.

Wendy and I moored the bath up on one of the Whitstable Yacht Club moorings and she took me into land. The yacht club offered me a room for the night and a shower. I went in under the jet, water hit my cuts and pain coursed through me. I went to scream but managed to bite my hand instead. I'd obviously developed new cuts between here and Margate and reopened older cuts too. I did my best not to curse while trying to wash myself as well as I could.

Bedraggled but clean I went out of the yacht club to find some food. After foraging, shattered and in pain, I went to bed. Oddly enough the cuts and dull thudding pains didn't seem as bad. I'd made it this far and had a warm bed and new friends around me. I liked Whitstable.

The pressure really had taken hold of me. I must make it to Tower Bridge. The bath trip was intended as a charity fundraising project that was supposed to last a month, a year and a half ago. Not only did I want to end it but also there were some other pressing concerns. Firstly, their bosses were beginning to ask my various sponsors exactly where the money they'd been giving me was going. In other words, without the shots of me coming under Tower Bridge they were getting nervous. This was fair enough, they'd kept faith with me for an extra year; it was time to prove them right. Secondly, rather rashly as it turned out, I'd booked a slot to do a show in the wonderful Pleasance Theatre at the Edinburgh Festival. Fifteen missed calls from the lovely (if put upon) artistic director of the Pleasance told me that the previews for that show kicked off in Edinburgh in just a few days. There was no way from my present position I'd make it to Edinburgh for that. Janette had been working hard and had managed to get them to scratch the previews. However, this meant refunding tickets, disgruntling audience members (I've put 'members' as amazingly there was more than one) and leaving an empty venue in the world's most over-subscribed arts festival. More depressing than that, scratching the previews only bought me an extra three days. Serious questions were being asked about my commitment to my day job. When your day job is making people laugh, serious questions are a bad thing. I currently had just seven days to get to the Festival on time.

All these thoughts vanished as a knock at the door woke me up. It was Wendy's husband with a cup of tea. I looked down with guilt at the milk and two-sugared marvel. As I sipped it, I couldn't quite work out why, in my dream, the artistic director of the Pleasance had been played by a giant bee; I wasn't sure why this was scary as, when awake, I quite like bees. He smiled and handed me a biscuit: I like Whitstable.

'Thought you might like this, you'll not be getting anywhere today.'
'What?'
'Look out of the window.'
I looked and saw nothing but a wall of mist.
'Where's the bath?'
'Exactly, there's no visibility, you'll not get away today. This happens here.'
'Come to that, where's the sea?'
'The support-boat skipper's radioed in, he's on his way back to Ramsgate.'

I got dressed and stumped off down to the yacht club bar. Nothing ever seems as bad when viewed through a pint glass in a bar.

I got talking to the barman. He'd been pulling pints in the bar for years. While we were nattering I noticed a chart on the wall. It was the most relevant one for Whitstable and also had on it the Isle of Sheppey. I looked at it and suddenly all the stuff Dom had been desperately trying to drum into me for weeks began to clear. I turned to the barman.

'Excuse me, but, from this, it looks like the tide comes in from both sides of the island and meets in the middle at the southern-most point of the Isle of Sheppey?'

'Yes, it's an odd thing that. You'd expect it to run in west to east and out east to west, but it doesn't. It's cos of the Medway meeting the Swale.'

'So hang on, I could row to the southern point of the island with the Swale tide coming in, put the anchor down, wait for the tide to turn and then row out the other side with the Medway tide going out.'

'Erm . . . yeah, I suppose you could. I've not seen it done but it must be possible.'

Straight away, I phoned Dom and explained my plan. He was at work and didn't have the charts in front of him but still responded.

'I'm not sure exactly how the currents work down there but just follow what we discussed about charts and I'm sure you're right. Sorry not to be more helpful but, on the plus side, if it works this is your first naval plan and it will have been a success. The responsibility for this is with you . . . good luck.'

I checked the charts again. People had started to gather in the bar. Word had got around that this was my thinking. The bar marshalled itself and managed to become several voices all saying the same thing: 'I'm not sure it'll work.'

'You'll have to get the currents just right.'

'If the anchor slips or if you get the tide wrong you'll end up in Herne Bay.'

'. . . Or Margate.'

I checked the charts and all the various voices agreed that my theory was technically possible, although they thought it mad and unworkable practically. In my head I substituted the words 'radical' and 'bold' for 'mad' and 'unworkable' and picked up the phone.

Until now I'd been taking guidance from the MCA (Maritime Coastguard Agency) and the Port of London (the PLA, who look after the Thames from Margate westwards). At no point did I think I'd need to contact the Head of the Medway Ports. However, I couldn't row on the Swale or the Medway without his permission. This was a very important phone call.

The man who runs the Port of London is a Rear Admiral and very senior. You don't get to speak to him, only the people way below him. It takes a few days for anything to get done, as there is a complex chain of command. A bit like a god or a djinn, the only way you know he actually exists is that the Port of London runs smoother than a lube factory.

I picked up the phone in the bar and phoned the Medway Port Authority. I'd have to talk to the person at the top, as I needed to get emergency permission to row today. I put on my very grown-up voice, as I'd need to circumvent the massive wall of bureaucracy fast. The receptionist picked up.

'Hello, Medway Ports?'

'Good morning, I'd like to speak to the person in charge. It's quite important.'

'Is it a maritime matter?'

'Yes.'

'You'll want the Harbourmaster. I'll put you straight through.'

'What? I mean . . . thank you.'

In all my long dealings with the Port of London this had never happened. My shock was compounded when on the other end of the line was the world's most affable man.

'Hello, I'm Steve. How can I help?'

'Erm . . . I need permission to row on the River Swale, around the south side of Sheppey.'

'Right, what sort of vessel is it?'

I took a breath. I really needed Steve's help. Without it I couldn't go round the south of Sheppey. More than that, if he chose to, he could delay his permission until I'd lost the tides and my chance of progressing. It wouldn't mean the end of the trip but it would mean I couldn't row any further today. Potentially, if the weather stayed bad, not having Steve's permission could hold me at Whitstable just as long as I'd been stuck in Ramsgate.

'It's a bath, well . . . more a sort of bathroom . . .'

'You've rowed it from France? I wondered when you'd call. When do you need to row round Sheppey?'

'Today?'

'No problem . . . where are you mooring for the night?'

I'd planned this. Sheerness is a really busy port so I knew I couldn't moor there. Previously, I contacted the Harbourmaster at Queenborough and got a mooring from him.

'Queenborough. I've got permission.'

'That's great, I'll look out for you when you come past me at Sheerness.'

I thanked Steve, put the phone down and turned to the bar.

'Right, we're on. What time does the tide turn today?'

Someone checked a tide table.

'It'll be starting about now.'

'Crikey. Right. We're going to have to move a bit.'

Auditioning to be head of the Port of London, I issued instructions. Everything had to be done fast. First, Dave and Phil were recalled from somewhere near Margate. Then I packed quickly and a RIB was made ready to take me out to the bath. The mist was still like a pea-souper and we couldn't see the bath till we were almost on it. I'd missed the start of the tide but if I didn't make best use of the rest of it, my plan would definitely fail.

I jumped into the bath, thanked Wendy, put the oars in the gate and locked them in. Taking out a compass and a chart I'd been given in the yacht club, I untied the bath, waved at where Wendy had been in the mist and pulled off.

I sculled as hard as I could up the estuary, very aware that I had to get over halfway round the south of the island for my plan to work. A motley assortment of vessels appeared out of the mist at me. People on board nervously dived toward drinks cabinets as they saw the bathroom looming out of the mist.

Rowing through the mist in the marshes south of the Isle of Sheppey reminded me of Magwitch and Pip in David Lean's *Great Expectations*. It was a very haunting and Dickensian morning on the river. I was all alone. Dave knew my plan and he and Phil were trying to catch me up, but both of us became aware that if I hadn't set off without him and kept with the tide, all would be lost.

People are unkind about Sheppey. They call the inhabitants of the island 'Swampies'. This is not a term of endearment, although like many previously derogatory terms some islanders are trying to reclaim it as cool. The guidebooks on Sheppey are equally uninspiring. One says: 'If Kent is the Garden of England, then Sheppey is the diseased cabbage in that garden.' Another: 'The economy of the Isle of Sheppey has been in consistent decline since the Viking invasion.'

As I rowed this stretch of water totally alone in the marshes, with only memories of the convict Magwitch to keep me company, I began to feel as though someone was watching me. It's not difficult to get paranoid, alone, rowing through a mist-filled marsh.

Suddenly a head popped out of the water just five feet from the bath. I missed a stroke. Perhaps it was the dead body of the man who'd written the guidebook? I looked again. Through the mist it was difficult to see but it seemed too hairy. Was it a Labrador? Again, through the mist, it was difficult to tell and if it was a Labrador, where was its owner? Another similar head popped out of the water nearer to the bath. It looked like a frogman. Would the world's longest bath trip end in murder? My breath stopped and I looked the frogman square in the eyes. He came towards me in the mist and as he got closer, turned into a seal.

More heads then joined the first two and swam playfully alongside the bath. I was entirely alone on a river by a marsh with only a seal colony for comfort. Sheppey was being stunning to me. One of the seals looked very like my flatmate from the sandbank yesterday: although it's quite hard to tell with seals as they all wear similar coats.

After an hour, Dave and Phil arrived to find the seal colony swimming entirely unabashed around the bath. Barking and frolicking, they were really beautiful. This was an incredible emotional experience: a sort of lower-budget chav version of swimming with dolphins.

Now with Dave, Phil and seal cheerleading-squad, my morale rocketed and I pulled as hard as I could round the south of the island to reach the magic halfway point. The main problem with the magic halfway point is that there's nothing there to tell you that you've reached it. How could I tell where the 'right' place to stop was to make the plan work? I had a vague idea but it was only vague.

I rounded a corner on the right side of the river; by that I mean the right side according to the guidelines. By coincidence, it is on the right side of the river, although as I faced it backwards it felt more like my left. Having rowed up and down the Thames training countless times I was well drilled on river etiquette. Rowers have to follow this more than most, as they can't often see what's ahead of them. Dave and Phil were a little way behind me at this stage. They couldn't see round the corner but saw me pull out of view around the bend and heard a massive ship's horn.

I heard the horn and saw Dave appear round the corner at some speed. I looked over my shoulder and saw the owner of the horn bearing down on me on the wrong side of the river. It was an implausibly large boat to be on that stretch of the river. A polite discussion about rights of way didn't seem possible. This was a very dangerous situation. The river was narrow, he was vast and on the wrong side of it (according to river etiquette) and I was in a bath. With all the misplaced confidence of a drunk major blowing off in a golf club, he sounded his horn again. My seal escort disappeared fast. Like the crew on the *Titanic*, they'd seen the iceberg. The horn noise echoed around the marshes of Sheppey and even the birds left.

Dom had taken me through horn signals we thought I might have needed in the Channel. Of course they'd proved to be pointless in the Channel as everyone uses GPS and radio. I racked every hole in the Swiss cheese of my brain. What did one blast mean? I sat there stunned. It definitely meant he was going to turn to port. Or perhaps it meant he was going to turn to starboard? Bother and one blast. As the ship continued to plough straight at me, I searched the washstand for the almanac. It had obviously gone overboard in the night. The ship sounded again, a single sharp indignant blast. Things were happening very fast. Then the ship sounded his horn five times.

Something clicked in my brain: five blasts definitely meant, 'I am doubtful you are taking sufficient avoiding action.'

The captain of that ship was very cross. Having remembered the meaning of five blasts, suddenly I was sure one blast meant he was going starboard. It made no sense in terms of his position on the river at all but I thought I just had to trust him and my own memory.

I swerved to my starboard and headed into the bank. This was all wrong, I'd been in the right all the way through this but he seemed so confident and had roughly 1,200 tons to back his opinion.

The tanker turned off into an unloading-type harbour to starboard. It was totally hidden from me and suddenly made sense of him wanting to go to starboard. His wash on the turn almost landed me in the middle of the field. As I bobbed violently next to the bank I saw a tiny sign covered in foliage. It explained how I had been totally right in my actions on every other stretch of river in the country; however, in this particular part of Sheppey, to accommodate the secret unloading-type harbour, the river regulations were reversed.

A breathless Dave and Phil caught up with me at the bank. Dave leant over.

'That was a close one. Weird he was on the wrong side . . .'

'Have you seen the thing covered in a bush?'

'Oh . . . they've reversed everything . . . right . . .'

I tried to row on away from the bank. It could have been the shock of nearly being scuttled but rowing here was like trying to run through concrete. I took a few strokes and seemed to get nowhere. Dave shouted again, 'I think the tide is turning! Best just put an anchor down and wait.'

'Are we halfway?'

'I'm not really sure . . . it's a bit tricky to tell . . .'

I'd travelled over 100 miles and never used the very heavy anchor; now, finally, I unclipped it from the bathroom floor and dropped it overboard. Dave shouted, 'You could have just tied off to me.'

'That's not the point.'

We all sat there waiting for hours. Dave and Phil on the support boat, me in the bath and the now-returned seal escort in the water. All was very calm. Despite the unflattering comments in the guidebooks Sheppey has some very pretty parts. Dave made cups of tea and even bacon butties, which Phil and I tucked into and the seals politely declined. We waited on. It was agonising, sitting there bobbing up and down, whistling, humming and waiting. Most agonising of all was not knowing if my plan had worked or failed. Had we made it halfway?

I was looking out over the water ruminating on all these things when I saw a reed turn in the water. The reed changed direction. I shouted to Dave.

'Mate, it's turned, the reed has turned!'

'What?'

'I think the tide has turned, I think we've done it! I think it's worked!'

Sometimes the tiniest thing can signal the mightiest change. After dropping a line in the water and trying some other tests, we both weighed anchor. I put the oars in the gate, screwed them down and pulled off.

We rounded a bend to see the tiny Kingsferry Bridge: the only thing that links Sheppey to the mainland. The showerhead cleared the underside of the bridge but there was no way Dave's boat would make it. The bridge keeper agreed to raise the bridge for Dave, which was kind, but said that it would take some time.

'Dave, I'm going to keep going as I don't want to lose this light and the current.'

With that, I sped off. In the deteriorating light I saw the Kingsferry Bridge being slowly raised and Sheppey once again being cut off from the mainland. The tide was being so helpful now. I'd obviously left the River Swale and was now on the mighty Medway.

I'd planned to get moorings at Queenborough. Dave and Phil caught up with me just upstream of the town.

'Where do you want to moor up?'

'I've still got some light and amazing current – I want to try and get to Sheerness so we don't have any current problems in the morning.'

'The light really is going but you've certainly got the current. Can you moor at Sheerness?'

Sheerness is one of the busiest ports in the country. It's a major centre for importing cars among other things. How or where we'd put a bath in there was anyone's guess.

'I'll phone someone.'

I picked up the gangsta phone and dialled Steve.

'Steve, hi, it's Tim. I've got light and wondered if there was anywhere I could moor in Sheerness?'

'You've made it round today?'

'Yes.'

'Good work. It's not been the best of days . . . erm . . . there's the inner harbour, I'll clear a berth for you . . .'

What a great man. Steve described where I needed to go as I narrowly avoided a buoy and its associated sailing ship upstream of Queenborough.

'Dave, we can moor in the inner harbour with the police boats.'

'I'm impressed.'

The tide picked up and I shot through Queenborough like Gonzo out of a cannon. As I came out downstream of Queenborough, darkness fell on the Thames. Dave flicked a switch and a bank of spotlights came on over the top of his cabin. I flicked a switch and two small and rather inadequate-looking lights sprang into action on the bath. It really was dark. The tide kept forcing me on, down towards Sheerness; soon vast shapes began to appear out of the darkness. Huge big ships, leviathans to the bath, loomed out of the dark, their mighty prows completely dominating me. They towered over me so utterly that they seemed to defy the basic laws of physics. Ranks of them appeared out of the night, all with names that sounded like a new and interesting sexual disease from ports with names like euphemisms for farting.

I saw a flash in the water, stopped and went cold.

'Dave! Get over here quick. I thought I saw a hand.'

Dave shone the light where I thought I saw the hand and we searched in the water. It was all so black.

'If you're sure we'll have to report it, Tim, but you'd better be sure, as searching for it in this will be a heck of a job . . .'

'I'm not, I couldn't say, it could have been a fish . . .'

Everything was so dark. Sheppey's busiest port was in total silence other than the gentle splosh of my oars in the water and the hum of Dave's engine on low revs. I rowed on past the *Gonnesyphilis* and found the tiny aperture that led to the inner harbour.

By now it was totally black and I pulled in through the massive thick walls of the inner harbour like a clandestine Napoleonic invader. Piratical-looking sailors crowed around the quayside above me. All eyes were trained at the new shiny thing that was coming in to dock alongside one of the Harbourmaster's boats.

One of the buccaneers on the quayside above shouted down in broken English, with an accent that would not have been out of place on a Bond baddie's henchman of the mid-1970s, 'Where you come from in bath?'

I stood in the bath and stared up at the faces illuminated in the harbour lights. 'France!' My shout echoed off the thick walls of the harbour.

'I tell you! It him!'

The regiment of corsairs cheered and waved. I was really shocked. Dave shouted over, 'They've heard about the bath!'

I pulled the oars from the gate, scrambled out of the bath and onto the quayside to have my hair ruffled and back patted by men who I'd never met and would probably never see again. That night, we all shared a common smile at the stupidness of the bath. As the men dispersed back to their various ships, I went back down to the bath, Dave, Phil and the support boat.

I was flushed with the happiness of the quayside above; Dave and Phil looked grave. Dave spoke first.

'Tim, I'm not sure I can come any further up. I have to keep going back down to Kent to refuel and I'm just aware that every time I do that, I slow you down. I know it's all tidal from here and I don't want to stuff it up for you. It's just that Ramsgate or even Herne Bay is miles from here and it takes me so long to get back . . . then you might have missed the tides . . .'

Dave had been through so much with us. He'd got me from seeming defeat in Ramsgate through the tricky waters of Margate and all the way to the western tip of the Isle of Sheppey. I didn't want to lose him. It had become as much his story as mine and I wanted him to finish it with me. I looked at him, much as Scott probably looked at Captain Oates: Dave was right, his need to refuel and the fact all his contacts and knowledge were in Ramsgate would slow me down. I'd assured the Port of London that I wouldn't come up the Thames without a support boat and with the very tidal nature of the rest of the journey a 'Dave refuelling' stop might cost me a tide, day's rowing or with added bad weather even longer. There was serious pressure mounting for me to get the trip finished and even a day now would make the pressure much worse.

'Dave, thank you . . . I . . .'

He smiled. 'Good luck, mate, it's been great being with you . . .'

He turned the key and his boat engines roared. He saw us looking down at him, smiled mischievously and said, 'I'm just going out . . . I may be some time . . .'

With that, Dave the remarkable cockle fisherman glided out of the inner harbour at Sheerness. Phil and I waved him off into the blackness. Phil turned to me.

'So, where are we going to stay tonight?'

Bugger. I hadn't really planned that. I took out the gangsta phone and dialled directories. 'No bother, I've got a plan.'

I arranged taxis and somewhere to store Phil and his plethora of kit. The main problem on my mind was my promise to the Port of London. The Thames from here up is a very busy, commercial stretch of water and they'd insisted I have a properly aware Thames support boat. Dave's decision was the right one but it did leave me unable to go any further without someone to take his place.

Without a support boat, I was stuck.

CHAPTER TWELVE

MONKEY STOPPED TO PULL UP HIS SOCK

'They had brought a large map representing the sea
Without the least vestige of land:
And the crew was much pleased when they found it to be
A map they could all understand.'

Edward Lear: 'The Hunting of the Snark'

I woke early the next morning. The way the tide was that day, if I could find a support-boat skipper I could still go on the late-morning tide.

'Hello, I need a support-boat skipper . . .'

'Sorry, I don't do that – got to go.'

The familiar tale started again . . .

'Hello, I need a support-boat skipper . . .'

'Where from?'

'Sheerness . . .'

'Sorry, I'm not there at the moment . . .'

'When will you be back?'

'No.'

'What? Hello?'

I was greeted with the blank dial tone. By phone I scoured Sheerness, Allhallows-on-Sea and even St Mary Hoo with no luck. I spread the field up to Tilbury with equal lack of success. I even tried Essex in the hope of finding someone but Southend, Shoeburyness and Canvey all turned out to be fruitless. It was clearly the closed season on lesser-spotted support-boat skippers.

I sat on the quay of the inner harbour at Sheerness, more stumped than the man standing in front of Adam Gilchrist. I was stuck.

A worm of thought popped its head out of a hole in my Swiss-cheese brain. The oath I'd taken with one arm at the Company of Watermen and Lightermen. I picked up the phone again.

'Hello, can I speak to the Clerk of the Watermen?'

'I'll put you through.'

'Hi, Colin, it's Tim. I need a support boat going from Sheerness to somewhere like Gravesend. Can you suggest anyone?'

'You'll want to finish at Gravesend . . . you'll be looking at someone like Mr Palmer, he's got a firm down there. I'll get you the number.'

Being a Waterman turned out to be great. I thanked Colin and hung up.

'Hello, is that Mr Palmer . . .'

I employed the technique I'd found the most helpful in the past. I explained the serious nature of the bath trip first: about Colin, my link to the Watermen and that I was trying to raise money for a charity. Then I took a deep breath and broke him into the full truth.

'It's a bath . . .'

'Oh, you're the nutter in the bath – have you really rowed from France?'

'Well, yes . . . sort of . . .'

'I wondered when you'd get this far.'

It was strange but the bath seemed to have become well known, at least among river people. I'd become 'the nutter in the bath', a mere sidekick to the star that I'd created. I felt like Ernie Wise.

'I need a support boat to get me from Sheerness to up near you.'

'It's quite a choppy day on the water. Are you sure the bath can take it?'

Now it seemed the bath was the one in charge. I felt like saying, 'I'll have to ask her,' but managed, 'I'm sure we'll be fine.'

'I'm not at Sheerness today but my brother's there as it turns out, running something up for me. I'll give him a shout and call you back.'

I pulled out of the sheltered inner harbour of Sheerness, past the vast prow of the *Herpemdyia* (Registered Port: Tundervelt) and out into wind swirling round my ears, dark sky and a very choppy wash. In increasingly bad visibility I saw the red-on-white lettering of Palmers' Marine. Mr Palmer's brother eyed me sceptically.

'You'd better keep up, I can't slow down too much cos of the freight.'

Ahead of me across the Medway Estuary was the dreamily titled Isle of Grain, which sounds like it plays host mellifluously to a stunning medieval farming community. A place where simple rural types take nature's finest and create bread that tastes like clouds. It doesn't. It is a single, massive, ugly power plant or at least that's what it appeared to be in the glimpses I caught of it through the mist: a mass of huge chimneys that probably, on a clearer day, would have belched smoke out into the sky. In a sky filled with mist, it was difficult to tell; I took the smoke belching as read and tried to battle on through the chop.

In the shadow of the dark satanic mills of Grain, the Medway Estuary had me in its power. Several problems were at work. Here, the Medway hits the Thames at right angles, which creates a chop. The prevailing winds can come from any number of angles and change at a second's notice. That meant that from having a following wind with the tide, I suddenly found myself the wrong way round with a wind going against the tide, creating more chop. There were also massive tankers coming in and out of Sheerness, Tilbury and all the other loading stations up the Thames. These things are huge: the friends and relations of, if not the actual ones, I met in the Channel over a month before. Their stopping distances are terrifying and in such a relatively confined area of water, any collision with them would end very badly. The other problem they created for me was throwing up huge amounts of wash, which only added to the chop. This leg of the row was not the stroll in the sunshine I'd been planning but turned out to be very difficult.

'It should get a bit easier once we get level with Grain.'

Mr Palmer was the first support-boat skipper I'd had who was involved in freight. All the others had been fishermen. I couldn't put my finger on what that difference meant but somehow it made a difference. He seemed somehow more urban and industrial. He also seemed fairly sure that I was a total waste of time.

I pulled hard and bailed out alternately as he shouted things at his son. His son also eyed me with suspicion. The dynamic between support-boat skipper and bath had found a new expression. From the uncontrolled excitement of Dave, the bath had moved to the hassled, inconvenienced monosyllabic responses of Mr Palmer's brother (also, of course, called Mr Palmer).

My seal escort reappeared just in time to maroon me on a sandbank. I saw Mr Palmer sigh and his son stifle a laugh. As an ablution mariner trying to impress a new support-boat skipper, there are better ways to show off than becoming marooned on a sandbank. A combination of wind and desperate flailing from me finally dislodged the bath. Mr Palmer's brother, Mr Palmer, sighed again, although the seals clapped.

I put in a supreme effort. I bailed out the bath, rowed on through the chop and spray and tried hard not to be capsized. It was a terrible day and I seriously considered giving up and pulling back towards Sheerness. The conditions in the water were very dangerous, especially in a bath. I'd not been out in anything like this since the first time I tried to cross the Channel. The bath pitched and rolled like I'd not seen her do in a year. Spray was everywhere but I determined not to give in. I paused in the rowing and fumbled for the road atlas. There didn't seem to be anything useful in terms of moorings near me; I'd just have to keep rowing. The waves tried to steal the oars from the gates and snatch them away from me several times. I simply pulled hard, bailed when needed and tried to keep the bath afloat. A year ago I would probably have gone under in this. Now, I'd had a year to practise.

I began to notice that the chop was getting better. The mist hadn't lifted exactly but it had improved. Mr Palmer's brother's son came out on deck.

'Dad says would you like a cup of tea?'

'Yes please.'

'Sugar?'

'Two.'

He disappeared again. I rowed through increasingly better-looking water. Clearly I'd made it through the worst.

The son reappeared and leant over the side of the boat.

'Here you go. That was quite rough.'

Then his dad appeared behind him and leaning over the side he cracked the first smile I'd seen from him all day.

'That's a great bit of rowing, I thought you'd go under . . . do you want a bacon sarnie?'

I would have pawned the Koh-I-Noor for a bacon sarnie right then and reached up to take it.

'You must have rowed quite a bit . . . did you ever do Doggets?'

'No, I'd never rowed before the bath trip, but it's taught me a bit . . .'

'I'll say . . . that was good work. It should get a bit easier for a bit now, you're out of the main chop.'

The seals shouted that they thought we should get a move on. I finished the sarnie and fumbled for the oars again. The strange dynamic of support-boat skipper and bath had entered another chapter. It seemed that through the tough water and near capsizing I'd earned their respect. Now they wanted the bath to succeed just as much as I did. I finished the dregs that proved it and handed back the mug before digging in and rowing off again.

The river was kind as I rowed past what the atlas told me was St Mary Hoo. My shoulder was painful. I'd been taking the very strong painkillers every day I'd been on the water and they seemed to be working but every now and then, usually shortly before I was meant to take the next dose, the pain would thud back through the happy numbness.

Large tankers passed me on the way out to sea and hooted their horns. I shouted up to Mr Palmer, 'I'm nowhere near in their way.'

'They're not cross with you, they're hooting to support you.'

'What?'

'The Port of London have enforced a slowdown on the river to try and help you.'

'What?'

I paused rowing to listen as Mr Palmer explained that someone from the Port of London had come on the radio earlier in the day and enforced a temporary slower speed limit on the Thames between Gravesend and Sheerness to help me with the bad weather. This meant that all the big tankers had to go at a maximum speed of five knots. Totally shocked by the enormity of the kindness, I pulled on the oars again and as the next tanker hooted at me I found I was crying. I looked over at the massive ship gliding majestically towards the sea at under five knots and waved. I was choked up; someone at the Port of London really wanted me to make it.

The river bent south as another tanker hooted. I turned to my right with the bend. The weather turned bloody again. The wind got up. The rain came back and the mist swept in again. I squeezed on the oars as hard as I could and begged the rain and wind to stop. This leg of the journey had just got hard again. Blood dripped off me and into the bath as all my cuts stung in the rain. The raindrops got larger as I rowed on. Finally they became hailstones: this was a classic British summertime. My shoulder felt even worse in the cold and hail and my back was in agony. Pulling something a third of a tonne is not easy at the best of times but in a hailstorm it was hideous.

I swore vigorously and rowed on. Eventually, after more Anglo-Saxon language than appears in the Chronicle, I saw a sign sticking out of the water on a pole. It simply read 'Higham Blight'. Through the tears, water, spray and hail, I laughed. I was a very Blighted Higham and the river had been waiting for me to turn up for hundreds of years. I rowed, swore, bled and bailed out as I crawled on upstream, desperate to reach Gravesend. It was a very tough time. All the while Mr Palmer and his son shouted encouragement from their boat as more tankers tooted on their way out to sea. I just had to make it to Gravesend.

Finally, the river bent west and I looked over my shoulder to see Gravesend. I rowed on, desperate to get to it. It was certainly not a very pretty bit of rowing but with every other stroke I moved closer towards it. The sun appeared briefly, warming the hail into rain and after a few moments a rainbow bent over Gravesend. It was stunning. Somewhere in the town centre, a leprechaun cartel plotted a bank heist.

Apparently, not much epic poetry has been written about Gravesend but as I looked at the town bathed in a rainbow I would gladly have written several sonnets, probably involving the rhymes 'river penned' 'rainbow's bend' and 'shelter lend'. Luckily for the poetic reputation of Britain, just as I was searching for a pen, the weather became appalling again. I shelved all thought of becoming the new Byron and had to concentrate on the more pressing issue of not capsizing. The waves, wind and stone-like hail were clearly on the side of poetry and set against me surviving long enough to murder any on to paper.

'Head for the pontoon!'

'But it's the Port of London one . . .'

Our conversation was made difficult through the spray.

'It's fine, you've got permission. Tie off and we'll see you in the pub.'

I tied off at the PLA pontoon in simply horrid weather. Mr Palmer and his son berthed slightly further upstream on another pontoon. My phone rang.

'Tim, it's Joe . . .'

I've known Joe since I was three and a half. He's now in IT and had kindly been running a website dedicated to the trip. On www.timstub.com were pages about the various legs of the journey and a link to the Comic Relief website where people could give money to support the trip.

'Tim, you're not going to believe this but the website has had over 50,000 hits.'

'What? So over 50,000 people have visited it?'

'Yeah. Well, it could just be one person who's a bit obsessive and has visited it 50,000 times, it's tricky to tell . . .'

'Crikey . . .'

'We've had emails from all over the world, from exotic places like Swaziland, Australia, even Cornwall saying that if you make it to Tower Bridge people are going to hold bath parties to try and raise even more money . . .'

'Wow – that's incredible . . .'

I sheltered under the roof of the PLA office on top of the pontoon as the hail died off to torrential rain again.

'You've even got the ultimate Internet accolade.'

'What?'

'Someone has created a website devoted to hating you.'

'Great news, mate . . .'

I'd had no news of how people were taking the bath trip and couldn't have cared if there was an army of sites dedicated to hating me. People were interested. We must have been raising money. That was great. Also, I'd made it to Gravesend and was safely moored on a PLA pontoon for the night.

I'd spoken to various experts on rowing and all of them had said it would definitely take at least five days to make it from Margate to Gravesend. However, as no one knew anyone who had actually rowed it, they couldn't be sure. In a third-of-a-tonne criminally heavy bath full of water, with a badly damaged shoulder and in less than great weather, I'd made it in just three.

I hung up the phone and, buoyed up by all the positives that now littered the project, returned to the bath. It was sinking. I jumped on board, pulled gaffer tape out of the washstand and did the best I could in the driving rain. If the bath would just hold up for a few more days I might just actually make it.

After liberally applying gaffer tape to the flotation tanks I headed up to join the Palmers at the Ship & Lobster. The room erupted into applause as I entered, then peals of laughter at my appearance – something like a drowned rat in lycra. Stories flooded out and very soon I discovered that my support-boat skipper had been born in the flat above the bar. The pub and pontoon had been his parents' business before he and his brother had taken it over. I relaxed and had a beer with them all. I'd not had an evening 'off' for ages. The bath was safe at the pontoon. The stories floated on and eventually flowed into the tale of our day rowing through the horrible weather. By the time Mr Palmer had started telling it, I was slumped soporifically in a chair near the window. The more he told the tale, the worse the storm of the day became and by the end we were all sure there was a whale somewhere near Higham Blight.

I slept really well that night. I was content, not just after a lovely evening in the pub, but also safe in the knowledge that although the weather could now slow me down, it could not stop me for a single day longer. Now, the weather would be dictated to by me and not the other way round. The Thames was narrow enough from this point westwards that I could row even if the weather was bad. The weather couldn't stop me . . . unless of course it was really fierce.

The next morning the weather was really fierce; like a vicious pride of lions it tore at the pontoon. For two days a thick Victorian fog descended on the Thames accompanied by dreadful rain and a lethal wind in totally the wrong direction. Every morning I'd turn on the radio in a deep funk, fully expecting to hear '. . . and now the weather forecast with Little Dorrit, before the breakfast news with Bill Sykes . . .'. This was weather straight out of Dickens. There was no way I could go out in that sort of storm. Mr Palmer wasn't even letting his own larger boats out. Lashed by rain, wind and in a huge fog, the Palmers and I manoeuvred the bath to the safer side of the pontoon. Water poured into my now-useless flotation devices as the gaffer tape came loose. The enormous difficulty we had in manhandling the bath round from one side of the pontoon to the other simply underlined the utter futility of any attempt to get out on the river that day.

Stuck in Gravesend, Phil arrived down with some post for me. Among the various things was another burgee: this time from Denmark. From the letter, it seemed that someone over there had read about the bath on the website and decided to send me a flag to fly. Drinking a Coke in the bar at the Ship & Lobster, I unfolded the small Danish flag and tied it to the Royal Temple and Whitstable Yacht Club ones. When the weather improved, it would fly proudly from my showerhead and we'd enter London, a terrifying Viking sanitary invasion force of one.

The next morning the weather improved. I missed the first tide in trying to get everyone organised. We left on the second. Joe, who'd been designing the website, and another mate of ours from Cambridge boarded the Palmers' support boat with Phil and the skipper.

I applied more gaffer tape, bailed out the flotation tanks and undertook the now-familiar routine of getting safety equipment, oars, attaching the showerhead, forgetting something (usually my compass or the atlas) before getting in the bath, attaching my shoes and rowing off. Gravesend still looked stunning in the light but I was glad to see the back of her. The day before in the horrid weather I'd begun to sense another Ramsgate.

Pulling out of Gravesend, various tankers streamed past on their way out to sea. Just as with the last leg, the Port of London had enforced a speed-limit slow down on the river to make it easier for me to continue and the tankers all hooted their horns in support. They could have been hooting in angry frustration at the slow down; it was impossible to tell complex emotions from hooting. Some tankers could even have been hooting in protest at the ambiguity of hoots as a method of communication.

To my shock, boats came out full of people cheering and waving.

I'm not sure if they had come specifically to see the bath or if they were just out on the river and happened to bump into us. Although the people who had signs with 'Tim' and 'Bath' written on them had either come to find us or were having a very surreal day out: 'I've been coming out on this river for the last 30 years with this sign, Enid . . .'

'The "Tim Bath" one . . . yeah . . .'

'And every week – nothing. Now some bloke has gone and rowed out in a bath from Gravesend just to support my sign.'

'Amazing what people will do when you make a sign.'

'Best give him a wave or he'll think I don't appreciate his effort.'

'How do you know he's called Tim?'

'Just a hunch.'

'Could be a sign . . . tea?'

As I left the boat full of people waving, the river narrowed radically. This was the narrowest point I'd seen so far. It also turned out to be one of the busiest. There was a huge number of ships coming from somewhere on the north bank. Checking the atlas I realised it was Tilbury Docks. Avoiding the tankers, I followed the river as it bent first north, then south. As I rounded the third bend to see it straighten up, I saw a truly majestic sight: the Queen Elizabeth II Bridge.

It is the most incredible piece of engineering. As I went under the massive arch I whistled up into the air. In the paper boat I'd rowed under every other bridge on the Thames and under all of them I'd whistled a bugle call my grandfather taught me. The QE II Bridge was the one I'd never been under and finally I'd managed it. On top of the bridge I could see people waving. It's a very busy stretch of road and how they'd managed to be there to wave I'm not sure, but it spurred me on once again to know that I must make it to Tower Bridge.

It was a difficult row, not as bad as others I'd faced but still very tricky. This was mainly due to the wind, which conspired all day with unerring accuracy to come from totally unhelpful directions. Also, oddly, my body felt worse having had a day off. I think perhaps it thought the ordeal was over and so had relaxed a bit only to be dragged kicking and bleeding back into the bath. The painkillers had my shoulder under control but the biting wind was unkind to my various cuts.

I rowed on in pain and looked back. Having gone under the QE II Bridge an odd feeling hit me that I was home. I'd not felt this quite so strongly before. All my focus had been on getting to London. When I'd crossed the Channel I'd not felt home as I'd been forced to row *to* France rather than to Folkestone. Folkestone, Ramsgate, Margate, Whitstable and Sheerness had all been temporary homes to me and the bath; like homes, I'd loved and hated them variously but never felt as I did now. The QE II carries the M25 and the M25 has always seemed to me like the boundary to Greater London. The bath had passed the outer marker and was preparing for the final approach.

My initial plan for the day was to make it to Erith Yacht Club by nightfall. The PLA were not keen on having the bath out on the river after dark and, having seen the size of the tankers and container ships around me, I agreed with them. Erith YC seemed very accommodating and said they'd love to have the bath moored up for the night, although there did seem to be some unclear issue relating to a gate and a key. The new support-boat skipper from Palmers', Mick, shouted down, 'You're never going to make Erith at this speed . . . we're going to have to look for some other mooring tonight.'

The wind had buffeted me more than a Women's Institute gathering. My progress had been radically slowed as a result and Mick was right. I scrambled for the atlas. I just couldn't find anywhere that seemed useful. Things were looking bleak. A return to Gravesend seemed the plan we'd have to adopt.

I rowed on a little despondently but began to realise that the wind was dropping. I still stood a chance. I speeded up and in a short time rounded a bend to my right. From the hanging glow of the evening sprang one of the most romantic, eccentric-looking sights on the river. A ship perched lightly on the muddy bank at a jaunty angle with a small flotilla of yachts at anchor bobbing around just yards from it. A red flag with a white crest and blue cross fluttered happily in the breeze. Mick shouted over, 'That's the yacht club. I don't believe it.'

At higher tide the boat probably floated impressively but sitting coquettishly on the silt there was something unbearably attractive about it. I pulled in, the Royal Temple, Whitstable and Danish flags fluttering from the showerhead, and hailed the yacht club in the traditional way. What was the point of Dom teaching me all that etiquette stuff if I never used it?

'Ahoy, Erith Yacht Club? Permission to come aboard?'

'You must be Tim. You're very welcome.'

A man appeared and finally answered the age-old question of where Santa lives in summer. A more mirthful, jocund, white-bearded man would be hard to find.

'Fancy a pint? We've a bar upstairs.'

Did I fancy a pint? Somewhere in a wood the Pope pulled down his pants and opened a newspaper, while in a church in Hornsey a bear took his first communion. I tied off the bath and bounded up the stairs. The gangsta phone rang.

'Hello, is that Tim?'

'Yes . . .'

'Good. This is President . . .'

'Pardon?' Something metaphysical punched me in the face; I reeled and almost fell down the steps I'd just bounded up. 'The President?'

'Yes.'

Thoughts mounted cars and drove a Formula One track in my head. The President of the United States was on my phone. This was unbelievable. I steadied myself and tried to make sense of things. If this was the President, why did he have an accent plummier than a jam factory?

'I'm phoning about an escort for a bath. This is HMS *President*.'

'Pardon?'

Just as the mist cleared and I realised it was not the President of the United States on the phone, smog billowed in. On the phone instead was the Royal Navy about providing an escort for the bath. I wasn't sure which was more surreal. I listened in awe as the officer explained what would be happening when I reached Tower Bridge. Some wondrous plotters had been very busy. There were plans afoot that I must start off on the right foot and not put the other one wrong.

Having pulled myself up the stairs, I was greeted by the not-very-cunningly disguised off-duty St Nick who'd just pulled me a pint. There were a few very merry people in the yacht club bar. When you've got Santa behind the bar everyone is happy; except on Christmas Eve: when he doesn't show up till late and getting a pint takes ages. We laughed a lot before they presented me with an Erith Yacht Club burgee. The gangsta phone rang; it was Phil.

'Mate, Mick wants to get you further up the river, he says he knows of a great mooring up a bit . . .'

I left the bar, got on the bath and rowed off upriver to find Mick, Phil and the support boat. As I rowed up with a pint of strong ale inside me I reflected that things were going well. Mine was a pot of ointment half full with just two small flies spoiling the picture by copulating in it.

The first fly was that I was due at the Palace soon and I only had one suit with me. The suit in question had been one of England's finer bits of tailoring when I'd inherited it but after a couple of outings with me it had somehow inexplicably become covered in a resolute mixture of chocolate, horse manure and car oil. I wasn't sure if Erith would have a dry cleaner and if it did, I'd only be here overnight (weather permitting) so how was I to collect the suit after the usual three days of cleaning?

The fly's girlfriend was that I simply could not find a mooring near Greenwich for the following night. I'd chosen Greenwich as it was controllably close to the Tower, so there was no chance I wouldn't make it under the Bridge the day after.

Up to that point in the journey people had been really kind with moorings. Vanquished Ramsgate fascist and disaster at Margate aside, everyone had offered me moorings for free to help keep the cost of the project down. London was sadly a very different story. I'd battled so hard to make it to London and was met with nothing but unhelpfulness. No one would give me a mooring. By that I mean no one would *allow* me to have a mooring even if I paid for it. Contrary to what I'd thought, most moorings and pontoons in London are privately owned and the owners did not seem friendly or helpful.

There'd been one exception to this in a lovely family-owned marina near Tower Bridge who kindly offered me a berth. Sadly their harbour was tidal so I couldn't take advantage of the offer. Due to the way the tide works, and the mechanism they use to keep water in the harbour at low tide, I would have been trapped there until very high tide. By the time I could have got out, I would have found it really quite tricky to battle up to Tower Bridge before the tide turned against me.

I'd been making dozens of frantic calls to anyone I could think of about this and none of them had turned up anything positive. I rowed on as my ointment looked a little less than half full and one of the flies rolled off the other and lit a cigarette.

I checked the atlas and realised I'd now made it level with the centre of Erith. I turned and up ahead, floating near some barges, was the support boat. I could see what Mick meant. Mooring up to one of the massive Thames barges was an inspired idea. Attached to one of these safe, sturdy, dependable Thames giants, the bath would be totally out of harm's way for the night.

'Here's your mooring, Tim.' He gestured behind him to the mighty Thames barge, in front of which was a small derelict sinking boat attached to an equally uninspiring precarious-looking buoy.

'You think I should moor up on the sinking … I mean … powder-blue boat?'

'It'll be fine, no one has moved this thing for years.'

'You don't say …'

Mick was an experienced man of the river. He was a Thames-approved skipper; I was a man in a bath so I took his advice. It didn't seem the best mooring I'd ever seen but perhaps I'd been spoilt with moorings in the past. The Royal Harbour of Ramsgate this was certainly not. What was certain, however, was that the bath would not get stolen from this mooring as it was right out in the middle of the river. Also, as long as my knots held up, the bath would not get loose. The proof of this was the gently rotting powder-blue spectre that floated alongside me. Clearly that hadn't been loosened from the buoy for several years.

I boarded the support boat and as Mick steered us towards the pier, checked the tide tables and did the various calculations that we'd need to make the journey tomorrow. Even up to a month and a half ago these various calculations had totally baffled me; I stood more chance of passing medical exams in Swahili than getting them right. Now they came as second nature. As I was doing them, I realised I hadn't phoned Dom for days. I had become the self-sufficient thing in the water that Dom had tried so very hard to create. I may not have become a salmon but I certainly felt I could pass for a newt.

I discussed the morning plan with Mick before saying goodbye to the others. Joe, Phil and the rest were going back with Mick in the full hope their cars would still be in Gravesend. I got all the kit I needed out of the support boat and jumped up onto the pier. I had the pressing issue of a couple of flies to deal with.

As I hit bed that night, my head was unbearably heavy. I was exhausted and had to lie in a specific position so as to stand any chance of sleeping without lying on or opening myself up to the pain of my various cuts. On the plus side, things were going well. Before bed I'd been kneeling (I still couldn't sit that well) and realised that finally after over a month of rowing I'd just entered the London *A to Z* on page 85. The bath had passed the middle marker; surely even a drunk pilot could land her from here. After months in the bath with it, I could finally put down the atlas. To celebrate I had a large glass of Irish whiskey and after all the rowing of the day, passed out as pissed as the best of the genus Salamandridae I now truly was.

Six hours later I was woken up by the sound of a castrated bee. I grabbed my phone.

'Hello?'

'What the fuck is that thing tied to my boat?'

Oh good, another day had started well.

CHAPTER FOURTEEN
[There is no Deck Thirteen on a Ship]

A POPOMASTICK SCULLER

'History will vindicate me: I shall write it myself.'

Winston S. Churchill

The earliness of the morning, coupled with the large intake of Ireland's finest the night before conspired to make me slower than a 20-stone sprinter.

'What?'

'There's some fucking thing tied to my boat. I phoned the Port of London to ask what the fuck is going on, and they give me your number.'

'What . . . it's half past . . . you're up early . . .'

'I work with my hands.'

I try charm. 'Are you a carpenter?'

'No, I'm a fucking boxer!' An already bad situation just got worse. 'What are you going to do about this?'

'Just give me one second . . .' On the other end of the phone was a very deep, gravelly voice belonging to an obviously furious sweary man. I had to think fast. 'Firstly, what's your name?'

'Let's say it's Mr Green – now what are you going to do about this?'

'Have you been boxing all night?'

'No, I've just got back from splitting up fights at the local night club – now what are you going to do about this problem?'

My pacifying charm offensive was not going well. How could I politely let the presumably enormous Mr Green know that we'd tied the bath to his powder-blue pride and joy as we'd assumed it was more deserted than the *Marie Celeste*?

'We thought it was scrap . . .'

At the school of politeness and charm my teacher had just handed in her notice before scouring the pages of *Stupidity Weekly* for a new job.

'What the fuck! Does it look like scrap to you?'

My mind raced. This was a crucial moment. 'Well . . . it could do with a bit of spring clean.'

'I'm down here now on the shore looking out at my boat and your thing tied to it!'

I stopped listening midway through that line. 'You're on the shore?'

'Yes.'

The already worse situation just got horrendous. He was within eyesight of the bath. Now, there was no way I could sneak down there, swim out and loosen it from the mooring without a bellicose pugilist using me as an innovative new way to measure up for opera gloves.

'How much money are you going to pay me to make this go away?'

'What?' The question startled me in its frankness.

'How much money are you going to give me to make me happy about this?'

'It's a project to raise money for a charity. There isn't any money to give to you . . .'

'I'm a charity. Now, again, I'm asking, how much money are you going to give me?'

There was something else trying to break through into my mind. Something he'd already said that I should have seen was important. As I thought of how to get out of this new hole, I re-ran the conversation in my mind. 'How did you say you got my number?'

'I phoned the Port of London, described your bath and they gave it to me.'

Brilliant. So now the Port of London were involved. Mike's fabulous mooring could not have turned out any worse.

'Look, I'll phone the Port of London and give you a call straight back.'

He protested for a while about me hanging up and made me write his number down twice, even though it had appeared on the window of my phone, before ending the conversation with, 'I want my money so make sure you call me back, or else . . .'

It was very early in the morning for this. I phoned the PLA.

'Hello, it's Tim, I need to speak to someone about a bath and a buoy near Erith.'

'It's been a morning for it. Someone else phoned up with those exact words earlier. Is it some kind of code?'

'Not exactly.'

'Oh I see . . .' she said conspiratorially. She clearly thought I was James Bond and there was a major operation going on that day code-named 'Bath, buoy, Erith'. 'I'll put you through to the man I put him, before you, through to.'

'Hello?'

'Hi, this is Tim FitzHigham, I'm phoning to apologise for any trouble I've caused with the bath.'

'Ah, I wondered when you'd call.'

'I really thought that boat was derelict and so . . .'

'Let me stop you there.' Uh-oh, this sounded a bit ominous. 'This sort of thing happens all the time on the river, skippers tying off on things they shouldn't. I would be surprised if the man who called you even owned that mooring himself . . .'

'So I shouldn't pay him for tying off there by mistake?'

He burst out laughing.

'I'll take that as a no . . .'

'Absolutely not. He sounded pretty aggressive but there's no way you should give him any money.'

'Right.'

'If you can get down there soon and sort it out I'd appreciate it as I don't really want to have him on the phone again this morning but other than that, really, think no more about it. We're all looking forward to seeing you go under that bridge. Best of luck.'

'Erm . . . thanks.'

I hung up. That had gone much better than expected. I'd gone from expecting to pay fines and a mooring fee to Mr Green to having a pat on the back and no extra cost. I phoned Mr Green. I'd had one of the shortest careers on record at the Foreign Office so this was not going to be easy. The smart money was on it going really, really badly. After a long and tricky chat with the husky, sweary, nightclub bouncer he gave up pressing me for money and our conversation turned to his new favourite preoccupation.

'OK, fine, you can have the mooring for free, but if you do any interviews you must make sure you thank me for having generously given it to you.'

'Right . . .'

'You tell anyone on the radio or whatever that you couldn't have made it to London without me . . . or else!'

'Well, thank you for being so understanding about the whole thing, Mr Green.'

'That's OK.'

'And good luck with the boxing.'

'I only do it to keep in training for the bouncer work.'

I hung up. I'd like to think I'd made a new friend but I couldn't be absolutely sure. On a radio station in Erith later that afternoon I thanked Mr Green and they played 'A Hard Day's Night', dedicated to him.

I'd missed the first tide of the day, so had to wait for the second. While Mike went out and shifted freight around, I made more phone calls to try and sort out a mooring near Greenwich.

No one was going to budge on the issue. It was becoming pretty desperate. Bizarrely I seemed to have come up against the Department of London Transport. They were *so* charming; I now know who trains traffic wardens in tact. Caesar would never have crossed the Rubicon if he'd had to deal with anyone at Ken Livingstone's office. There was simply no reasoning with them. The conversation can be summed up in two lines:

'Can I moor on the pontoon near the National Maritime Museum?'

'No.'

It took 20 minutes to exhaust all the possible ways of saying this. The obnoxious man on the phone said he could not have cared if I'd rowed from Cape Horn to Greenwich. He said he hated charity; except his own, devoted to the care of pontoon managers in the Greenwich area. Nothing I could say would change his mind. I hung up totally frustrated. His was the only pontoon I could realistically use and he was not going to budge.

My phone flashed and the friendly voice of the Clerk of the Watermen graced my ear.

'Hello Tim, how's it going? I'm really looking forward to seeing you come under Tower Bridge.'

'Rowing is going great. I'm having trouble with getting a mooring near Greenwich.'

'Who have you tried?'

I took him through all the options I'd exhausted.

'My, you have been busy. Why don't you give him half an hour and call him back?'

We talked a bit more about the various things that had been going on. People on the river, my issues with Mr Green and the fact I was trying to leave with the second tide that day before I hung up.

Half an hour later my phone rang. It was the obnoxious man from Greenwich Pier.

'I'm sorry not to have got this sorted earlier but of course you can come and moor here.'

I couldn't quite believe what I was hearing. Perhaps this was some sort of cruel trick.

'What? Er . . . thank you. That's very kind of you. I'll only be there overnight and be gone in the morning.'

'Apparently you can stay as long as you like. I've had the Royal Navy, Port of London and the Watermen on the phone. You've got some friends, you have. I've never heard my boss use language like that to me. It seems I owe you an apology.'

'Think nothing of it. I'm sure you were just doing your job. I look forward to seeing you later.'

With that, the former mooring moron turned into a friend. One fly had finally bitten the dust. Now there was just a suit to deal with.

Mike arrived with his usual bluster. He was really pleased we were on the second tide as he'd been able to move freight around all morning. On such good form he was almost ready to burst he shouted over, 'I hear you got into trouble for choosing that mooring! I did warn you!' He smiled mischievously. 'Your name'll be mud on the river if you're not careful! You know . . . like the banks . . .

get it?' He let out a laugh stained with years of cigarettes and early frosty mornings. I smiled and loaded kit onto the support boat ready for the off. Phil arrived and loaded his masses of kit bags containing all sorts of cameras, lenses, tripods etc. Mike upped the revs and we chugged off into the middle of the Thames to arrive at the powder-blue *Marie Celeste* and the bathroom that floated next to it.

I jumped aboard. Mike handed down the kit. I strapped myself into the shoes, popped the oars into their gates and we headed off upstream with the tide. It was not a long row up to Greenwich and the river was much narrower which made things easier for me.

I rowed on up through what was and sort of still is London's industrial heart: lots of factories making stuff, supplying something somebody needs to somewhere. The river winds basically north-west at this stretch so the wind blowing south-east was less than helpful but luckily it was not as ferocious as it had been in the past. The river straightened and I found I was rowing more or less due west before it wound and meandered again, taking me south-west. The Romans certainly hadn't designed the River Thames, or if they had, the normally sober architect of the straight roads had drawn up the plans while spending the afternoon in a taverna after winning heavily, betting on the lions versus the Christians cup match. The river wiggled on and finally I saw the Woolwich Arsenal Ferry as it narrowly missed me.

I'd actually made it to Woolwich. When I'd been sitting in Ramsgate, bailing out water, Woolwich had seemed a distant dream. Now I was there, I knew how the Spanish felt having dreamt for so long of finding gold-filled El Dorado only to arrive and discover it looking less like the bullion vault of fable and more like the rough end of, well, Woolwich.

You don't realise how close to the Woolwich Ferry the Thames Barrier is until you've rowed it by river. In under 300 strokes I'd almost crashed into it. It is some piece of engineering; like a very small Sydney Opera House. This polite-looking piece of architecture serves a mighty purpose. Finally, I understood it fully; it protects London from the power of the elements and mighty sea I'd just rowed through and also regulates the flow of water going east out to sea. Without it, Gravesend and Erith would be distant flooded memories, or towns inhabited by people wading through their daily lives on stilts.

Again, it's shocking how close the Millennium Dome is to the Thames Barrier. For the first time on the trip I wanted the elements to slow me down. I'd been looking forward to this part of the trip since I'd made it to France. In my head (not having checked the charts of course), I thought I'd see the Woolwich Arsenal Ferry one day and Thames Barrier the next, before setting out on the third to pass the Dome in a blaze of sunshine. Now we were rushing past them all so fast. I had become a sightseeing glutton. As I reached the Dome finally I got perfect weather. It was the first time since before Ramsgate. The sun came out, filling the sky with a massive orange orb. It was like rowing home. Suddenly things seemed tropical. In my head, a tune reappeared that used to wake me up every morning when I lived abroad. I looked over my shoulder at the sun-filled sky, the Dome in the foreground and smiled; the familiar drum roll started in my mind and the first line kicked off, 'Hail Grenada, land of ours we pledge ourselves to thee . . .'

The Dome is on a promontory. I rounded it beneath a perfect peach sky and saw the pyramid roof of Canary Wharf. I was finally in London. People waved and shouted down from windows on the Thames. As I went past Nelson Docks, sailing boats and kayaks came out and followed me as I rowed on.

Finally, as the sun entered its final stages of setting in the sky I arrived at the jetty next to the Royal Naval College at Greenwich. A man in more uniform than an admiral came out onto the pontoon and shouted over, 'We spoke on the phone. Can you moor on the inside as that would be more helpful to us?'

Oh good, the initially unhelpful man was there to watch me moor up.

I pulled the bath round to the inside of the pontoon. The tide was really racing on that side. It was funnelled like wind in a test tunnel. Trying to moor the bath in that was as tricky as navigating rapids in a bin bag, wearing clown shoes made of boulders. I had to pull really hard to get up to the mooring position and when there, the bath wanted to slip out again and go with the current, away from the pontoon. Once, when I got up to it successfully, I threw the line over to the ostentatiously dressed man only for him to shout back, 'I'm not really sure how to tie you off . . .'

The line slipped gently off the pontoon and back into the water. Finally I came up with what seemed to be the only viable plan. I pulled hard and got the bath into position. Then, holding the line, I jumped from the bath onto the deck of the jetty and looped the line around a fixing as the bath jerked off and tried to leave me to go off downstream. Via some jostling of the line around the fixing I finally got the bath to a position where I could jump back onto her and get another line. Jumping back with that one, I tied it to another fixed point of the pontoon. It was possibly the worst plan I'd come up with to tie off. Dangerous and incredibly risky but it had worked.

Mike was having similar problems with the support boat as he thrashed the engine to try and get it into the pontoon. At one point he reversed and trapped the bath between the metal hull of his boat and the metal of the pontoon. This was very dangerous. In this position the bath would be snapped in an instant. Desperate and worried I shouted, 'Move out! Go forward!'

'What?'

Under the sound of his thrashing engines, there was a crack from the bath.

'You're crushing the bath! Move!'

He thrashed the throttle and the support boat jolted forward away from the bath. I looked at the bath, waiting to see her go under. I exhaled all the breath in my lungs. To have dragged a third-of-a-tonne piece of plumbing all the way from France only to have it crushed by the very boat that was meant to be supporting it less than five miles from target would have been utterly heart breaking. Tentatively I stepped onto the bathroom floor and began checking the hulls. Luckily, it seemed it was just a tiny crack above the waterline. Less than ideal but a lot better than it could have been.

I stepped back up on to the pontoon deck to see a fast orange boat mooring alongside it on the other side. As it pulled level one of the men removed his helmet.

'Which tide are you going to go with for Tower Bridge tomorrow?'

'Erm . . . I think the second one.'

'OK, thanks and we'll see you there. Sorry, must go, we've got to be further downriver . . .'

With that, he re-helmeted and the RNLI speedboat hacked off downriver leaving me bemused on the pontoon.

The sun had really gone now. As I stood on the bath watching the lights dancing off the river I tried to analyse why I was suddenly taking so long. I could have gone on the first tide tomorrow, I could have probably made it under Tower Bridge today, if Mike had arrived on time and I'd rowed faster. I followed the line of the green laser marking the Greenwich Meridian up into the sky. If anywhere was the place to reflect on time, this was it. Weirdly, now I was so very close to Tower Bridge, I wanted it to be further away. Very often we have so little purpose in life and for so long getting the bath to the Tower had been mine. Now it was nearly over, I wanted it to last for ever.

The sun came up the next morning. It was a glorious English summer day as I walked across the lawn amid Wren's magical buildings. Feeling like a mid-18th-century midshipman I pushed the massive doors and came to a halt at the reception desk of the National Maritime Museum. Heroic naval scenes and ships in cases surrounded the reception desk; behind it, a woman sat talking on the phone. She finished.

'Can I help you?'

'I was told to ask for Deirdre.'

'I'll phone her. You can take a seat.'

Deirdre was someone I'd been speaking to on the phone for a while. She was running a campaign based in the Maritime Museum and had kindly said I should call in on my way through that part of London.

'Ah, Tim, there you are. Do come upstairs.'

I followed Deirdre through passages and corridors, up staircases and under atriums until we ended up in a tiny office at the end of a long corridor. On the way I realised my phone was running low on power. There were calls I needed to make, things that had to be organised.

'Does anyone in your office have a phone charger for this?'

'Yes, I've got one and better still, I've got to pop out for a bit. Why don't you have a seat at my desk and make calls. I'm sure you've got a lot to organise.'

The view from the desk was stunning. I stared out over the sun-drenched lawns I'd just walked across. There was little time for wistful romantic glazing over; there was a lot to organise. I picked up the phone and began to deal with all the various things that needed to come together later that day like some admiral planning a battle. I worked on from the now-empty, tiny broom cupboard feeling increasingly like a cross between Nelson and Gordon the Gopher. Deirdre arrived back.

'Right, let's go to the bath. There's some people who want to take pictures.'

As we wandered back out to the lawns past the portraits of the great mariners of the past, I was sure they seemed to smirk. Quite what men like Hardy, St Vincent and Collingwood would have made of the bath would be anyone's guess. Deirdre's pace was vigorous but on the way back to the bath she still had me giggling as I trotted alongside her at stories of polo matches in Ulan Bator when she was younger.

We arrived at the bath and did photos before going back up to the broom-cupboard office. Surrounded by Deirdre and her stunning team, I made more calls.

Before leaving the NMM I went down to the lavatory and gaffer-taped up my hands again before applying more surgical spirit to my still-lacerated swollen plums. When I'd first applied it after crossing the Channel, I'd passed out with the pain. Later in the trip around Margate, I'd applied it to my nethers and it felt very painful but I'd at least managed to stay conscious. Around Gravesend, when applying it, it burnt and I felt vaguely morally dirty. Now when I applied it, it felt warm and oddly comfortable. I made a mental note to go through surgical spirit plum cold turkey the moment today was over or seek help. Whimpering, I pulled up my rowing lycra and waddled gingerly out of the lavatory.

The last tide of the day did not obey Naval time. Contrary to everything the Navy and I wanted and expected of it, the tide was late. I paced up and down on the tiled bathroom floor waiting for it to turn.

We all waited for the tide. Once again nature had stopped me. A grey launch arrived at the pontoon with two sailors on top and a White Ensign flapping in the breeze. One shouted over, 'We thought we'd meet you on the way down, you still here?'

'The tide's being slow today . . .'

The grey launch pulled into the pontoon. I started.

'Andy?' A boyish-looking sailor grinned in a way that would have made Just William justifiably proud. 'I thought you wouldn't remember . . .'

Andy had been the Navy coxswain who'd escorted me down the Thames in the paper boat two years previously.

'I wouldn't have missed this. I asked to change shifts to be here.'

I grinned in a way that would have made an idiot justifiably proud. I was very touched.

More boats arrived. The RNLI, the Port of London, various marine companies and Thames Watermen all sent boats. Everything was going really well. Boats were assembling for the off. This was going to be a top evening. Finally, a gorgeous wooden launch built by 'Uncle Bill' who has the boathouse next to Mark's came bombing down the river. At its helm was Uncle Bill himself.

'Thank goodness, I thought I'd missed you!'

'Is Mark coming?'

'No, he's had to go up to Henley today. There's been some sort of emergency. He told me to say well done.'

I felt a bit down that Mark couldn't be there to see the completion of everything we'd worked so hard for. Still, at least Uncle Bill was there so someone from the boathouse would get to see it. Phil handed me my phone.

'It's Comic Relief, mate, I think you'd better take this . . .'

My sadness at Mark's unavailability was compounded by the following conversation. Comic Relief couldn't send anyone down to the river either. This was a blow. I understood how busy everyone in the organisation must have been but it was a real shame. They'd promised that someone would be there to give me my other sock. Silly as it may sound, I really wanted to get it. I'd been trying so hard to reach London and raise money for them and the thought of eventually making a pair of Sport Relief socks (albeit a year late) had kept me going at times. Eventually they agreed to send someone down to pick up any money that might be donated that evening but as for anyone officially coming down to present me with a sock, no one could make it.

I hung up feeling a bit glum. Perhaps no one would be turning up. Maybe there would just be me and a bunch of boats?

A photographer and reporter arrived from Kenny. The reporter was the same one who had crossed the Channel with me.

'Hope the journey is a bit less painful for you today . . .' He grinned. 'Kenny can't be here, he's got to make sure tomorrow's paper goes out, but he sent you this . . .' He handed me a large bottle of champagne and an envelope. Inside the envelope was a sticker with 'Well done, you made it, Kenny'. I peeled the back off the sticker and stuck it to the roll top. At least Kenny would sort of be there when I went under the bridge.

I had a huge moment of doubt. I'd always thought that people would turn up to welcome the bath but these key members of the team not being there gave me a real pause for thought. People had been going on with their lives while I'd been faffing around on the river. Would anyone bother to show up? I could have set up one of the most embarrassing moments of my life: to arrive in London and be greeted by no one. Perhaps it would have been better not to have bothered coming round Kent at all. I was suddenly struck with fear. I'd not been afraid at any point in the trip before but suddenly it was a fear of rejection by a city I love that made me stop. I stared into the water. Mike broke me out of it.

'Tim! The tide's turned!'

There was no time to dwell any more on this rather depressing series of thoughts. I'd set this up. I had to go through with it.

This stretch of the river is familiar to anyone who watches *EastEnders*. In the official technical maritime description: it's the really wiggly looking bit you see on the credits just after they kick off. I leant over the side and checked the gaffer tape on the flotation tanks. If it could just hold up for another few hours I would get to see the Tower.

I lowered my skinless bottom into the sliding seat of the bath and winced a little as the cheeks hit the wood. On the plus side, however, finally, it was nearly all over.

The sun was turning to set as I pulled off from the pontoon at Greenwich. Its rays glinted off the Victorian showerhead. The plumbing below was shot to pieces and it couldn't suck water up any more but it still looked splendid in the half-light. Flying from the showerhead of the bath were all the yacht club burgees and the one Danish one that I'd been presented with. Behind them, towards the stern, on its own masthead, flew the Red Ensign that had been with me since the start.

As I pulled on the oars with gaffer-taped hands, I looked around me. The bath, in the half-light, with her escort boats and the sun setting behind was like some haunting sanitaryware parody of

Turner's *The Fighting Temeraire*. I smiled at the wonderful ridicu-
lousness of the scene. The bath was as battered as the pictures of
the *Suhaili* when Robin Knox-Johnston pulled her into Falmouth.
A craft, ill-designed for her purpose which had held up against the
odds to make it. I was shot to pieces, with gaffer-taped hands,
surgical-spirit-numbed plums and a still-broken shoulder, but if both
of us just held together for the next hour or so, we would make it.

As I rowed up the last short hop to Tower Bridge I noticed that
people began to appear on the riverbank taking pictures, shouting
and waving. Sailing boats and kayaks again came alongside the
bath: as well as the support boats that had already joined us, a
small flotilla was gradually gathering, splayed out behind a Thomas
Crapper bath.

I relaxed into the row. Never had the conditions been this good.
It seemed finally even the weather conceded that I stood a chance
of making it. Yet as I took the curve around Rotherhithe something
took hold of me. True, I was in pain but I wanted to make this. A
focus suddenly clicked in. I increased the stroke rate. I'd become a
man in command of rowing, rather than the useless master of capsize
that had started this project.

I rounded the final bend near Wapping and looked over my
shoulder. There it was, in front of me: Tower Bridge.

I turned back to face the taps, dug in and increased the pace
again. Nothing would stop me now. I heard various voices screaming
into the darkening sky: 'Come on Tim!' I pulled as though nothing
else in my life had ever mattered before. I was going to make this.

Upriver of me, aboard HMS *President*, sailors stood to attention
on deck, flags flapping in the breeze. People crowded the bank
under Tower Bridge cheering and shouting; people lined up on top
of the bridge and leant over the side craning to see what was
happening.

The noise told me all I wanted to hear: London had turned up.
A lump welled up in my throat. The gaffer tape had started to come
loose; I wrapped blood-drenched hands around the oars, looked
into the reflection in the taps and pulled on, getting faster and faster
as I sensed the end was near. The bath voyage would end with a
racing finish.

For a year and a half of my life I'd been a man in ill-fitting,
blood-stained lycra, defined by my total failure to get here. It had

obsessed me, hospitalised me twice and almost killed me, but now I could see Tower Bridge.

People shouted and cheered. I pulled on. To the lasting shame of all my antecedents my stiff upper lip collapsed altogether and as I pulled, tears rolled down my cheeks. I wasn't crying at the pain, although it was intense, but at the fact that people cared. It seemed that for once a random lot of people had come together, forgotten all the aggravating things in their lives and united to celebrate something very silly. In the final strokes of the bath, I cried with a sheer unadulterated sense of joy.

Before I realised it, I was under Tower Bridge. Horns on all the escort boats around me sounded off. One of the mighty Thames Fire Ships, an updated version of those that had been used for Winston Churchill's funeral, sucked up water from the Thames and spewed it out in a massive victory arch. Even people on the bridge were soaked. Everything seemed to slow down. I pulled under Tower Bridge and sank back into the roll top of the bath. All I could manage was to gasp between breaths, 'Yes, yes . . .'

I removed the remainder of the gaffer tape from my hands – most of it had already come off – and raised my exhausted arms up in the sky. Still breathless, I shouted again, 'Yes! Yes!'

I'd done it. Boats criss-crossed around me as the Navy escort tried to help keep the flotilla in order. I pulled a couple of extra strokes just to check I really had made it under the bridge. The Thames Fire Ship carried on spewing water everywhere, boats sounded their horns and I undid my fixed shoes in the bath. Within seconds I had the Red Ensign flag and its masthead in my battered hands, held it aloft and waved it victorious at the people on the bank, those on the bridge and to anyone who might have been watching from outer space. The first person to row the Channel in a bathroom was indefatigably British.

Putting the flag down for a second, I remembered the champagne from Kenny in the washstand. Very soon, to cheering from the bridge and bank, I'd sprayed *Lilibet II*, myself and the Navy, before feeding some to the river and drinking the few mouthfuls that remained.

The moment of victory is so short compared to the length of time an achievement has taken. With the last drop of champagne gone, I flourished the Red Ensign again before turning the bath towards the Tower of London and rowing back under the bridge to the mooring I had at HMS *President*. In all of its grizzly history, no one had ever been as pleased to see the Tower of London as I was that evening. As I rowed back, now against the tide, towards *President*, the Fire Ship went off again. The shower of the bath looked on impotent and jealous at the massive power shower being given to the people on the bridge.

I stepped off the bath. This is a crucial moment for anyone involved in maritime. The journey was over and leaving the bath filled me with an overwhelming sadness. Simply put: I did not want to leave her. She had been my home for a month and a half and, more than that, she'd been the focus of my life for nearly two years, and now our journey was at an end.

Stepping up onto the pontoon, I was greeted by the second-in-command of *President*. He saluted very smartly, shook me by the hand and broke into a huge grin.

'Welcome aboard, Tim, well done. There are some people to see you.'

Coming down the gangplank to the pontoon was the Alderman of Tower Ward. He's called Richard and is a very kind man indeed. Aldermen are the next rank down from the Lord Mayor of London (in fact all Lord Mayors must be Aldermen first), so he's also quite senior. He looked splendid in the traditional full regalia of the Alderman: a red fur-lined gown, black bicorn fur-lined hat and white gloves. He grinned.

'I understand there's no one else to give you this.' He pulled out the Sport Relief sock that would make my pair. 'You've very richly deserved it. Well done.'

I shook him by the hand and felt very special. Someone from Comic Relief had obviously been thinking of me after all. Finally, a year and a half after getting the first one, I now had a second Sport Relief sock.

'Where are Mum and Dad?'

Richard smiled. 'Your parents are probably drenched, they're on that Fire Ship.'

Dom appeared on the pontoon and, much to his old-style British embarrassment, had to suffer me flinging my arms around him. Then Simon, Managing Director of Thomas Crapper & Company, arrived next to us on the pontoon. It was genuinely a treat to have them next to me in the moment of triumph. Simon grinned.

'Tim, you should be Grade Two Listed and preserved for the nation.'

Richard the Alderman turned to him and smiling said, 'Surely you mean Grade One, with a star!'

The Fire Ship arrived at the other side of the pontoon and the smart sailor who had greeted me helped my mum, dad, sister, brother-in-law and three friends off it. Hugging my family was one of the greatest moments of the bath journey. The smart sailor said to Mum, 'You must be very proud of him.'

Dad grinned as water dripped off him. Mum simply smiled quietly. 'More relieved he's made it back safely . . .'

My three friends Clare, Charlotte and Jane formed a collective, beaming from ear to ear; they'd become very giggly with hoards of buff firemen to play with and, although wearing their kit, had somehow still managed to get soaking wet. The newly formed trio of the women's auxiliary fire service gave me a big excited hug. If A.A. Milne had bumped into them, there would have been three Tiggers in *Winnie the Pooh* instead of just the one.

'We got to use the hoses, we got to use the hoses! Did you see us soaking the bridge?'

Finally, with my family, friends and the second-in-command in tow, I walked up the gangplank of *President* and onto the deck. I was totally blown away; the deck was crammed with people. So many friends had turned up. It was very moving. Coming forward from the crowd was the Officer Commanding of *President*. The smart second-in-command stiffened, saluted and introduced me. At first she looked very grave and serious. I wasn't sure she liked having all this nonsense on her command. Then, there was a twinkle in her eye, she burst into a smile and shook me by the hand.

'Welcome to *President*, very well done. I'd like to offer you the Ward Room to celebrate with your friends. You deserve it, rowing all that way is a heck of an effort . . . and in a bath. Come in.'

I took to her immediately. I'd never been allowed in the Ward Room before. This was an honour and to have it for the night to celebrate was very kind.

It was a truly great evening, with people from all stages of the bath trip now colliding, reunited over drinks and laughter. I introduced Wendy and her husband to my mum and dad, met the people who'd been with my friend Rich on the QE II Bridge in Kent before finally owning up to Ollie and the Mumblers why I'd had to leave the field so fast that afternoon after the match.

With horns sounding, people shouting and cheering, Fire Ships going off, flags flying and Royal Navy saluting, the bath had come home to a most beautiful and peculiarly British celebration of the epic absurd. All the threads of my plumbing odyssey had come together as London celebrated one of the most eccentric happenings on the Thames in years. The bath had finally reached the finish.

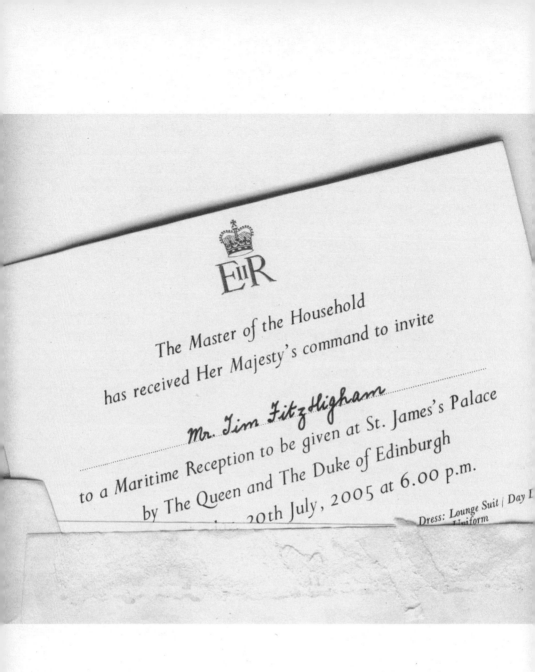

E II R

The Master of the Household
has received Her Majesty's command to invite

Mr. Tim FitzHigham

to a Maritime Reception to be given at St. James's Palace
by The Queen and The Duke of Edinburgh
20th July, 2005 at 6.00 p.m.

Dress: Lounge Suit / Day ...
Uniform

WRAPPED UP WARM IN THE ODCOMBIAN BLANKET

'It is the duty of everyone to protect those less fortunate than themselves.'

David Kent Anns

It is easier to teach piano to a swarm of bees than to attempt to Windsor-knot a tie while sprinting down Pall Mall. Running as fast as I could, one of England's formerly decent pieces of tailoring became a blur to onlookers as an errant tie flapped in the breeze behind me. I finally managed to get the short bit of my tie through the hole just as my phone rang. It was a cousin of mine.

'Hi Tim?'

'Yes.'

'It's me.'

'Hi, I can't talk for long, I'm late for the Palace thing . . .'

'I heard it was today. You're always late for everything. Could you not have made sure you were on time today for once? She is the Queen, you know.'

'I'm nearly there . . .'

I broke into a trot – the Aethaneum up ahead.

'Right ho, thought you should know, you're in the newspaper, there's a cartoon and everything . . .'

I stopped. 'What?'

'I'll read it, if you like. I'm not sure you've got time for all of it, so I'll just give you the best bits. It's under the headline "Bath-time at Buckingham Palace". "The Queen champions British explorers, no matter what frontier they push. Tomorrow, Tim FitzHigham will dine at Buckingham Palace . . ."'

'It's actually St James's and I'm not really dining as such, just sort of nibbling, really . . .'

'That's the least of your worries. You've obviously spoken to them as they quote you.'

'Yes, I remember talking to him when I was around Margate stuck in a storm. We talked about lots of stuff, the letter from the Queen, the paper boat, all sorts, he was a nice guy.'

'That bit's all fine . . .'

'What's the problem then?'

'Let me finish. "Tim's panicking as the only suit he owns is covered in horse manure."'

'D'oh! Me and my big mouth . . .'

'Great work, cuz.'

'What if the Palace have seen it? That could make it a tricky afternoon.'

'Have you had the suit cleaned?'

'Of course.'

'I shouldn't worry about the Palace, it's the *Independent*, I'd bet you five quid the Palace staff all read the *Telegraph*, except the socialists among them – they'll read the *Mail*! So no one will have seen it. Just thought you should know in case.'

'More alarmingly, what happens if my mother's seen it?'

'That's more of a worry.'

'Thanks for the heads-up, mate – what's the cartoon like?'

'Hilarious. It's you in a suit made of dung.'

'Oh good . . . hang on, why are you reading the *Independent*?'

'Remember why your grandfather always took the *Mirror*?'

'Erm . . .'

'It's always good to know what the other side are up to!'

'Oh . . . er . . . right . . . I'd better . . .'

'Yes, sure, off you go . . . have a great time.'

What other side? I left confusion aside and concentrated on other matters. I never thought there'd be a cartoon of me in a newspaper. I suspect like everyone who's ever had a cartoon of themselves in a paper, I couldn't wait to see it. However, before I could get to the newsstand there was the not-insignificant matter of the Royal reception I was late for. Cantering now, I finally completed my tie as I passed the Reform. Moments later I drew level with Crown Passage and rounded the corner into Marlborough Road. In a whirl, I pulled out my invite and cleared security, trotted along a few corridors, bounded up a gilded stairway and finally found myself in a red gilt-trimmed room across a large table from a member of the Palace staff.

Even though I must have looked smart, facing the gimlet-eyed gaze of a member of Her Majesty's finest, I felt scruffier than my old dog. There was a list of the people that were allowed into the Palace that day; I froze. I've hated lists since I first heard of them behind a desk in a small classroom in Derbyshire. Suddenly I was paralysed by not knowing which letter I'd be under. Stentorian tones emerged from the mouth beneath the gimlet eyes.

'Name?'

'Erm . . . I'm not really sure . . .'

'What?'

'Well, I could be under T for Tim or F or C for Channel, or something else.'

A cheerful-looking member of staff then emerged.

'You must be Tim FitzHigham, suit's looking good – you can't even smell the dung!'

My heart sank. 'Oh good, you've seen it . . .'

'Yes, very funny, this way.'

With a smile that brightened the room she pushed open a door at the end of the one we were in and suddenly in front of me was a room of people looking as nervous and excited as I felt.

'The boss will be along in a mo, someone will find you with refreshments . . .'

With that she handed me a very smart badge with my name on it and left the room. I looked around and, like an experienced croupier, shuffled my feet. I was in the first of three interconnecting rooms. All of them were exquisitely decorated in the same red and gilt colourings of the room before. Candelabras larger than small children sat near the windows and everything glistened beneath the enormous sparkling chandeliers. The furthest room from me contained a throne. It was obvious to even the dimmest intellect that if it was a palace you were searching for, this was a pretty good place to look. I whispered to myself, 'We're not in Kansas now, Toto . . .'

A naval officer in uniform spun round. 'What?'

'Oh . . . er . . . nothing, I was just . . . er . . .'

Not sure how to explain I was momentarily playing a small girl called Dorothy, I thought I'd better try something else. 'Sorry, hi, I'm Tim . . .'

We started chatting away about the Navy, how long he'd been in and what ships he'd been on. While we were doing this I caught sight of the Queen across the room. The good thing about being a rower in a room of sailors was that I was by far the tallest man there. I'm not freakishly tall; it's just that sailors are traditionally quite short. My eye halted and sprung to attention: gazing at Her Majesty, all other noise became a blur. It was a lot to take in. Just across the room from me was a person I'd sincerely admired since I was tiny. Not only had I admired Her, my entire family admired Her and had been trying for years to die for Her in a variety of imaginative ways. Before Her they'd been trying to die for Her father, grandfather etc., and the ideals they believed in.

I became predictably nervous but also, and this was baffling, a huge feeling of protectiveness swept over me. I was sure that the room was teeming with Royal Protection Officers filling every crack in every door, lurking behind every curtain, banging their heads beneath every tablecloth but a strange feeling appeared in my stomach: I felt protective of the Queen. I've had the feeling before around my grandmother, sister (when she's sick), mother and also when friends of mine have been pregnant, but quite why it hit me then was weird. Across the room, above the heads of the others, the Queen saw me and seemed to smile at me. I could just have projected that on to Her in my own mind; she could just have been smiling at the room decoration in general; not knowing Her well, it was impossible to tell. Instinctively, I bowed my head in Her direction. Looking back up from bowing my head I saw Her smile again. The first piece of instinctive pre-decimal etiquette I'd knee-jerked into had seemingly been correct. I turned my gaze back down to the officer in uniform; he'd obviously just asked me a question that I'd missed.

'I'm sorry?'

'It says "cross-Channel rower" on your badge, what did you do? Other than the obvious of course . . .'

This was a question I'd been trying really hard to avoid. In the room waiting patiently to meet the Queen were the truly great heroes of current British Maritime. Men like the First Sea Lord, the Second Sea Lord, round the world yachtsmen and -women and the heads of various illustrious maritime bodies, the Coastguard, RNLI and other senior organisations. I had rowed the Channel in a piece of ablution equipment. The longer I could keep that secret, the better.

'Erm . . .' My mind floundered around desperate for something to say other than mention the bath, 'Erm . . .' This was getting awkward. '. . . I sort of rowed the Channel in a bath . . .'

The officer looked stunned. 'What?'

'I sort of took a bath and rowed the Channel . . .'

'That was you?'

'Er . . . yes . . .'

'You'd better come with me, She wants to see you.'

'What?'

It turned out that the smartly dressed naval man was an equerry at the Palace. Equerries are serving military officers who attend on the members of the Royal Family.

Suddenly, from loitering near a curtain at the back, I found myself at the front of the queue to be presented to the Queen. The equerry handed a card with my name on to one of the stunning ladies-in-waiting who surrounded the Queen and whispered something in Her ear before withdrawing to stand smartly beside me.

One of the many things my grandfather decided I needed to grasp at the age of five was a total command of absolutely correct royal etiquette. We would spend many happy hours in one of his enormous greenhouses with him drilling me in the correct way to greet and address various members of the Royal Family, Ducal lines and all aristocratic stations south. As the Queen was often unavailable for these important tutorials, she would normally be played by one of his prize marrows or a large pumpkin.

During the second local difficulty, as my grandfather called it, or, as it's more commonly known by history, World War II, my grandfather was running back to barracks after some military exercise or other. He was running alone; the ability to act as an individual was one of the hallmarks of the regiment he was in. A large black car, a Rolls-Royce or something similar, glided past him before coming to a stop up ahead of him in the road. The driver's door opened and a man in a smart uniform got out, approached him and demanded to see his papers. My grandfather presented them. The man inspected them and went to the back window of the car. The man in the smart uniform opened the back door of the car and out stepped Queen Mary (wife of George V[15], grandmother of Elizabeth II). Shocked, Grandfather followed the rigid codes of etiquette that had been taught to him and the Queen-Empress was kind enough to offer him a lift back to barracks in Her car. Sitting in the back of the Royal car the first thing She asked him was, 'How is the war going?'

---

[15]By an odd coincidence, the man whose travel bath I'd tried to auction the previous year.

He looked at Her and always said his eyes widened. He felt that in one question She had taken the entire fate of civilised Europe and rested it on his shoulders. At the time my grandfather was just a young soldier and his grasp of high command policy would have been sketchy but he did his best to enlighten Her Majesty as to the things he knew and the morale of the regiment. He was a great storyteller and the bit at the end was my favourite. He got on well with Queen Mary and they chatted for quite some time. Before the car stopped he'd been ahead in the exercise but due to his delightful conversation with the Queen-Empress he arrived back at barracks much later than the rest of the regiment. When questioned by his senior officer as to why he was so late, he replied that he'd been unavoidably delayed as he'd got a lift with Queen Mary in Her Rolls-Royce. The senior officer looked him squarely in the eye and said, 'Come on David, if you're going to make excuses at least make them believable.'

The moral of this story, he felt, was that you never knew when absolutely correct Royal etiquette would be needed. He clearly resolved then that his grandson would never be found wanting, as the marrows and I later found out.

Now faced with the Queen and not a marrow, suddenly my lessons in the greenhouses came good. Never speak to the Queen until She speaks to you. Never ask Her questions. The first time you speak to Her, call Her 'Your Majesty', after that always 'Ma'am'. Never say, 'It's a pleasure to meet you,' it is taken as read that it's a pleasure to meet the Queen. Never shake hands with the Queen; that could be correct or could just have been as the marrow had no arms. If She offers you Her hand, touch it only briefly. Never turn your back on Her for a second and bow from the chest or, if you have a bad back, the neck. Of course, like any good set of rules there are hundreds of exceptions, for example, as a Waterman, you *are* allowed to touch the arm of the sovereign in a special tradition going back centuries. There were a whole lot of rules and exceptions like this that I'd been taken through day after long happy summer day in the greenhouses and that's why grandparents are great. I bowed at the chest. The Queen offered me Her hand.

'So you rowed the Channel did you?'

'Your Majesty, how kind of you to ask, yes I did . . . in a bathtub.'

The Queen has very stunning blue eyes and on hearing this they distinctly twinkled and She broke into a smile. For the next ten to 20 minutes we giggled with each other. She is a very funny lady.

One moment the conversation was straight out of a Bond film.

'A copper bath, with a floor, it must have weighed half a tonne.'

I smoothed my hair slightly, not wishing to miss the chance. 'It was actually only a third of a tonne, Ma'am, but it was still really rather heavy.'

The next minute it was out of the *Goon Show*.

'Did you not think of putting a sail on the bath and sailing it?'

'I did consider a shower curtain, Ma'am, but I couldn't decide on the colour . . .'

Towards the end of our time together I thanked Her for Her constant support in my attempts to raise money for charity. She smiled and modestly mumbled something about how She wasn't sure exactly why Her support had helped but if it had, She was pleased. Very kindly, She thanked me for coming before She moved on to talk to the Head of the Coastguard and I was left with a stunning lady-in-waiting wearing a beautifully cut pink dress.

'Thanks for coming, Tim.'

'Erm . . . I was just very shocked to be asked.'

'We don't often get to see the boss laugh like that.'

'Erm . . . my pleasure.'

'And may I say, very well done.'

Then she was gone too and I was left, feeling just a little shaken (and not unstirred) with only a glass of Bollinger for company. It's not every day you get to see the most easily recognisable face in the world looking directly into your own. The face I'd just been looking at is on the stamps, I reflected as I admired the taste of whoever had chosen the Bollinger. All the marrows in Berkshire hadn't prepared me for this. I tried to get out of the limelight that surrounded the Queen only to find I'd been expertly guided by the officer equerry into the company of the Duke of Edinburgh.

His Royal Highness initially appeared to be under the impression that I was some sort of war hero. Initially, I put this down to vagueness but then realised it was actually due to some very shrewd observation by the Duke. I was wearing an old family tie of some long-disbanded regiment, which my great-grandfather had worn throughout the First World War. The Duke recognised the tie instantly and was clearly wondering why I was wearing it. Sheepishly I explained that I had been asked to attend the event not for being a war hero but for rowing the English Channel in a bath. The Duke looked stunned and thundered, 'What?'

'I rowed the English Channel in a bath ... well, more a sort of bathroom ...'

'What?'

I could see he thought I was teasing him. Behind his eyes I perceived he was trying to work out how best to deal with me. Any minute I feared the cantankerous, irascible spirit for which the Duke is so famous would obliterate me more completely than fast-flowing lava. Like an Exocet missile his eyes locked on to mine. I gulped like a compromised ship about to take the final hit. Luckily for me just as he was about to bury me, the First Sea Lord appeared at his arm.

'The tragic thing is – it's actually true; he did row the Channel in a bath.'

The Duke smiled, then chuckled, and then he laughed before swinging into the conversation with gusto. He asked lots of questions about the weather, journey round Kent, speed of the bath, type of oars etc. Somewhere on the other side of London, Dom must have been beaming with pride as I trotted out all the information the Duke requested, none of which I'd have known without Dom. The Duke turned out to be a very funny, clever and knowledgeable man. It's impossible on meeting him to reconcile the dynamic, polite, kind and hilarious man with the image of him I'd read about in the press.

After a while, the Duke and Sea Lord left me to resume my post near the curtain and practice foot shuffling. I took another sip of Bollinger and mused that it was a very surreal day. A youngish man standing next to me said hello and we got into conversation. It wasn't until we'd exchanged a few stories and made each other laugh a few times that I realised the funny, charming, mischievous man in front of me was Prince Edward. Either he was on the best form of his life that day or has been as much abused in the popular imagination as his father. He was so very funny.

The Queen was joined by Prince Philip and they left the room. After they'd left I made to leave too but on my way out a man approached me.

'Hello Tim, I'm Brigadier Black, one of the equerries . . .'

His name wasn't Black but I can't remember what it was, also he may not have said equerry but some other Palace posting. I would blame discretion but probably a more likely explanation is the excellent Bollinger. What was certain was that he was a senior member of Palace staff and a brigadier.

'. . . just thought you'd like to know: when the boss left the room, She turned to Prince Philip and said She thought She'd just met the maddest man in Her Kingdom. Well done, and thanks again for making Her smile.'

As I finished the day barside at a hotel in St James's (predictably, after having had to spend part of the day as Bond, sipping one of London's finest Martinis) I knew what line would replace James Cracknell's to be written on my tomb.

In the days that followed the bath trip various letters arrived including one from Number Ten signed 'with best wishes' and 'yours sincerely Tony Blair'. I also had a very kind letter from the chairman of Comic Relief. It seemed that a single blood-inducing piece of stupidity I'd thought up in the bath had made a lot more people smile than I thought it would. The bath had completed around 200 miles from France to Tower Bridge and the timstub.com website had received in excess of 50,000 hits.

Matthew Pinsent, James Cracknell and Steve Williams did treat the rest of the world as they had treated the bath and won gold in the Olympics at Athens. The margin was much closer and there was no time for pitch and putt.

A mere six days after stepping off the bath under Tower Bridge in London I stepped onto the stage at the Pleasance Theatre in Edinburgh. Would the audiences be as relieved as the Pleasance artistic director that I'd finally turned up?

I'd had no time to prepare the show or try it out. Most comics like to start trying out material in March, before beginning the process of honing it until the Festival in August. I'd had four days to recover and tend to my wounds, one day to pack my stuff and another to drive north to Scotland. During this, there had not been much time to think of something to say.

I walked out on stage with no clue what to say other than a

vague idea I should tell the bath story in my own way as truthfully as possible. In my undecided mind, the show would be an acoustic stand-up storytelling hour called *In the Bath: Unplugged*, as I hate show titles with puns in them. Still haunted by the critical mauling I'd taken the year before I was very apprehensive about doing anything but the slot had been booked and it would have been very bad manners of me to have wasted it.

The first show was a very curious experience. I arrived on stage with a couple of sheets of paper to help me remember the thread of the story and started to talk. I finished telling the stupidity of the truth before the audience sat totally silent at the end. The CD of music that was meant to kick in had failed. The lights went down and I realised a tear had rolled down my face. That doesn't normally happen to me in shows that are meant to be funny. I stood silent on stage not really sure exactly what I'd just said before one person started to clap. Almost immediately the whole audience started to clap, before standing up. I stood frozen and faced a standing ovation. People on the front row even got on stage and gathered around me in a big group hug. It was a comedy show that made people happy to cry at the end. Before I knew what had happened the bath show had kindly become critics' choice in the *Evening Standard,* the *Guardian, London Metro* and *Edinburgh Three Weeks* and sold out for the rest of the run at Edinburgh. The show was not eligible for most of the awards, as I fell foul of various eligibility rules because I'd been stuck out at sea and missed bits of the Festival, but amazingly in the final week it won the *Three Weeks* Editor's Award. *In the Bath: Unplugged* has now played in hundreds of theatres, barns, places and palaces all over the UK and abroad. From the first day, there's not been a music CD at the end. Some mistakes work better than the plans they destroy.

What about the bath herself? After the incredible reception at Tower Bridge, Uncle Bill Colley arrived the next morning to tow the bath back up to Mark in Richmond. I wanted somewhere for the bath to go that would be warm and comfortable for her but after phone calls to every museum or gallery I could think of, it was obvious that no one had the room or inclination to take in the star of our double act. The bath spent a year falling into disrepair on a mooring near Richmond, of interest to only the most dedicated sailors, rowers and people that came to the bath shows. Throughout all of that time I kept trying to find someone to take the bath. Despite all my efforts nothing seemed to be possible. Then one day my phone rang.

'Tim, it's Ben at the National Maritime Museum in Cornwall.'

The National Maritime Museum in Cornwall is one of my favourites. From 2003 to 2007 it was home to the paper boat, so I'd got to know the staff quite well.

'We're staging a new exhibition called "Mad Dogs and Englishmen" and we were wondering if we could have the bath.'

From a dilapidated state at her mooring in Richmond, *Lilibet II* was plucked for stardom. Many people: Mark, the apprentices, the restoration team at the National Maritime Museum and I, worked really hard to clean up and restore her to the shining state she was when she first floated off the boat ramp in 2004. After all the hard work, in late 2006, *Lilibet II* took her place as the centrepiece of the new exhibition. It was a lovely moment to pan around the main gallery of the National Maritime Museum, Cornwall, looking at all the famous mastheads and see, sparkling in the middle of them, a Thomas Crapper showerhead.

It is difficult to say exactly how much money the bath project raised for Comic Relief as, incredibly, in the years since I stepped off the bath money has still been coming into the fund, but the last time anyone checked it was in excess of £30,000. Wherever the bath is, there is normally a Comic Relief collecting bucket not too far away.

After its narrow scrape with international fraud Simon and I decided not to auction off George V's travel bath. We were both uneasy about it even before the attempted fraud as we felt something that stunning should be enjoyed by as many people as possible. We took the decision to make it available for everyone to see and so it's now on display at the small ablution museum near the head offices of Thomas Crapper & Company.

Just as Shackleton had been knighted and Nelson made a viscount for their heroic deeds, I was made Waterman to the Mayor and Unitary Authority of Swindon. Other honours and laurels followed swiftly after that. I was made Commodore of Sudbury Town Quay in the County of Suffolk. Normally the Commodore of a Quayside is responsible for the safe landing of large ocean-going vessels; since Sudbury is 25 miles inland, my main problem is the car parking. Although I do get a rather natty pennant (flag) that I can fly from any ship or boat I happen to be on, and a big hat. If something is worth doing, it's worth doing wearing a very big hat.

In Selby, a stunning market town in Yorkshire, I was given a title first used in the time of William Rufus (son of William the Conqueror): Pittancer of Selby in the Ridings (which sounds like something out of Tolkien). The title of Pittancer gives me various medieval rights and privileges. On Maundy Thursday every year I attend the Pittancer's service in the Abbey in Selby. After it, I am obliged to give the Prebandry of the Abbey (the priest who runs the place) one pound in order to help him maintain himself throughout the year. In addition to this, if there are any stray Benedictine monks found wandering in the Abbey grounds on that day, I am obliged to give them the medieval measurement of a pittance of eggs and cheese to feed themselves. My main concern every year is that a coach trip of Benedictine monks will randomly happen to be passing through Selby that day and I'll have to cook up the world's largest cheesy omelette in the market place.

In 2006 I was asked by the UK Environment Agency to team up with the TV impressionist Alistair McGowan. We were both made spokespeople for the United Nations World Environment Day. My part of this was to try and get people to spend less time in the bath and take a shower instead.

I was really overwhelmed by the kindness of the various Mayors, Town Councils and Boroughs that wanted to show their support for the bath project. To be a spokesperson with the UN and Environment Agency was something I never thought possible but still there was one even greater honour in store.

Simon phoned up from Thomas Crapper & Company.

'Tim, in honour of the Channel crossing by bath, we at Thomas Crapper and Company are going to release a commemorative lavatory named after you: *The FitzHigham*.'

Finally, my family seat: I was flushed with pride, couldn't get it out of my *cistern*; this was the zenith of toilet humour. A loo named after a fool, Simon had created genuine Comic Relief.

'It will have a little picture of you rowing the Channel in the bath, inlaid into the porcelain for people to aim at . . .'

Simon believes that *The FitzHigham* is only the second commemorative lavatory issued in the entire history of sanitaryware and he's a relentlessly enthusiastic sanarack.

'The first commemorative lavatory was produced in celebration of Queen Victoria's Jubilee . . .'

The FitzHigham turned out to look as stunning as it was eccentric. When people buy them, some of the money goes to Comic Relief. All Thomas Crapper loos have the company seal on them with 'Made in Great Britain' written round the edges of it. All except *The FitzHigham*; Simon left an 'e' off, so it reads 'Mad in Great Britain' instead. A few weeks after the first one was made I got a call from Simon.

'You've got a very strange bunch of friends. They all appear to want to go to the loo on you. I've got a waiting list for them now . . .'

The official position of the French government has never changed. Their position is very clear: to them, officially, the bath crossing of the English Channel never took place. The logic they use to justify this staggeringly silly position is that if it had happened, the French Navy would have been duty-bound to arrest me. Gallic logic dictates that as I was not arrested, the bath crossing must not have taken place.

It is a customary courtesy to any foreign nation in whose waters you find yourself to fly a small national flag of that country next to the larger one of your own. For the first failed attempt to cross the English Channel in the bath I happily flew a small courtesy *Tricolore* with my larger Red Ensign when in French waters. That *Tricolore* was lost in the storm during the first attempt. Due to the very unhelpful behaviour of the French government, with sadness at the death of *fraternité*, I refused to fly the *Tricolore* again. The successful crossing and subsequent trip round Kent to Tower Bridge was made with no French courtesy flag.

My time in the bath taught me something that I have been trying hard to share: we live in a nation where you can say, 'I'm going to do something really, really hard – like climb Everest, row the English Channel or run to Timbuktu.' Rather than being encouraging, the great British people will stoically stare you in the eye and say, 'It's not that hard.'

Or, 'What are you complaining about?'

Or, 'Get a hair cut.'

Perhaps the last one is just what they say to me. These discussions often carry on even after people have completed their achievements and fulfilled their dreams. There seems to be a tendency to look to discredit rather than support. But, if you say to those same stoic, staring-eyed Britons, 'I'm going to do something really, really hard – like climb Everest, row the English Channel or run to Timbuktu . . . *dressed up as a badger, wearing a diving outfit, or in a bathtub*', then they'll back you to the hilt. I'm not sure what it says about us as a nation in the 21st century but I offer it up as something I've found to be undeniably true. However, what this wonderful trait in our national character does mean is that if a Briton attempts something absurdly stupid with the unerring enthusiasm of a manic five-year-old they will be supported, encouraged and given every assistance the country has to offer.

It was September after the Edinburgh Festival had finished and somewhere in a pub in Hertfordshire I sat down. In front of me was the pint I'd rowed 170 extra miles to win.

'There you go, mate. Well earned.'

'Thanks.'

As I wrapped my lips around the cool glass and the delicious brown liquid hit the back of my throat I closed my eyes. Sometimes attempting the absurdly stupid can help achieve the impossible.

Afterword

By Simon Kirby
Managing Director of
Thomas Crapper & Company

When Tim telephoned to explain his ridiculous idea, we assumed that my friend Ronnie Wootton was on the line. Ronnie is a well-known character in the architectural salvage trade who delights in making spoof telephone calls. My long-suffering secretary, a Czech girl called Radka, has dealt with many of his ludicrous enquiries, each delivered in one of a variety of accents. In addition he normally gives an 'interesting' name, for example: 'Edward Heath'; 'Rhett Butler'; 'Harry Lime' or 'Don Keebles'. (Say the latter out loud.)

Therefore when she heard the moniker 'Tim FitzHigham', she perhaps assumed it was another example of British humour. Crapper & Co seems to attract eccentrics like an antiques shop attracts VAT inspectors, so I expect it was inevitable that Tim would pitch up here one day. Warrick (our General Manager) and I decided instantly to support Tim in his heroic and very British endeavour, so we did what we could, having explained that we were rather financially over-committed.

We are based as far from the coast as it is possible to be within these islands, and none of us has any maritime experience. Hence we had no idea how terribly dangerous was his plan; had we known, we would have tried to dissuade him!

Not that we could have succeeded. Even during the grim period after his first attempt, it was clear to us that he would try again. This despite his having been confounded (and nearly killed) by violent storms and the spite of bureaucrats. I am sure I would not survive even the training so I cannot begin to comprehend spending two years on such a project, including the performance of TWO Herculean rowing feats in hostile conditions. Whenever I see film of the first storm, I have to look away. Then I take two aspirin, and having prostrated myself, grasp the floorboards until the giddiness subsides.

The eccentric Tim FitzHigham is an inspiration: he accepts daunting challenges, he stands up for his beliefs and principles, he entertains everyone around him (as well as the paying public) and he raises huge sums for charities. For us, it was an honour to be of some assistance. Thank heaven there are still folk like him.

I am concerned that there are simply not enough of these people, so I decided to develop the impromptu declaration I made upon Tim's victorious embarkation of HMS *President*. Crapper & Co have been holding discussions with the Art Fund, the Tate Modern and English Heritage. Our joint proposal is that after he has been formally listed (Grade One, definitely) then that nice Mr Hirst will be commissioned to mount him in a Victorian bath full of aspic, and thus he will be preserved for posterity.

Sorry, Tim. I am aware that this is a little hard on you. But remember: once again, you are doing it for Britain!

THE APPENDICES

You've made it. Hope you enjoyed the book. I thought I'd include a few appendices – think of them as DVD extras for a book. So you can either read them or just turn off now . . . up to you, but if you are going to turn off, may I take this moment to thank you for reading my story. Thank you.

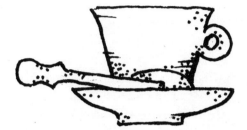

Appendix A

A WORD FROM CHRIS GILMARTIN

Chris was on the support boat for the successful attempt and has kindly written this so it's over to him for his bit . . .

'Here's how I remember the bath affair. I was having an entertaining year off work, meeting up with Tim. During one long inebriated afternoon I agreed to help. I have a vague recollection of a few false starts, with Tim explaining the various weather, tide, crew issues . . . there seemed to be quite a few issues . . . but then there was a call where Tim said it all looked good.

'In Richmond I was introduced to a most important activity in boatyards: that of confused waiting. Eventually Tim backed the battered diesel estate car and trailer down the slip ramp and rowed the bath over to it, where the boatyard chaps manhandled it onto the trailer. I had to drive the car back up the ramp. Doing a hill start in an unfamiliar car with a third-of-a-tonne bath trying to pull you backwards into the Thames isn't recommended, but we got away with it, and a scant three hours late we were away. Stopping only to buy a mobile phone (previous one "got wet" which seemed a bit ominous) we headed down to Kent.

'We arrived in Folkestone, put the bath in the water and checked into the Hotel of Doom. The clientele looked like zombies, and the whole place had a faintly bizarre air about it, as if nobody actually expected paying guests to turn up. We were running very late though; I think we got to sleep about midnight, after setting alarms for 3 a.m.

'The morning started with Tim wolfing Weetabix as I prepped a bag for the support boat. The part where sunrise started was beautiful. Following this, things on the support boat settled into a routine. Essentially: have a cup of tea, chat, have another cup of tea, chat, and every now and then a gingernut biscuit (good for seasickness, Tim said) to break things up a bit.

'There were times when the sea was glassy smooth, and times we were getting bounced up and down so much that people got seasick. First it was cold, later everyone got sunburnt. Conditions were changeable, and at one point it looked like Tim was caught by the tide and would be swept too far south.

'Towards the end, I shouted "row like a bastard!" Clearly motivated by my exceptional coaching, he pulled through and all of a sudden it looked possible, probable, that he would make it. The shouts of support grew more strident. We'd helped him get this far, we weren't going to quit now, and neither was he.

'After about nine hours, he made it to the French coast. Unfortunately for him I think everyone shook Tim's hands, which probably hurt a bit. I recall he was unable to hold a phone, he seemed slightly delirious and rambling (yes, more than normal), and obviously overjoyed. Back in Folkestone we'd missed high tide so were unable to get the bath out of the water so Tim and I dropped into a local pub for a few well-earned beers.

'Tim hadn't changed out of his rowing outfit and it's fair to say this attracted attention. Attention turned into a rapt audience as Tim explained what he'd been doing that day. The locals turned out to be impressed, and Tim promptly recruited them to assist getting the bath out of the water at closing time. How Tim thought we'd have managed if we'd not chanced on a pub, I've no idea. I'm not entirely convinced he does either! Lashing it to the trailer was much harder than before as, due to a leak, the pontoons were half full of water.

'A short time later the phone call came: we were good to go again. I elected not to spend another day confined in the support boat, but instead drive the car and trailer up the coast taking pictures and videoing on the way.

'I was drinking tea then figured I should check out Deal before Tim arrived. As I got to the shore, there was Tim and the support boat, making great headway. Too much headway in fact, he was really moving. I ran shouting for people to get out of the way. I thundered down to the end of the pier, nearly fumbled the camcorder into the water, and caught the sight of Tim majestically sweeping past to a smattering of applause from some little old ladies.

'At Ramsgate there was some further slipway fun: this one really was slippery. I proudly donned my Wellingtons and waded in to assist. My Wellingtons leaked. We then went to the pub for a pint.

'I went back to my year off as whenever I was free Tim couldn't row, and when he could I wasn't around. In the end I had to head off before Tim made it to Tower Bridge. Tim finally finished his epic journey just after I'd started mine, albeit with more traditional transports . . . and much drier feet.'

THE BATH AND HISTORY

When I started rowing my bath I wasn't aware of the unsung but pivotal role in human history of that lowly piece of plumbing. While lowering our buttocks, how many of us have realised the bath or associated sanitaryware below us has been used variously as a grizzly weapon of death, kingmaker and even the hand of God. Things nearly ended badly for me. I believe the reason I survived is to put the record straight. Here are some of the most important times that humble ablution equipment has shaped the course of human history.

Eglon

The first time the lavatory was definitely used as an instrument of death is not recorded. Perhaps two cavemen got into a fight over which was the softest loo roll. However, the really brutal bit of the Bible (Judges 3:12–30), before God invented political correctness and mercy came to Him, has the lurid tale of Eglon, the very fat King of Moab who conquered Israel and went to the lavatory there for 18 years.

The Israelites wore out handkerchiefs crying to God for a deliverer.

God said the deliverer must be left-handed. Ehud was the son of Gera the Benjamite (isn't that a type of yeast-based sandwich spread?), a flourishing lefthander and the school lazy-rounders champion.

The Israelites sent Ehud to Eglon with a nice pressie to say how much they enjoyed him ruling them despotically. It was a double-edged sword a foot-and-a-half long. Eglon was not suspicious at this. Ehud said he had a message from God. Eglon was bursting to defecate so Eglon and Ehud went to the loo together. The last time anyone even mentioned double-edged swords and coming to the loo with me I discovered he'd also been putting Rohypnol in my Guinness for the previous two hours. But again Eglon was not suspicious. Eglon sat to evacuate his bowels and Ehud stabbed him so deep the handle went in after the blade and Eglon's blubber closed around it. Ehud scarpered out of the window.

By the time Eglon's servants crashed the door in, Ehud had taken up the trumpet in Seirah. After playing solos in a Dixieland jazz combo he led the armies of Israel against the people of Moab and murdered about 10,000 of them. Israel then took control of Moab and the bathroom had altered history's epic ebb for ever.

Agamemnon

Greek history was changed by one bath. Agamemnon was a classic Greek classical hero from one of the most distinguished families in Greece: notable ancestors included a murderer, a rapist, several cousin marriages and at least three raging pederasts. He became King of Mycenae and possibly Argos too. He'd ordered the Kingship of Mycenae from a catalogue but the one from Argos came by mistake. He wasn't sure if the mix up had occurred at the post office or in dispatch so ruled them both just in case.

He married Clytemnestra who was, in ancient Greek terms, a bit of a hottie (she does look quite stunning on the vases). Things were going well before Agamemnon said, 'Someone has to work in this relationship, darling,' and left to lead the Greeks in the Trojan War. It took a while and he missed his wife, so saying to himself 'what happens in war, stays in war' took a doomed prophetess called Cassandra for a bit of fun on the dark nights.

Eventually the war finished and he and Cassandra returned home to find Clytemnestra had also been a bit lonesome so had been ravaging Aegisthus.

Aegisthus was a sort of a cousin of Agamemnon's – with that much incest, bigamy, rape, murder and pederasty in the family, most people were. Aegisthus thought the best way to sort it out was to have Agamemnon round for tea. Nothing is ever so bad after a nice cup of tea. It was a long journey to Aegisthus's and Agamemnon fancied a bath. Clytemnestra fancied Aegisthus so went to the bathroom, seductively popped a blanket on Agamemnon as he dozed in the bath and brutally murdered him with an axe.

Cassandra the doomed prophetess waited for Agamemnon to finish in the bath, again cursing the mix up at the labour exchange. She'd actually applied to be a normal prophetess but they'd ticked the wrong box and she ended up a doomed one instead. Clytemnestra came out of the bathroom and killed Cassandra. 'The lives of doomed prophetesses never end well,' thought Clytemnestra as she and Aegisthus ruled Mycenae until family tradition got out of control in a party game and her son Orestes savagely murdered them both.

Seneca the Younger

Son of Seneca the Elder, Seneca the Younger was one of the greatest orators, statesman and stoic philosophers of Rome.

In his writings Seneca the Younger emphasised the need to live a moral life. In his life he slept with anything that moved: women, men, livestock and the wives of his friends being his favourites.

Eventually after a life of chronic excess he got caught up in the Pisonian Conspiracy – a plot to kill Nero who'd gone a bit far even for a Roman Emperor. Nero caught the conspirators and ordered his loyal friend Seneca to do the decent thing and slit his wrists.

Seneca had led such a life of excess that slitting his wrists didn't kill him; the blood (mainly alcohol) came out too slowly which only caused him minor irritation. With wrists bleeding Seneca then drank poison, which didn't work either, as it tasted better than the home brew at his local. He then jumped into a hot bath in an attempt to scald himself to death. That failed so he used the hot water to try and make the blood flow faster. This didn't work. Seneca next tried drowning himself. Even that didn't work. Slitting his wrists, downing poison, burning himself to death and drowning himself had failed. Finally he accidentally suffocated on the steam rising from the hot bath while trying to drown himself again.

Commodus

Lucius Aelius Aurelius Commodus Augustus Herculeus Romanus Exsuperatorius Amazonius Invictus Felix Pius (or Commodus as he was known to his cousin-mum) was the last of the Nervan-Antonian dynasty of Roman Emperors. Like all great Emperors, instead of eight great-grandparents he made do with six. He's the one played by Joaquin Phoenix in the film *Gladiator* with Russell Crowe. There's a few things in the film that don't totally reflect history but one major one that we must correct here.

Previous Roman Emperors had married horses but in 192 AD Commodus went madder than the rest. He re-named Rome the 'Colonia Lucia Annia Commodiana' and put defenceless wounded soldiers and people with no feet in the arena and clubbed them to death believing they were giants.

The Romans had had enough. Marrying horses was encouraged in Emperors, changing the name of Rome and beating unarmed amputees was not. As if to prove the Romans right, the Temple of Vesta burnt down. No one was anywhere near it with the matches, all of them said so. Commodus held Plebian games and had a Swan Vesta amnesty. He fought as a gladiator every afternoon. It was a bad year for the bookies as it was impossible for him to lose and treason for them not to give odds on him.

Eventually the bookies plotted to get rid of him. They poisoned his food but Commodus simply threw it up. The Romans remembered the trouble they'd had with Seneca Jr so decided to rely on the old failsafe.

In a tradition still alive and well in certain hotels in Rome, Commodus was sharing a bath with a nude wrestler called Narcissus, who was in the pay of the bookies. Commodus and Narcissus were on the third round of 'hunt the soap' when Narcissus strangled him to death.

All statues of him were toppled and Rome became Rome again thanks to two naked men wrestling in the bath. This didn't make the final cut of the film and they went with the slushy historically inaccurate stuff in the arena instead.

Elagabalus

Following the 'if it ain't broke . . .' school of politics, Elagabalus was another Roman Emperor who died in the bathroom. He was as bad and as mad as Commodus. Whereas Commodus offended Rome as a gladiator in the ring, Elagabalus offended Rome with an entirely different ring, working as a prostitute in the temples of Rome, taking all comers. His granny eventually had enough of this and had him murdered in the loo with his mum Julia Soaemias before replacing him as Emperor with another of his cousins less inclined to prostitution.

James the First

James I was King of Scotland from 1406-ish to 1437 (not officially crowned in 1406 but 1424. Easter was late that year). In 1437, on a routine trip to the bathroom while staying with some monks, Sir Robert Graham and a bunch of people battered on the loo door to kill him. A lady-in-waiting bravely stuck her arm through the clasps where the door bolt should have been and the King jumped into the loo to escape through the sewer. Loos didn't have U-bends in those days. Unfortunately for James he was a big fan of tennis.

He kept losing tennis balls down a drain near the tennis court so had the drain outlet blocked up. To his horror it turned out to be the outlet of the very drain he was trying to escape in. Stuck down the loo in the sewer, Robert Graham and the others brought his life to a very messy end.

Marat

Perhaps the most famous of all bath-based deaths. Jean-Paul Marat was born in Switzerland but became a great mate of Robespierre and gamely joined in with the French Revolution. Marat had to spend hours each day when he wasn't running France in the bath due to a mysterious skin complaint.

At that time things were more confused in Paris than usual and trying to simplify anyone's belief was impossible. The young Charlotte Corday, a Girondin (in favour of democratic revolution) with Royalist sympathies, used the old rouse from Ehud in the Bible and arrived at Marat's house with a message for him. She knew it wouldn't work if she said it was from God as the Revolutionaries weren't keen on Him. Cunningly she said it was from the townspeople of Caen. Marat never stopped thinking about politics or tottie so let her into the bathroom. She stabbed him to death. The French have been wary of baths ever since. Luckily the very famous artist Jacques-Louis David happened to be in Marat's bathroom at the time too and painted the most famous picture of a bath-based death in history.

Other important historical events involving bath.

Show-business people have had an even worse time with bathrooms than Roman Emperors.

The great comedian Lenny Bruce was found dead in the bathroom of an overdose. Charlie Chaplin's son, imaginatively called Charlie Chaplin Jr, also an actor, died in his grandma's bathroom. Judy Garland died in the bath of an overdose. Jim Morrison, the Doors singer, died in a bath in Paris of unknown causes. Elvis Presley died in the bathroom of Graceland of a heart attack: although he's been sighted and cited as a bathroom attendant many times since.

That bath . . .

As the world's leading bathtub mariner, there's one bath that people always mention: history's most positive event involving plumbing.

King Hiero II of Syracuse had a new crown made in the shape of a laurel wreath. He wanted to know if it was made of solid gold or if the goldsmith had tricked him. At the time people could only measure the density of things if they were cube-shaped. The King didn't want to melt his new crown into a cube but was troubled by the shifty-looking goldsmith. Luckily the King was related to the greatest mathematician of all time: Archimedes.

Archimedes was taking a bath at the time and had realised, as he got in, that the water rose relative to his mass, discovering displacement. This effect could be used to determine the volume of the crown and therefore its density after it had been weighed. The more cheap metals had been added to the gold, the lower the density of the crown. Keen to tell his cousin, he jumped out of the bath and ran through the streets shouting 'Eureka' or 'εύρηκα!' in Greek. Being a maths genius he was tolerated by the King, dripping wet and stark-naked in the throne room. The goldsmith had been cheating and Archimedes was given a towel. Archimedes is quiet on what happened to the goldsmith but the fairly smart money is on his business not going awfully well after that. The very smart money is always on a horse called Flirty Jill.

A COCKTAIL LIST . . .

BIBO ERGO SUM

It's drinking things like these that led to the messy trip you've just read about. I'm not an alcoholic, I drink less than my doctor; but seeing his corpulent, heart-attack-primed form rolling around the surgery leads me to think that drinking in moderation is probably the best way to be. However, that said, here are a couple of belters for you to enjoy if you want to end up like my doctor. If I had a dream job it would be being a booze chef.

Shandy

I like ginger a lot. Between capsizing at university, losing the myriad temp jobs mentioned earlier and attempting to float in a paper boat, I lived abroad. A lot of my time there was spent farming. Ginger was one of the things that grew on the farm. It's also good for seasickness.

Before the Second World War if you ordered a shandy in a pub it would be made of beer and ginger ale. Then war came and ginger was scarce so they went over to making it with lemonade. That's why if you order it in a pub now, they will instinctively make it using lemonade, spilling it everywhere, as no barperson ever seems to have been taught to let it settle first.

My recipe for a really good shandy is to take three quarters of a pint of bitter and top the rest up with Stone's or Crabbie's Green Ginger Wine. I'd recommend not drinking more than a few of these as it turns out to be fairly potent.

When tucked up next to a fire on a cold winter night, this drink is great for two as you can have half pints each.

If it's the hot day in summer then you can apply it to lager too. Three quarters of a pint of lager and a quarter green ginger wine.

The Stir and Drink

I found this one when I was living abroad, too. I lived in a shed on stilts down a track cut into the hillside by goats running along it over the years. A little further up the track, where it hit the bigger track, was a rum shop run by a lovely lady called Miss Louie. I'd go there most nights after work. We'd tell stories, make each other laugh and play dominoes. Together we created a variant of something they used to drink in that village a long time before I arrived. It involves very strong dark rum: something around the 80% volume (160% proof) mark. Put a generous measure of dark rum into a glass. Add twice as much milk as the rum and enough Angostura Bitters to make the liquid go a chocolate colour. Just before the milk congeals, starts to turn to cheese or begins to look like a weather front in the glass stir briskly and drink. Do not drink this if you are lactose intolerant.

Another tip I got while I was abroad was from my grandfather. If you're ever worried about impure water, just add a spot of whiskey (or whisky), swill it round and that will kill most bugs.

The Polish

The Edinburgh Festival Fringe has changed quite a bit over the last few years from being one big fire-juggling party where people went to try new things out to becoming much more of a corporate trade fair for jokes.

Before the change there was a big party every night. Many of them were parties where no one knew who they knew, where they were or why they were partying. Edinburgh used to be like Lent but with the focus on taking up everything and creating excess for 40 nights rather than giving it up. It was the ultimate hedonists' playpen.

At one of these parties we realised that the bar was free and to celebrate I invented a new cocktail. The result was The Polish, named after the nice lady who was pouring the drinks. Again, it's got a touch of the ginger about it as one of the people I was with had flaming red hair.

I'm going to give you the amounts that make up a pint as that's the best thing to mix it in. Take half a pint of whisky (Scottish), add a quarter of a pint of green ginger wine and a quarter of a pint of ginger vodka. This is a drink designed for the professional debauchee and anyone wanting to invest in a serious hangover, guilt, remorse and denial the next morning.

Pimm's Casino Royal

This is a lovely drink for the summer but not mid- or high-afternoon. It is the late-afternoon sister of the Pimm's Royal. Simply put. Make all the loveliness of a Pimm's Royal with Pimm's, champagne and lashings of fruit then simply add sherry to taste. When people are falling away after a hot afternoon of playing, the introduction of something new to the taste buds will perk them up or lead them happily to a disco nap before the evening.

The Lancaster Bomber

This was an old naval favourite and was taught to me by my favourite Commander (now retired). It's called the Lancaster Bomber because it writes you off. The instructions were handed to me as follows. 'First find a large fermenting bucket or vat of some sort: empty into it one bottle of vodka, one bottle of Cointreau, one bottle of Grand Marnier. Add three litres of orange juice and four litres of lemonade. Gather team, finish vat and then you're ready for the Mess Dinner.' You don't have to be in the Navy to attempt this but I'd suggest any dinner after this will be messy.

MORE BATH-BASED SKULDUGGERY

Having rowed a bath people often ask about other bath-related things. This is another of those. It's on a par with Marat's death as another infamous episode in the history of sanitaryware. I've lifted the details on this from the Scotland Yard files. This is the case of the Bride of Bath Murders.

On 13 July 1912, Bessie Williams was found dead in her bath at 80 High Street, Herne Bay. Five days beforehand she'd made a new will in favour of her husband, Henry Williams. The doctor who examined Bessie convinced the inquest jury it was epilepsy and the cause of death was asphyxia brought about by drowning. The jury returned the verdict: 'Death by misadventure'.

Meanwhile George Joseph Smith was trying hard to please his future parents-in-law. Alice's father Mr Burnham said George was of a 'very evil appearance' so totally suitable to marry his daughter. On 12 December 1913 Alice went for a bath at the apartments she shared with her husband in Blackpool. She never returned. Her body was found much later. Her kindly landlord, Mr Crossley, noted that her head, unusually, was, at the foot of the bath. Alice had insured herself for £500; the beneficiary was her new husband. The inquest jury's verdict was that Alice had 'Accidentally drowned through heart failure when in the bath.'

On 18 December 1914, Margaret Elizabeth Lloyd (nee Lofty) was found dead in the bath at 14 Bismark Road, Highgate, London. Earlier that afternoon Margaret had made a will in favour of her husband John Lloyd. The verdict of the inquest jury was accidental death.

No one saw a pattern, until on 3 January 1915, Alice Smith's former landlord Mr Crossley wrote to the Metropolitan Police. He enclosed a newspaper cutting about the death of Margaret Lloyd, and remarked how similar it was to the death of Alice.

The Yard's finest sprang into action. Divisional Detective Inspector Neil went back to Herne Bay, Blackpool and Highgate and inspected the baths with pathologist Dr Sir Bernard H. Spilsbury (of the Crippen Case) who concluded all three baths were too small to allow grown women the space to drown.

Det. Insp. Neil was beginning to suspect that this was one of his most intricate cases yet. He came to the groundbreaking conclusion that Henry Williams, George Joseph Smith and John Lloyd might be the same person. He investigated Williams-Smith-Lloyd and found that he'd been born George Joseph Smith in Bethnal Green on 11 January 1872. In 1898 he married Caroline Beatrice Thornhill. Thornhill had been the Bonnie to his Clyde but got scared of him and fled to Canada in 1903. He then simultaneously married a widow Florence Wilson, Edith Peglar (under the name Oliver George Love), Sarah Freeman (under the name George Rose Smith) and Alice Reid (under the name Charles Oliver James). He cleaned out their savings and left them before marrying the first of his ill-fated brides: Bessie. How anyone at the Yard or more importantly Williams-Smith-Lloyd-Love-Smith-James was able to keep track of this is remarkable.

Det. Insp. Neil stopped Williams-Smith-Lloyd-Love-Smith-James on 1 February 1915 in Uxbridge Road. He appeared at Bow Street and was charged with 'causing a false entry to [be] made in a marriage register'.

But Williams-Smith-Lloyd-Love-Smith-James had more to worry about than bigamy. Although under British law at the time he could only be tried for the first murder, the court was informed of the other two to establish a pattern. The clinching evidence came from the 1915 Highgate funeral. The undertaker H.F. Beckett told the court he distinctly heard Williams-Smith-Lloyd-Love-Smith-James say to him, 'Get it over as quick as you can,' and after the funeral, 'Thank goodness that's all over.' Punctual or devious? The court went for the latter. He was found guilty of the murder of Bessie Williams, found dead in a bath, with Alice Burnham and Margaret Elizabeth Lofty taken into account. He was sentenced to death and executed at Maidstone Gaol on 13 August 1915.

Divisional Det. Insp. Neil, the Yard's finest, had won the day.

APPENDIX E

SOME POEMS . . .

Not sure including a poem by me is the best way to finish this off (see chapter 12 for details). Thankfully neither does Trevor the publisher.

Picture Credits for the Plate Section